First World War
and Army of Occupation
War Diary
France, Belgium and Germany

19 DIVISION
56 Infantry Brigade
East Lancashire Regiment
7th Battalion
6 July 1915 - 31 January 1918

WO95/2079/2

The Naval & Military Press Ltd
www.nmarchive.com

Published in association with The National Archives

Published by

The Naval & Military Press Ltd

Unit 10 Ridgewood Industrial Park,

Uckfield, East Sussex,

TN22 5QE England

Tel: +44 (0) 1825 749494

www.naval-military-press.com

www.nmarchive.com

This diary has been reprinted in facsimile from the original. Any imperfections are inevitably reproduced and the quality may fall short of modern type and cartographic standards.

© Crown Copyright
Images reproduced by permission of The National Archives, London, England, 2015.

Contents

Document type	Place/Title	Date From	Date To
Heading	WO95/2079/2		
Heading	7th Bn East Lancs Regt Jly 1915-Jan 1918		
Heading	7th Battn. The East Lancashire Regiment. July (6.7.15-31.7.14) 1915 Jan 18		
War Diary	Perham Down	06/07/1915	17/07/1915
War Diary	Boulogne	18/07/1915	18/07/1915
War Diary	Eperlecques	19/07/1915	23/07/1915
War Diary	Wallon Cappel	24/07/1915	24/07/1915
War Diary	Guarbecque	25/07/1915	29/07/1915
War Diary	Merville 1 Mile North Of	30/07/1915	31/07/1915
Heading	7th Battn. The East Lancashire Regiment. August 1915		
War Diary	Merville 1 Mile North Of	01/08/1915	12/08/1915
War Diary	Vielle Chapelle	12/08/1915	20/08/1915
War Diary	Merville	21/08/1915	30/08/1915
War Diary	Lacon	31/08/1915	31/08/1915
Miscellaneous	Appendix "A"		
Heading	7th Battn. The East Lancashire Regiment. September 1915		
War Diary	Lacon	01/09/1915	12/09/1915
War Diary	Trenches Line Approx Quinque Rue Pipe Trench	13/09/1915	15/09/1915
War Diary	Trenches	15/09/1915	30/09/1915
Operation(al) Order(s)	Operation Order No. 1 Col. M.V. Hilton Cmdg 7th East Lanc Regt Appendix B	24/09/1915	24/09/1915
Miscellaneous	A Form Messages And Signals.	24/09/1915	24/09/1915
Heading	7th Battn. The East Lancashire Regiment. October 1915		
War Diary	Trenches Conlines	01/10/1915	04/10/1915
War Diary	Rue des Chavattes	05/10/1915	07/10/1915
War Diary	Leszelobes	08/10/1915	11/10/1915
War Diary	Rue des Chavattes	13/10/1915	15/10/1915
War Diary	In Trenches	16/10/1915	24/10/1915
War Diary	Locon	25/10/1915	31/10/1915
Heading	7th Battn. The East Lancashire Regiment. November 1915		
War Diary	Locon	01/11/1915	08/11/1915
War Diary	Le Hamel	09/11/1915	12/11/1915
War Diary	Festubert	13/11/1915	13/11/1915
War Diary	Le Plantin	14/11/1915	19/11/1915
War Diary	Trenches	20/11/1915	23/11/1915
War Diary	Trenches To Locon	24/11/1915	24/11/1915
War Diary	Merville	25/11/1915	30/11/1915
Heading	7th Battn. The East Lancashire Regiment. December 1915		
War Diary	Merville	01/12/1915	07/12/1915
War Diary	Trenches	08/12/1915	15/12/1915
War Diary	St Vaast	16/12/1915	22/12/1915
War Diary	Le Touret	23/12/1915	31/12/1915
Heading	7th E. Lancs Vol 3 January 1916		
War Diary	Trenches	01/01/1916	04/01/1916
War Diary	Merville	05/01/1916	11/01/1916
War Diary	Robecq	12/01/1916	30/01/1916

War Diary	Serny	31/01/1916	31/01/1916
War Diary	Estree Blanche (Serny)	01/02/1916	02/02/1916
War Diary	Robecq	03/02/1916	17/02/1916
War Diary	In The Frenches	18/02/1916	19/02/1916
War Diary	Croix Barbee	20/02/1916	24/02/1916
War Diary	In The Line	24/02/1916	26/02/1916
War Diary	Croix Barbee	27/02/1916	27/02/1916
War Diary	In The Line	28/02/1916	29/02/1916
War Diary	In The Trenches	01/03/1916	01/03/1916
War Diary	Croix Barbee	02/03/1916	03/03/1916
War Diary	In The Trenches	04/03/1916	07/03/1916
War Diary	Croix Barbee	08/03/1916	11/03/1916
War Diary	In The Trenches	12/03/1916	13/03/1916
War Diary	Merville	14/03/1916	23/03/1916
War Diary	Croix Barbee	24/03/1916	27/03/1916
War Diary	In The Trenches	28/03/1916	31/03/1916
War Diary	Croix Barbee	01/04/1916	03/04/1916
War Diary	In The Trenches	04/04/1916	08/04/1916
War Diary	Croix Barbee	09/04/1916	13/04/1916
War Diary	In The Trenches	14/04/1916	16/04/1916
War Diary	La Gorgue	17/04/1916	17/04/1916
War Diary	Robecq	18/04/1916	18/04/1916
War Diary	Rely	19/04/1916	08/05/1916
War Diary	S Vast	09/05/1916	26/05/1916
War Diary	Frechencourt	27/05/1916	27/05/1916
War Diary	Albert	28/05/1916	02/06/1916
War Diary	Frechencourt	03/06/1916	03/06/1916
War Diary	St Vast En Chaussee	04/06/1916	06/06/1916
War Diary	Flesselles	07/06/1916	15/06/1916
War Diary	Molliens an Bois	16/06/1916	26/06/1916
War Diary	Baizeux	27/06/1916	27/06/1916
War Diary	Henencourt	28/06/1916	30/06/1916
Heading	7th Battn. The East Lancashire Regiment. July 1916		
Miscellaneous		04/08/1916	04/08/1916
War Diary	Albert	01/07/1916	08/07/1916
War Diary	Millen Court	09/07/1916	09/07/1916
War Diary	Henencourt Wood	10/07/1916	19/07/1916
War Diary	Bazentin-Le-Petit Wood	20/07/1916	23/07/1916
War Diary	Sq.X. 23.b	24/07/1916	29/07/1916
War Diary	Becourt	30/07/1916	30/07/1916
War Diary	Franvillers	31/07/1916	31/07/1916
Miscellaneous	Appendices I, II, III & IV.		
Miscellaneous	App I	14/07/1916	14/07/1916
Miscellaneous	Appendix II	00/07/1916	00/07/1916
Miscellaneous	Appendix III 56th Infantry Brigade	21/07/1916	21/07/1916
Diagram etc			
Operation(al) Order(s)	7th East Lancashire Regt. Operation Order No. Appendix IV	21/07/1916	21/07/1916
Heading	War Diary 7/East Lancs Reg August 16		
War Diary	Franvillers	01/08/1916	03/08/1916
War Diary	Gorenflos	04/08/1916	05/08/1916
War Diary	Pont Remy	06/08/1916	06/08/1916
War Diary	Bailleul	07/08/1916	08/08/1916
War Diary	Piccadilly To N.29.B.9.6 1/2	08/08/1916	14/08/1916
War Diary	Locre	15/08/1916	20/08/1916
War Diary	Piccadilly (exclusive) to N 29.B.9.61/2	21/08/1916	26/08/1916

War Diary	Kemmel Shelters	27/08/1916	31/08/1916
War Diary	Trenches	01/09/1916	01/09/1916
War Diary	Piccadilly N 29 B 9.4	02/09/1916	02/09/1916
War Diary	Le Romarin	03/09/1916	03/09/1916
War Diary	Ploegsteert Wood	04/09/1916	30/09/1916
Miscellaneous	56th Infantry Bgde	16/09/1916	16/09/1916
Miscellaneous	Report on Raid Effected Night	15/09/1916	15/09/1916
Miscellaneous	Narrative of Raid		
Diagram etc	Rough Sketch To Illustrate	15/09/1916	15/09/1916
Operation(al) Order(s)	7th East Lancashire Regiment Operation Order No 2	21/09/1916	21/09/1916
War Diary	Doulieu	01/10/1916	05/10/1916
War Diary	Couin	06/10/1916	10/10/1916
War Diary	Sailly Au Bois	11/10/1916	12/10/1916
War Diary	Hebuterne	13/10/1916	15/10/1916
War Diary	Rossignol Fme	16/10/1916	16/10/1916
War Diary	Vadencourt Wood	17/10/1916	21/10/1916
War Diary	Bivouacs At N.20a.9.4	22/10/1916	22/10/1916
War Diary	Wood Post & Leipzig Redoubt	23/10/1916	23/10/1916
War Diary	Stuff Trench	24/10/1916	26/10/1916
War Diary	Donnet Post	27/10/1916	30/10/1916
War Diary	Aveluy	31/10/1916	01/11/1916
War Diary	In The Trenches	02/11/1916	02/11/1916
War Diary	Donnet Post	03/11/1916	05/11/1916
War Diary	In the Turecle	06/11/1916	09/11/1916
War Diary	Old German Front Line	10/11/1916	11/11/1916
War Diary	Ovillers Post	12/11/1916	12/11/1916
War Diary	In the Trenches	13/11/1916	15/11/1916
War Diary	Marlborough Huts-Aveluy	16/11/1916	17/11/1916
War Diary	Hansa Line	18/11/1916	18/11/1916
War Diary	Gnoutskiets Of Grandcourt	19/11/1916	19/11/1916
War Diary	Reserve Dug-Outs	20/11/1916	21/11/1916
War Diary	Athuille	22/11/1916	22/11/1916
War Diary	Warloy	23/11/1916	23/11/1916
War Diary	Harponville	24/11/1916	24/11/1916
War Diary	Longuevillette	25/11/1916	25/11/1916
War Diary	Fienvillers	26/11/1916	30/11/1916
Miscellaneous	A account of Operation caused and by 7th East Lancashire Regt on 13th 14th November 1916		
Operation(al) Order(s)	7th East Lancashire Regiment. Operation Order No. 5	12/11/1916	12/11/1916
Miscellaneous	Narrative Of Operations During 18th November		
Operation(al) Order(s)	Battalion East Lancashire Operation Order No 8	18/11/1916	18/11/1916
War Diary	Fienvillers	01/12/1916	09/01/1917
War Diary	Raincheval	10/01/1917	10/01/1917
War Diary	Coigneux	11/01/1917	25/01/1917
War Diary	Bayencourt	26/01/1917	31/01/1917
War Diary	Sailly	01/02/1917	02/02/1917
War Diary	Trenches	03/02/1917	06/02/1917
War Diary	Bayencourt	07/02/1917	09/02/1917
War Diary	Trenches	10/02/1917	13/02/1917
War Diary	Sailly	14/02/1917	17/02/1917
War Diary	Trenches	18/02/1917	21/02/1917
War Diary	Bus	22/02/1917	25/02/1917
War Diary	Bus Courcelles	26/02/1917	27/02/1917
War Diary	Lealvillers	28/02/1917	04/03/1917
War Diary	Bertrancourt	05/03/1917	08/03/1917
War Diary	Bertrancourt Authie	09/03/1917	09/03/1917

War Diary	Longuevillette	10/03/1917	10/03/1917
War Diary	Neuvillette	11/03/1917	13/03/1917
War Diary	Hericourt And Guinecourt	14/03/1917	14/03/1917
War Diary	Monchy Cayeux	15/03/1917	15/03/1917
War Diary	Laires	16/03/1917	17/03/1917
War Diary	Lambres	18/03/1917	19/03/1917
War Diary	Ebblinghem	20/03/1917	20/03/1917
War Diary	Zouafques	21/03/1917	02/04/1917
War Diary	Longueness	03/04/1917	03/04/1917
War Diary	Hazebrouck	04/04/1917	04/04/1917
War Diary	Caestre	05/04/1917	06/04/1917
War Diary	Weston Camp	07/04/1917	08/04/1917
War Diary	Murrumbidgee Camp	09/04/1917	12/04/1917
War Diary	Trenches (Diependaal Sector)	13/04/1917	16/04/1917
War Diary	Ridge Wood	17/04/1917	20/04/1917
War Diary	Right Subsector	21/04/1917	24/04/1917
War Diary	Murrumbidgee Camp	25/04/1917	30/04/1917
Miscellaneous	Relief Orders No 1.	11/04/1917	11/04/1917
Operation(al) Order(s)	7th East Lancashire Regiment. Operation Order No 2	15/04/1917	15/04/1917
Operation(al) Order(s)	East Lancashire Regiment. Operation Order No 3	19/04/1917	19/04/1917
Operation(al) Order(s)	East Lancashire Regiment. Operation Order No 4	23/04/1917	23/04/1917
War Diary	Murrumbidgee Camp Nr La Clytte Belgium	01/05/1917	01/05/1917
War Diary	Carnarvon Camp	02/05/1917	02/05/1917
War Diary	St Lawrence Camp	03/05/1917	09/05/1917
War Diary	Trenches Right Subsector Diependaal Sector	10/05/1917	13/05/1917
War Diary	Ridge Wood	14/05/1917	17/05/1917
War Diary	Trenches	18/05/1917	20/05/1917
War Diary	Weston Camp	21/05/1917	21/05/1917
War Diary	Kampton Camp	22/05/1917	31/05/1917
Operation(al) Order(s)	East Lancashire Regiment Operation Order No 5 Appendix 1		
Operation(al) Order(s)	East Lancashire Regiment Operation Order No 6 Appendix 2	01/05/1917	01/05/1917
Operation(al) Order(s)	East Lancashire Regiment Operation Order No 7 Appendix 3	08/05/1917	08/05/1917
Operation(al) Order(s)	East Lancashire Regiment Operation Order No 8 Appendix 4	09/05/1917	09/05/1917
Operation(al) Order(s)	East Lancashire Regiment Operation Order No 9	12/05/1917	12/05/1917
Operation(al) Order(s)	East Lancashire Regiment Operation Order No 10 Appendix 6	17/05/1917	17/05/1917
Operation(al) Order(s)	East Lancashire Regiment Operation Order No 11 Appendix 7	30/05/1917	30/05/1917
Operation(al) Order(s)	East Lancashire Regiment Operation Order No 12 Appendix 8	31/05/1917	31/05/1917
Operation(al) Order(s)	East Lancashire Regiment Operation Order No 13 Appendix 9	29/05/1917	29/05/1917
Miscellaneous	Report on Raid on Nags Support Trench on Morning	19/05/1917	19/05/1917
Heading	On His Majesty's Service. 7th East Lancashire Regt. Vol 20		
War Diary	Nr La Clytte M.12.a.9.5 Sheet 28 SW 1/20000	01/06/1917	02/06/1917
War Diary	Curragh Camp	03/06/1917	06/06/1917
War Diary	Nr Carre Bois (Plan Attached)	07/06/1917	15/06/1917
War Diary	Birr Barracks	16/06/1917	18/06/1917
War Diary	Red Line	19/06/1917	19/06/1917
War Diary	Kemmel Hill	20/06/1917	30/06/1917
Operation(al) Order(s)	East Lancashire Regiment Operation Order No. 14	01/06/1917	01/06/1917

Type	Description	Date From	Date To
Operation(al) Order(s)	East Lancashire Regiment Operation Order No. 16	06/06/1917	06/06/1917
Miscellaneous	7th East Lancashire Regiment Instructions For The Offensive		
Map			
Miscellaneous	Situation Map.		
Miscellaneous	Additions To Instructions For The Offensive		
Miscellaneous	19th. Division. No. G 123/24/27		
Operation(al) Order(s)	East Lancashire Regiment. Operation Order No. 16	19/06/1917	19/06/1917
Operation(al) Order(s)	East Lancashire Regiment. X Operation Order No. 16	19/06/1917	19/06/1917
War Diary	Doncaster Huts and Bivouacs Kemmell Slopes	01/07/1917	01/07/1917
War Diary	Birr Barracks Locre	02/07/1917	18/07/1917
War Diary	Blue and Red Lines	19/07/1917	20/07/1917
War Diary	Trenches O.17 a 4c	21/07/1917	22/07/1917
War Diary	Camp N. 16.b.9.3	23/07/1917	23/07/1917
War Diary	Camp N.15.c.9.9	24/07/1917	29/07/1917
War Diary	In The Line	30/07/1917	31/07/1917
Operation(al) Order(s)	East Lancashire Regiment. Operation Order No. 17 Appendix I		
Operation(al) Order(s)	East Lancashire Regiment. Operation Order No. 18 Appendix 2	18/07/1917	18/07/1917
Operation(al) Order(s)	East Lancashire Regiment. Operation Order No. 19 Appendix 3		
Operation(al) Order(s)	East Lancashire Regiment. Operation Order No. 20 Appendix 4	28/07/1917	28/07/1917
Miscellaneous	B Dome House		
Miscellaneous	8th Bn East Lancashire Regiment Instructions For The Offensive Appendix 5	26/07/1917	26/07/1917
Map	Appendix 6		
Miscellaneous	Make Use Of Paragraphs As Required Give Map Reference Or Mark On Map At Back		
War Diary	In The Line	01/08/1917	03/08/1917
War Diary	Birr Barracks Locre	04/08/1917	05/08/1917
War Diary	Camp M.13.b.8.9 Nr Westoutre Sheet 28 1/40,000	06/08/1917	09/08/1917
War Diary	Nielles En Blequin	10/08/1917	10/08/1917
War Diary	Henneveux	11/08/1917	22/08/1917
War Diary	Quesques	23/08/1917	29/08/1917
War Diary	M.20.d.5.5 Sheet 28 1/40,000	30/08/1917	31/08/1917
Operation(al) Order(s)	East Lancashire Regiment. Operation Order No. 21	03/08/1917	03/08/1917
Operation(al) Order(s)	East Lancashire Regiment. Operation Order No. 22	06/08/1917	06/08/1917
Operation(al) Order(s)	Operation Order No. 23 East Lancashire Regiment.	09/08/1917	09/08/1917
Operation(al) Order(s)	East Lancashire Regiment. Operation Order No. 24	10/08/1917	10/08/1917
Operation(al) Order(s)	East Lancashire Regiment. Operation Order No. 25	21/08/1917	21/08/1917
Operation(al) Order(s)	East Lancashire Regiment. Operation Order No. 26	26/08/1917	26/08/1917
War Diary	Inkerman Camp Near Westoutre M.20.d.5.5 Sheet 28.S.W.	01/09/1917	05/09/1917
War Diary	Wakefield Huts Locre M.29 A.61	06/09/1917	17/09/1917
War Diary	Wakefield Huts Locre	18/09/1917	18/09/1917
War Diary	Irish House	19/09/1917	19/09/1917
War Diary	Bois Confluent	20/09/1917	20/09/1917
War Diary	Centre Sector I36	21/09/1917	21/09/1917
War Diary	Line	22/09/1917	22/09/1917
War Diary	Right Sector I 36	23/09/1917	28/09/1917
War Diary	N 22.a.2.4 Sheet 28.S.W.	29/09/1917	30/09/1917
Operation(al) Order(s)	East Lancashire Regiment. Operation Order No. 27 Appendix 1	05/09/1917	05/09/1917
Operation(al) Order(s)	East Lancashire Regiment. Operation Order No. 28	11/09/1917	11/09/1917

Operation(al) Order(s)	East Lancashire Regiment. Operation Order No. 29 Appendix 3	18/09/1917	18/09/1917
Miscellaneous	Appendix 4		
Operation(al) Order(s)	East Lancashire Regiment. Operation Order No. 30	30/09/1917	30/09/1917
Operation(al) Order(s)	East Lancashire Regiment. Operation Order No. 31 Appendix 5	23/09/1917	23/09/1917
Operation(al) Order(s)	East Lancashire Regiment. Operation Order No. 32 Appendix No 6	26/09/1917	26/09/1917
Operation(al) Order(s)	East Lancashire Regiment. Operation Order No. 33 Appendix 7	29/09/1917	29/09/1917
War Diary	Rossignol Wood	01/10/1917	05/10/1917
War Diary	Right Subsector	06/10/1917	08/10/1917
War Diary	Support (Right)	09/10/1917	11/10/1917
War Diary	Right Subsector	12/10/1917	14/10/1917
War Diary	Camp N.6.d.1.7	15/10/1917	19/10/1917
War Diary	Kemmel Shelters	20/10/1917	26/10/1917
War Diary	Left Support	27/10/1917	30/10/1917
War Diary	Left Subsector	31/10/1917	31/10/1917
Operation(al) Order(s)	East Lancashire Regiment. Operation Order No. 34 Appendix No 1	04/10/1917	04/10/1917
Miscellaneous	Administrative Instructions. With reference to Operation Order No. 34 Appendix No 1		
Operation(al) Order(s)	East Lancashire Regiment. Operation Order No. 36 Appendix No 3	07/10/1917	07/10/1917
Operation(al) Order(s)	East Lancashire Regiment. Operation Order No. 38 Appendix No 3	11/10/1917	11/10/1917
Operation(al) Order(s)	East Lancashire Regiment. Operation Order No. 37 Appendix No 4	14/10/1917	14/10/1917
Operation(al) Order(s)	East Lancashire Regiment. Operation Order No. 38 Appendix No 5	18/10/1917	18/10/1917
Operation(al) Order(s)	East Lancashire Regiment. Operation Order No. 39 Appendix No 6	26/10/1917	26/10/1917
Operation(al) Order(s)	East Lancashire Regiment. Operation Order No. 40 Appendix 7	30/10/1917	30/10/1917
War Diary	In The Line Shrewsbury Forest Sheet 28 N.W.	01/11/1917	04/11/1917
War Diary	Beggar's Rest Sheet 28 SW 1/20000	05/11/1917	08/11/1917
War Diary	Wakefield Huts Nr Locre	09/11/1917	09/11/1917
War Diary	Inkerman Camp	10/11/1917	10/11/1917
War Diary	Sercus	11/11/1917	30/11/1917
Operation(al) Order(s)	East Lancashire Regiment. Operation Order No. 41 Appendix No 1	03/11/1917	03/11/1917
Operation(al) Order(s)	East Lancashire Regiment. Operation Order No. 42 Appendix No 2	07/11/1917	07/11/1917
Operation(al) Order(s)	East Lancashire Regiment. Operation Order No. 43	08/11/1917	08/11/1917
Operation(al) Order(s)	East Lancashire Regiment. Operation Order No. 44 Appendix No 4	09/11/1917	09/11/1917
War Diary	Sercus	01/12/1917	07/12/1917
War Diary	Bailleulmont	08/12/1917	08/12/1917
War Diary	Courcelles	09/12/1917	09/12/1917
War Diary	Le Comte Etricourt	10/12/1917	12/12/1917
War Diary	Ribecourt Sheet 5/c	13/12/1917	31/12/1917
War Diary	France	01/01/1918	08/01/1918
War Diary	In The Field	09/01/1918	31/01/1918
Heading	E Lan R. WD. Jan 1918		

WO 95/2079/2

19TH DIVISION
56TH INFY BDE

7TH BN EAST LANCS REGT

JLY 1915 - JAN 1918

DISBANDED

56th Inf.Bde.
19th Div.

Battn. disembarked
Boulogne from
England 18.7.15.

WAR DIARY

7th BATTN. THE EAST LANCASHIRE REGIMENT.

J U L Y

(6.7.15 - 31.7.15)

1915

Jan '18

Army Form C. 2118

WAR DIARY or INTELLIGENCE SUMMARY
(Erase heading not required.)

7th (Ser) Bn. East Lancashire Regt.

Instructions regarding War Diaries and Intelligence Summaries are contained in F. S. Regs., Part II. and the Staff Manual respectively. Title Pages will be prepared in manuscript.

Place	Date	Hour	Summary of Events and Information	Remarks and references to Appendices
Perham Down	6 July 1915	3 pm	1. Battalion received orders to mobilize. — Strength of Battalion 38 officers and 1039 O.R.	
"	7 July	7 am	All ranks medically inspected. 2/Lt Hallsize proceeded to France for embarkation duties and entraining	
"	7 July 15 July		Mobilization orders carried out in accordance with instructions.	
			Battalion mobilized at midnight 15th July. Rgms and others received.	
"	16 July	8.5 am	1st Line transport 2 officers and 104 other Ranks proceeded by 8.5 am train to Southampton under Major E. A. Sanders for embarkation to France landing at Havre	
"	17 July	10.15 pm	10.9/4 Followed 2nd Lieuts Supernumerary to the establishment of the Batt'n – 2/Lt J.W. Marr	
			2/Lt R.N. Morse; 2/Lt C.E. Carswell; 2/Lt C.A. Hickson; 2/Lt P. Davis	
			(iii) Capt. P.L. Brierley left at Group Hospital, London (appendicitis)	
			(iv) 2/Lt L.W. Shaw allegedly commissioned (N. Lanc)	
			(iv) Capt. H.D. Collyer Seconded Brigade Machine Gun Officer	
"	19 July	7.15 pm	The Battalion strength as under entrained for Boulogne for active service. 273 officers and 859 O.R.	
Boulogne	18 July	4 am	Battalion disembarked at Boulogne, and went into Rest Camp.	
"	18 July		2/Lt Bailey "D" Coy left at Boulogne to Clark for 3rd Echelon, Pte Crook "B" Coy admitted to Hospital	
"		8.10 pm	Battalion entrained at Pont Aubergue station where it free and 1st line transport for Watton, arriving at midnight.	
Eperlecques	19 July	12.45 am	Battalion marched to Eperlecques (3 miles) into Billets	
"	20 July	—	30m men admitted to Hospital at St Omer. Pte 16 Coy left Pte Rance, Ho/11(19016) Scott, 13549 Pt Moore and 13669 Pt Regas	

1875 Wt. W593/826 1,000,000 7/15 J.B.C. & A. A.D.S.S./Forms/C. 2118.

WAR DIARY or INTELLIGENCE SUMMARY

Army Form C. 2118

Place	Date	Hour	Summary of Events and Information	Remarks and references to Appendices
EPERLEQUES	20 July	—	Inspection of Billets by D.A.M.S. Instructions received to boil water for drinking purposes.	
"	21 July	—	Battalion carried out route march 7 miles. 4 men absentees arrived from England under Sergt Savill — travelled over latter by P.B.M.	
"	22 July	—	Battalion carried out route march ordr. 7 miles. No 12744 Pte Kyne A. Pvt. escorter No 9 Inf. Bt. Train (Amentiers) to where 2/Off Baillie 3/Cur left at Boulogne C/Regt Nevin (GR Bn) proceeds Rouen to join 3rd Echelon to where 2/Off Baillie 3/Cur left at Boulogne to attestation	
"	23 July	7 am	Battalion moved into billets at HALLON CAPPEL abt 18 miles; 6 men under Sergt Bolland were left behind to follow the Battalion under this arrangements. Roughly 100 men fell out on line of march and Battalion was issued with new boots 2 days previous. finished he some feet is attestation	
HALLON CAPPEL	24 July	5.25	Battalion moved into billets at GUARBECQUES abt 10 miles: — 110 men fell out owing to sore feet. 85 men under A. Commander were left at HALLON CAPPEL whilst remainder (some feet) the bought on under Div: Arrangements: Officer held Cadr + 2 men to train arrived GUARBECQUE next day.	
GUARBECQUE	25 July	—	Parade under OC Coys. Inspection of Respirators. Iron ration. Ammn: etc. Pte Davis No 12,288 "A" Coy could not turn out at R. Veronk by Bttn outing all ranks were warned not to carry letter by Lt. Give information to the Enemy. — 4 Comrades a 85 men (appl) arrived from HALLON CAPPEL — Sergt Bolland & 6 men arrived from EPERLECQUE.	
"	26 July	—	Battalion Parade — then checked by CO. to fallin out — Battalion roll checked — throughly 31 officers 967 — OR. (including no. 44 RFC driving) — 2 Absentees	

Army Form C. 2118

WAR DIARY
or
INTELLIGENCE SUMMARY
(Erase heading not required.)

Instructions regarding War Diaries and Intelligence Summaries are contained in F.S. Regs., Part II and the Staff Manual respectively. Title Pages will be prepared in manuscript.

Place	Date	Hour	Summary of Events and Information	Remarks and references to Appendices
GUARBECQUE	27/7/14		Battalion paraded for a short route march – 6 miles – No men fell out 2 attended who fell out on march. WATTEN CAPPEL – GUARBECQUE informed – but few fishes up by Armt Column. Battalion issued with Shoots Whistle. Tribal Idicy Pl. 31 off. cadre. OR.	
"			Capt. Kelly II Opr. admitted Hosp. Lt. Im/s Lt. Brennan, A.Coy Lt. 13494 Pt. Harris. Pt. 16970 Pt. Mullen heavy Sgt. Ch. for desertion, with vape orders for Active Service, award 28 Days Field Pun. No.1 for 28 Days	
"	28/7/14		Battalion inspection of respirators etc. L/Cpl. Bailey rejoined from 3rd Echelon.	
"	29/7/14		Battalion paraded for short route march. About 7 miles. – machine Gunners, 1st Signallers paraded for instruction under their own officers	
MERVILLE 1 mile North of.	30/7/14		Battalion moved into billets. 1 mile North of MERVILLE – Very hot march, men suffered by several butter lorries passed on side of road – 25 men fell out – and chiefly to heat and weight carried. Billets chiefly farms – Battalion HQ not properly settled upon by billeting party, consequently had to be passed. Also two Coys. (A & D) had no horses being long out in 5½ Bde. area. – Battalions T/ Cpl. attended Hospital Parade under Coy. Corps.	P. & Hayashi Officer. R.G.
"	31/7/14		definition of references etc.	

56th Inf.Bde.
19th Div.

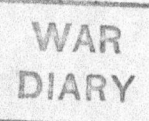

7th BATTN. THE EAST LANCASHIRE REGIMENT.

A U G U S T

1 9 1 5

Attached:

Appendix "A".

WAR DIARY
or
INTELLIGENCE SUMMARY. 7/East Lancashire Regt.

(Erase heading not required.)

Army Form C. 2118.

Place	Date	Hour	Summary of Events and Information	Remarks and references to Appendices
MERVILLE [Rue de Noote B]	1st Aug.		Battalion inspected by Corps Commander.	
"	2nd Aug.		Coys. paraded for Physical training etc. — No 14758 Pte Bowman A Coy convicted Kingfisher on hand shot down Lower Angeltt Capt H.S. attendances to be kept. Major Reefe 20 Aug 1915. — Water in Billets Area found to be unfit for drinking. — Given to find all water facilities.	
"	3rd Aug.		Coys. paraded for Physical training etc. — 4 NCOs + 24 men detailed for Divisional Guard.	
"	4th Aug.		Battalion marched for short Route march — to have fell out — O.C. Coys received a certificate that these were to absence in the possession of the Officers NCOs or men of his Company.	

Army Form C. 2118

WAR DIARY
or
INTELLIGENCE SUMMARY
(Erase heading not required.)

Instructions regarding War Diaries and Intelligence Summaries are contained in F. S. Regs., Part II and the Staff Manual respectively. Title Pages will be prepared in manuscript.

Place	Date	Hour	Summary of Events and Information	Remarks and references to Appendices
MERVILLE 1 mile North of.	5th Aug		Capts Pinches for Physical Training. Pte Genoux Pinches. C'Coy admitted to Hospital – Corpl Kelly & Corp and Sto Sams A Coy injured too Hospital.	
	6 Aug		Battalion paraded for Route March – to men fell out – No 13702 Pte Cooper 2 Coy admitted to Hospital.	
	7 Aug		Coys paraded for Physical Training – Drill etc. Inspection of Smoke Helmets & several were found broken and Gas emit to follow. – No 14321 Pte E. Collins admitted Hospital – Regt Stores proceeded to HINGES for 16 Amn Carres Machine Gun	
	8 Aug		Voluntary Church Parade in MERVILLE – few men went – It would be better if the parade would have been taken to a Church Parade and to Billet.	
	9 Aug		Battalion paraded for Route March – 2 men fell out – Very hot – Men did not take packs. Notification was received that Lie 18293 Pte L. Howe C Coy. Embarked for England struck off strength.	
	10 Aug		Coys paraded for Physical Training etc. Orders received to move into billets at which 11th & 13th FIELD COMPANIES were to billeted. No 18th North Lanc Regt in Trench – one Coy to go into trenches at a time – one platoon from each Company	
	11 Aug		No 8097 Corpl H. WHITEHEAD A Coy & L 16988 Pte J. Lawley B Coy admitted into Hospital. Battalion paraded at 11.45 am for funeral of Hartley of VIEILE CHAPELLE – buried at 12.30 in Chuyard. MERVILLE where he died on the 10th by 7th Bn E. Lanc Regt – 7th Bn WILTS to HINT & were fired upon by enemy by Trench Mortar.	
	12 Aug		Old Estaminet arrived at 11.15 fell in at VIEILE CHAPELLE at 3 am – Bullets were – 2 Platoon was to return into a on the place.	

WAR DIARY or INTELLIGENCE SUMMARY

Army Form C. 2118

Place	Date	Hour	Summary of Events and Information	Remarks and references to Appendices
NEUVE CHAPELLE	1915 12 Aug	10 a.m.	The C.O. and Adjutant, at Bn Station Commanders who were going into the trenches that night, left for the Brigade Hqrs of the Jullundur Brigade at headqrs of the Sirhind Bde who were relieving the 8th Infantry Bde of the 3rd Divn. The Battalion was then transport for trench warfare and to the Sirhind Bn.H.Q. Shewn round.	See App.[?]
		12 noon	The Bn Stations Commanders proceeded to CROIX BARBEE when Guides met them and took them to H.Q.s of the 1st Hampshires and H.Bn Surrey — one Officer and Guide only being sent up to what had been seen in the trenches to arrange for all arrangement to the Bn Stations were given Special Guides & Officers & also [illegible] to be made in the trenches.	
		3 p.m.	Some Officers went down the trenches as Guides. Lieuts Cochrane & [?] went to what had been the trenches that night and platoon Commanders.	
		7 p.m.	Bn marched to CROIX BARBEE and ROUGE CROIX to platoon, 1 H + B Coy and B. ROUGE CROIX and Hd Qrs of C + D Coys £ Croix BARBEE. Men halted but had one Coy were then taken to the trenches and relieved the Hampshires. A relief Officer was sent with each platoon for instruction. The relief was carried out without incident. The Hampshires were also sent up the trenches for instruction.	
	13 Aug	12 noon	The Lieut Col and B.H.Qs. to Bn Hqrs in Lansdowne Post Subbing into the O.C. and personnel to gain advantage from our experience. Successor returns to trench Hqtrs. All the Battalion officers from scraped one by one.	
	14 Aug	10 a.m.	The Brigadier General inspected trenches in process. Some ... [illegible]	
			...POPES NOSE... [illegible]	

1875 Wt. W5993/826 1,000,000 4/15 J.B.C. & A. A.D.S.S./Forms/C. 2118.

WAR DIARY or INTELLIGENCE SUMMARY

Army Form C. 2118

Place	Date	Hour	Summary of Events and Information	Remarks and references to Appendices
VIELLE CHAPELLE	1915 15 Aug		Pte Bryant's body recovered and brought into VIELLE CHAPELLE, where it was buried in the Soldiers Cemetery. (Grave No 12 Sword)	
			1 Officer and 6 NCOs of Bn attached at R.E. Stores for instruction in sand bag bayonet.	
	18 Aug		The Medical Officer made Coy inspection & wished to relieve Pte McIlroy - by Canadian Lt Bernardo as unfit for hospital.	
	19 Aug		Lieut Hay of Signal Wireless returned to duties Batt.	
	18 Aug		CO and Coy Commanders attended a demonstration of MERRIGON given by the 17 Army Corps experts. Also smoke which is more than in a trench gases with gas shell fumes very satisfactory.	
		4 pm	OC (a) Halves Coys reconned company reliefs to posts in the trenches - when went to observation of battles & relief.	
	19 Aug		Inspection of transport by GOC 8 Div team - Inspection passed by the Battalion. Horses not that suitable at MERVILLE.	
			No 11658 Pte W. Irwin 'B' Coy Killed in action - No 13643 L/Cpl T.R. Wilkinson 'B' Coy wounded Left Casualties form Bhopal – 1st Lieut Agar - NPA 19 ton	
	20 Aug		Battalion paraded at 6.15 & ADO handed in bullets 1 mile north of MERVILLE. John Settiers bankoff while in the trenches were Capt Kingston to follow on not being able any	

WAR DIARY or INTELLIGENCE SUMMARY

Army Form C. 2118

Instructions regarding War Diaries and Intelligence Summaries are contained in F. S. Regs., Part II. and the Staff Manual respectively. Title Pages will be prepared in manuscript.

(Erase heading not required.)

Place	Date	Hour	Summary of Events and Information	Remarks and references to Appendices
MERVILLE	21st Aug		Battalion arrived at MERVILLE at 10.30 pm in light of 20°. — 2 men fell out sick – sent to Hos. Bombing Platoons arrived from the trenches. Heavy suffering to the their casualties. Apparently patrols very inactive & gaining ground.	
	22nd Aug		10 officers & 6 men attached to the units for tuition. 6 men instruction were for arrangement made for MEERUT Signalling Section for instruction to the Infantry. — 6 Quarters to HQ. 6 Signallers sent to Bn H.Q./15 Brigade.	
	23rd Aug		SHOUT. — They were attached to 9th Gurkhas for H.E. Hrs. — 6 Signallers sent to Bn H.Q./15 Infantry training for musketry & drill inspection. Battalion received that the Battalions of the B.E.F. have to ask for Bomb hour in so instructions Co. Commdrs attended & officers attended lecture — 2 men admitted to Hospital — 3 men discharge from hospital. Captn Snuffin returns from Front. Lt Cammidge returns to duty from hospital.	
	24th Aug		Battalion paraded for Route March. 1 man fell out — sick. A Party of 10 officers proceeded to Trenches & forward line. Its first party to lorries. Cars 1st line Transport inspected by B.G. Transport officer. Bn Vet officer. Inspection is good Rations. — 2 men reported from Hospital. — Regl Sergt Major Collins returned from Mil Gun course & resumed to him on Q. M. Staff	
	25th Aug		Battalion paraded for Route March — No man fell out — Ho men returned from Hospital. 1 Platoon for A.B. Co. inducted to Bomb throwing.	
	26th Aug		100 men from A Coy & Bo from B.C. + D. proceed to Casarne for a hot bath. New cold exchange under clothing for clean — 1 Platoon of B Co & 1/2 Platoon each of A & B Cos instructed in Bomb throwing. Remnt of Coy's paraded for Concentration trench — clothing & Kit. — No man fell out.	

WAR DIARY or INTELLIGENCE SUMMARY.

Army Form C. 2118

(Erase heading not required.)

Place	Date	Hour	Summary of Events and Information	Remarks and references to Appendices
MERVILLE	27 Aug		Battalion paraded for Route march - distance 6 miles - Warning Orders for aircraft (instruction) issued to Coys	
	28 Aug		Major A.S. Mghelvene Comdg. "B" Coy and 2 men admitted to Hospital - 2 Stations instructors in Bomb Throwing. All officers start a Lewis Gun Course	
	29 Aug		Sunday - Church Parade.	
	30		Continuous old Physical Training and Bayonet fighting - 3 men admitted to Hospital - 2 men wounded	
			Loss Hospital.	
LACON	31		Battalion marched to LACON - Billets fair - 2 Lt. Halliday and 4 men admitted to hospital. Hit by wind	

Appdx No "A"

Ref War Diary page 5.

At VIELLE CHAPELLE on 10th Aug 1915 the CO ??? inspected ... the
Brigade-Major ??????? ???, who showed him the hostile trench held
by that Bde. and gave him a ?????? information as regards details
?????? ... of Instruction

1. The officer in charge of a Platoon that was going into the trenches at
night was to reconnoitre the work by day in order of his own ??
trenches by day so as to acquaint himself with the work going
on — details of Sentries, reliefs, location of the MG, bombs for the Coy,
Platoon ... latrines etc.

2. Night — Every man to get a spell in the ??? Platoon on full duty in
??? the defences.

3. The OC and ??? Coy Coˢᵗ Offⁱᶜᵉˢ would instruct officers and N.Cos.
in loopholing, Sandbagging and bombing.

4. That the CO inspected ??? ? ??? the ??? ? ??? Platoon which instructed
??? to be the ??? when from were coming in.

5. The Bde ??? ? Officer held give instruction to the scale his own
team.

This course of instruction was of the greatest value. All ranks
gained great benefit by it — as here, going up a Platoon at a time
our officers amongst old soldiers, got experience we were even able
to ??? it himself. They claim the greatest ??? and
thoroughly enjoyed the experience.

All the officers ??? up ???, the trenches and were able to pick up
a lot of useful information which will be of the greatest use when
the Battalion takes it turn to hold the trenches.

The Coy and Platoon Commanders went into the trenches again from
22nd Aug for 48 hours. They were attached to the MEERUT Divⁿ and
were able to see how the native troops held the trenches. Further
experience was gained. The idea of seeing different regiments ...
at work is good, as the officer can ??? ??? ??? pick out the
best bits and therefore was able to carry out a proper organization
of defect when it is their turn to go into the trenches.

56th Inf.Bde.
19th Div.

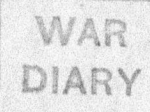

7th BATTN. THE EAST LANCASHIRE REGIMENT.

S E P T E M B E R

1 9 1 5

Attached:

Appendix "B".

Army Form C. 2118.

WAR DIARY
or
INTELLIGENCE SUMMARY.   7/East Lancashire Regt.
September 1917
(Erase heading not required.)

Instructions regarding War Diaries and Intelligence Summaries are contained in F. S. Regs., Part II. and the Staff Manual respectively. Title pages will be prepared in manuscript.

Place	Date	Hour	Summary of Events and Information	Remarks and references to Appendices
[LACON]	1st Sept		Nothing of any importance — Coys cleaned up billets etc	
	2nd Sept		Battalion paraded for Route march — 7 miles — Instructions received for Coys to be Battalions except that kilts worn now — Packed Trained 16 men as snipers.	
"	3rd Sept		Coys paraded in the evening to dig trial communication up at the trenches — 1 hour at water & spade off Halfpenny at men to dig as team from hospital	
	4th Sept		A+C Coys have into front billets on account of flying a few hundred not amongst civilians in the billets area.	
	5th Sept		Raining — no Church parade held.	

1875 Wt. W593/826 1,000,000 4/15 J.B.C.&A.   A.D.S.S./Forms/C. 2118.

T/131. Wt. W.708-776. 500000. 4/16.   Sir J. C. & S.

WAR DIARY or INTELLIGENCE SUMMARY

Army Form C. 2118

Place	Date	Hour	Summary of Events and Information	Remarks and references to Appendices
LoCoN	1915 6 Sept		Battalion paraded for Route March. Cast off boots. In the afternoon Companies paraded for Route March bayonet fighting. - 5 men detailed to proceed today to Béthune for A.S.C. Supply Column.	
	7 Sept		Battalion addresses to affixed. In 2nd in parts, new Supples list to be issued.	
	8 Sept		Companies paraded for Inspection.	
	9 Sept		Companies paraded for Battn. Transport fighting.	
	10 Sept		Battalion paraded for Inspection by C.O. and arms drill. 41 men inoculated for Cholera.	
	11 Sept		Battalion detailed for digging at trio II. No casualties - Orders received to return to 10th Warwicks in 2nd in.	
	12 Sept		C.O. and Coy Commanders went into the trenches to have a look round. — Orders received to transfer Horse into tes lines when to Brigade Transport depot in Le Sars.	

WAR DIARY or INTELLIGENCE SUMMARY

Army Form C. 2118

Place: Trenches line of Rue — Rouge Rue — Pipe Trench

Date	Hour	Summary of Events and Information	Remarks and references to Appendices
14th March /15	11:10 pm	At 11.10 pm on the night of 13th Day the Battn took over the trenches from B: 10" Brigade — 2 Co's and One Officer went previously into the line to be told — Battn HQrs were in last of huts also — the report had that his HQ Aid Post in Rouge Rue was Tube Station Communication trench to the rear of the trench — Whole trench clear. There had a considerable amount of Sniping Shortage Now Standards been built of Rifles as Sgt Major for Coys in front on the ready to receive attack etc. Platoons were brought up for 200 nights or thirty hours to from Rue 21 at Tube Station — which occurred on England. A Coy was nearest — D. Battalion with HQ in as follows: on the right A Coy with HQ Station in dugout — B Coy B Co with HQ Station in dugout in left of the line with 2 platoons in Support — C Co held in reserve in trenches and dug-outs near Battn HQ. Communication by telephone was established between the Coys and the HQ also between HQ and Brigade HQ.	[notes in margin]
14.	2 am	At 2 am the enemy show a burst of H.B. and rifle fire for about 15 minutes in our trenches and his enemy shot a flare. During the day firing from a few Battle HB on line — Casualties: 1 killed and 1 wounded. In front of the left of the line held by the Battalion there is a house known farm called COUR D'AVOUÉ battalion reported work going on at by hostile working parties. They also reported that it was near to Brigade Snipers.	
15.		During the night hostile enemy shelled our line from our right practically enfilade our line — shells fell between front and Support trenches — No casualties. Work reported going on at the FARM COUR D'AVOUÉ	

WAR DIARY or INTELLIGENCE SUMMARY

Army Form C. 2118

Place	Date	Hour	Summary of Events and Information	Remarks and references to Appendices
Trenches (Continued)	15 Sept		Enemy also infantry working on a trench extending from E of H.5 Southerly direction from the farm. A great barricade was observed opposite our left Company. At a distance it resembles the broken tree with its branches bent back. The plot which was about 18 miles from the left was quite overwrought, and at times the flash was seen there. The periscope commanded the whole of our left and reserve trenches. In the Indian Corps Summary 6) 13" well. It was reported destroyed by our still fire. But it is still in the same place and apparently undamaged.	
	16"		Enemy shelled our lines during the night 15/16. Did did no damage. Work still proceeded at the Farm. During the day our line was again shelled. Little damage done. One man was wounded. One man was killed by a sniper. Briefed by the enemy was active during the night and day. A fresh s.p. appears than one began tunnel from the Farm in a S.W. direction. Our front police claim wood on other tunny. A judge of a German cloth who picks up in the there seems be none of an American firm R. Stock & Co. During the night 16/17 enemy opened 3 burets of refer to H. Gun fire lasting about 10 minutes each. During the day a few shells were fired. One casualties one killed and one wounded. 2/fft. Cox and Slade slightly wounded by shell September. Not been able to resume duty. Work infantry going on at the FARM. Patrols actively being found 2 little advanced posts in front of our right Company which were used for sniping purposes. A little to keep	
	17"		post was broken. Really unknown - probably some damage was done as no horses come from it afterwards.	

WAR DIARY or INTELLIGENCE SUMMARY

Army Form C. 2118

Place	Date	Hour	Summary of Events and Information	Remarks and references to Appendices
Trenches Continued	18th		Usual Sniping and artillery fire — Casualties Nil – 2 of our Snipers got 15 which up to the FARM at about 3:30pm. They fought to snipe at. At about 10 pm our rifle and artillery opened rapid fire on enemy's trench. — They were also replied to from guns — Rifle fire done in retaliation for the fight before. Result was that the enemy were very quiet for the remainder of the night. We brought the enemy some active again. Works going on at the FARM.	
"	19th		Usual sniping by day & night but rather less active. Our lines were shelled especially the trench left by me some 60 yds. Patrols reports work going on N.E.S. of the FARM and also on advanced posts in front of our Right Company.	
"	20th		The Battalion moved its position in the line and took over the trenches held by 10th R.W. Surrenders before the CANADIAN ORCHARD. — The old line left by the Battalion being taken over by 9th South Lancs Regt. at 4 pm. — The Battalion relieved the Royals at 9.10 pm. The trenches are not so good as the former ones and require a lot of improvement. 'B' Company moved up into the fire trench. 'A' Company coming back into support. No. 05 Rifle in fire trench 354, in support 163; in reserve 108 –	
"	21st		Our guns opened a bombardment on enemy's front companies at 8 am. – enemy return were quiet — only a few rifle grenades were fired into our lines.	

WAR DIARY or INTELLIGENCE SUMMARY

Army Form C. 2118

Place	Date	Hour	Summary of Events and Information	Remarks and references to Appendices
Trenches Continued	22/8/15		The Bombardment was continued - Enemy trench bombardment were quiet, but as soon as his types a full enemy opens with shells, rifle grenades, trench mortars - some bag-on-here fires in - Casualties 6 highly wounded - O.R. 1 killed and 2 wounded.	
	23/8/15		Continuation of Bombardment - Enemy periodically shelled our trenches with Whizz-bangs, trench-mortars, rifle grenades - 4 men wounded. During the night of 22/23rd a working party was dispersed by our fire - Part of the right coy. parapet was blown in -	
	24/8/15		Continuation of Bombardment - Enemy continues to annoy our companies with brisk shrapnel etc. One man accidentally shot himself whilst cleaning a rifle - Enemy rifling more actively than our bombardment. His shells burst over Battn. H.Q. and bursting behind it. two batteries that search if this shells did not burst. Orders received for 1st Army to resume the offensive. See appendix B	Capt Beavis B. Battn Orderly Order No.1.
			The 24th was the last day of this Bombardment trenches - most of this fire was directed on our right - during the bombardment part of the guns been directed on his enemy were and the companies during the nights 21-24 - Buffs left, N.Q. and left of Coy on his enemy wire where it was suspected it have been cut to prevent enemy repairing the wire	
	25th	5.50 a.m.	Our guns opened a very heavy bombard next on the enemy's position and smoke candles were out all across the line - Our enemy began heavy fire on our trenches with mortars + shells - our casualties were 4 officers and 1 man killed (Capt. Hampton, 2nd Lieut and 15 OR wounded -	
		4.35 a.m.	At 6.30 am a detail of Royal Scots Fusiliers to attack by the SEE Barn on our right - Heavy fighting on our right was carried on all day - 2nd Battalion remained in the trenches us the SEE Barn remaining trenches to press their attack -	

WAR DIARY
or
INTELLIGENCE SUMMARY

(Erase heading not required.)

Army Form C. 2118

Place	Date	Hour	Summary of Events and Information	Remarks and references to Appendices
Trenches Sect B	26th Sept		Lieut Heard returns to battn & fires a Light Infy to ensure his safety and to protect his kindred. Lis pine - Enemy Snipers were very active. Slung night 25/26 and during morning 26.26 for him the platter again (?) but had damage done. - Casualties - Capt Llewelyn accidentally wounded in the arm - obtained a automatic pistol - and 1 man wounded. 4 Coy relieved D Coy in the fine trench - D Coy back into Reserve.	
	27th Sept		Usual Sniping and shelling with trench mortars - 12.433 Evans. Sent to his grenade which exploded a portion of the line. He was so injured at night. There was no casualties	
	28th Sept		Enemy shelled our front behind than usual - also two guns well shells fell when Lis and Rifle trenches are but little damage. No one was in one or two places were hit. No one saved wounded at night. Sta batt'n fetched 67-5 men has been seen in front of our lines - they were heavily shot on and apparently not seemed to be dead and seem of firm. - He has been wounded during the day.	
	29th Sept		Our Battalion heard orders to be relieved. Position which is held from the 14th Sept - 16th Oct inclusive - tobay the place as though Battalion relieves us at 8 (?) Sept Regt - Relief took place after 8am 30th - She relief was a very long time owing to the State of the trenches complete at 3 am 30th - The relief was the heavy and slippery also it has been a distance much. - Very wet and maddy - & parts of the trench were nearly knee deep in water.	
	30th Sept		During my quiet - all turn to have good rest. The men lay down - being bitte and there to have comfortable - 2 men of the Battalion have gone to Somerville on (?)(?) R.E.	P. Cliffords have sent ??? signed

1875 Wt. W593/826 1,000,000 4/15 J.B.C. & A. A.D.S.S./Forms/C. 2118.

Appendix B

OPERATION ORDER No. 1
By Col.M.V.Hilton   Cmdg
7th East Lanc Regt

INFORMATION   The 1st Army is to assume the offensive tomorrow the 25th Septr. The Corps south of LA BASSEE CANAL is to advance eastward on to the line   TONT -A-VENHIN -BAUVIN

The second Division on the right of the 19th Division is to assault the enemy if weather conditions are favourable for a gas attack

The LAHORE Davision on left of 19th Division is to play a role similar to that of this Brigade (see below)

The MEERUT Division on left of Lahore is to assume the offensive and advance on ILLIES & BAVVIN.

The 57th Brigade in Army Reserve is to move to vicinity of LE HAMEL.

The 58th Brigade is to prepare to attack in cooperation with 2nd Division

The 56th Infantry Brigade is to play a defensive role in first instance and as our offensive operations elsewhere progress to make every effort to detect any signs of weakening on part of the enemy. If and when the enemy retires to press forward on left of 58th Brigade.

The 7th L.N.Lanc R. are to remain in Divisional Reserve between CAILLOUX and EPINETTE Posts

INTENTION 2p   The 56th Brigade if attacked will hold its trenches at all costs and will make arrangements for the subsequent role it has to play.

DISTRIBUTION 3. Battalions in the trenches will remain as at present distributed

Transport will remain as at present

The Brigade Ammunition Reserve at CSE-du-RAUK under Brigade Transport Officer

1 N.C.O & 10 Sappers to each Bn in trenches also 1 Officer R.E

Distinguishing flags on scale of 2 per Coy will be issued - 19th Division rear face yellow with red St Andrews Cross - front face khaki

LAHORE Division Yellow with black central verticle stripes - They will be used to assist in shewing localities reached by our troops

Each Coy will be prepared to send out when ordered by the C.O a patrol consisting of :- 1 Officer,6 selected men , 2 grenadiers,2 Sappers,and 2 Signallers.

Early information negative or positive as tothe

enemys action is of the greatest value.

An advance by the Battalion is only to be made if and when our patrols report that the enemy is retreating.

The Battalion will have two Coys finding firing line and support and two Coys in Battn reserve - Detail of Coys will be issued later

6 Machine Guns will be allotted to leading line and 6 Machine Guns to Battalion reserve line. One Platoon Grenadier Coy will be on extreme right of the Brigade and one on extreme left in the leading line

METHOD OF ADVANCE

4. On the advance being ordered the leading Coms will advance by the right direction VIOLLAINES - SALOME

The Battn Reserve Coys will xxxxxxxxx occupy our front line trenches and will not advance without reference to Brigade Headquarters

The Battalion will direct - touch to be kept with Battalion on right if possible. Every opportunity will be taken to employ oblique fire

Information must constantly be passed laterally as well as from front to rear. Guides and connecting files must be used to keep touch from front to rear

Signed P.C.W.Goodwyn Major & Adjt
7th E.Lanc Regt

7 p.m

Copy No 1   Filed
2   O.C "A" Coy
3   O.C "B" Coy
4   O.C "C" Coy
5   O.C "D" Coy
6.   2nd in Command.

24 Sept 1915.

"A" Form.   Army Form C. 2121.
MESSAGES AND SIGNALS.

| TO | O.C. Coy. (Copy of message to O.C. Bn) |

Day of Month: 24   AAA

Ref Operation Order No 1 para 4 aaa B & D Companies will furnish firing line and Suffolk aaa B Coy. will direct aaa A & C Companies will be in Reserve being on front line trenches aaa General line of advance being E.S.E. approximately 116 degrees.

From: Capt.

(Z) P. Cox

56th Inf.Bde.
19th Div.

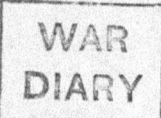

7th BATTN. THE EAST LANCASHIRE REGIMENT.

O C T O B E R

1 9 1 5

WAR DIARY or INTELLIGENCE SUMMARY

Army Form C. 2118

Place	Date	Hour	Summary of Events and Information	Remarks and references to Appendices
Trenches Cuinchy	28th Oct		Enemy on the whole were quiet — On right the explosion by a falling of 70 m.m guns but no damage was done — On the left we had a burst on our right front line corner over and greatly strengthened — One man was killed by a sniper and another wounded by a bomb.	
	29th Oct		Enemy Snipers were considerably more active and their 70 m.m guns fired a good deal during the night and morning. Our guns could give little support as they had orders not to fire except in case of an attack. 1 man killed.	
	30th Oct		Enemy Snipers were still very active — their guns in camps shelled the line frequently the casualties being 1 killed and 5 wounded. On periodic reports his soft approach the right company has been very short — a regular blockhouse.	
	1st Oct		Enemy guns were very active — some big shells fell near Battn H.Qrs — in the evening and during the day enemy fired salvos from their 70 m.m guns — 3 men wounded. At 11.50 p.m the Battalion was relieved by 2nd Kings Own and went into billets at Rue du Chapitres — after having been 22 days in the trenches. The men were taken over and very glad to get some hot baths in the trenches. The men had to do a lot of work in the Barnfeld — dug outs etc, so it has been more greatly hampered by the want of Sandbags and timber. Total number of casualties since his Battalion went into the trenches is 10 off & 9 OR killed and 4 officers & 33 OR wounded.	

WAR DIARY or INTELLIGENCE SUMMARY

Army Form C. 2118

Instructions regarding War Diaries and Intelligence Summaries are contained in F. S. Regs., Part II. and the Staff Manual respectively. Title Pages will be prepared in manuscript.

(Erase heading not required.)

Place	Date 1915	Hour	Summary of Events and Information	Remarks and references to Appendices
RUE du CHAVATTES	5 Oct	—	Battalion arrived in billets in RUE du CHAVATTES at about 10 P.M. "A" Coy took over billets in RUE du BOIS and RUE de L'EPINETTE. Junior 7 tools in all. The men were chiefly in dugouts — On the 5th Companies paraded under Company arrangements — fitted them fresh clothing etc.	
	6 Oct		Commanding Officer inspected the Battalion — being clothing in a bad state — took only give them clothing — Draft of 9 Sergt. — 1 Corpl. — of 39 men joined from England.	
	7 Oct		Inspection of Draft: — 1 Platoon of a few inspected in Bonzay — have seen to fight duty of bombing. owing to number of accidents have been reported. Orders received to move into billets at LES ZELOBES on main road BETHUNE — ZESTREM to relieve 9/S/ump	
LES ZELOBES	8 Oct		Battalion billets in good quarters by 3.30 p.m. — 2/Lt Lowe posted from C/K'S Lt G.W. to report to Casualties — Billets good and clean.	
	9 Oct		Men got clean underclothing — Companies paraded to Physical Training —	
	10 Oct		Battalion marches to LA GORGUE for bath etc —	
	11 Oct		Coys paraded for arms Drill and Physical Training — Orders received to return to old billets.	
RUE du CHAVATTES	12 Oct		Battalion returned billets at RUE du CHAVATTES — have completed by 2 p.m.	
	13 Oct		Battalion stood to arms early to have in case of eventuality, the line — a feint attack on enemy trenches in front of Jean Belle town made by 2/S Bn between an attack further South.	

1875 Wt. W593/826 1,000,000 4/15 J.B.C. & A. A.D.S.S./Forms/C. 2118.

WAR DIARY or INTELLIGENCE SUMMARY

Army Form C. 2118

(Erase heading not required.)

Place	Date 1915	Hour	Summary of Events and Information	Remarks and references to Appendices
RUE DU CHAVATTES	14th Oct.		Companies paraded for medical inspection – 2 men of draft here found medically unfit	
"	"	16.00	Battalion paraded at 5 p.m. to move into his trenches and relieve 7th Kings Own. Relief completed at 7.30 p.m. One man of B. HQ. wounded whilst Battn. was getting into trenches.	
In Trenches	16 Oct.		Enemy on the whole very quiet. Usual sniping. One man of R. Bn. killed – whilst a party was working on ROPE KEEP.	
	17 Oct.		Enemy was very active with rifle grenades & trench mortars. 1 killed & 3 wounded proper was day of wounds after operation. On open retaliation and on a line enemy were quiet. Battalion issued with a new steel helmets. Fired on parapet against shell splinters.	
	18 Oct.		Enemy were again active and one casualties were again increased by 2 Sergeants – 1 killed and 1 wounded.	
	19 Oct.		Enemy on the whole was quiet but sent open several rifle grenades, which also the most damage. Casualties 4 men wounded.	
	20 Oct.		Colonel H.W. Hilton was killed by a rifle grenade whilst visiting the trench of 'A' Coy. Enemy here active with rifle grenades & sniping – 1 man of A Coy killed. Anna visited to retaliate which they did with 16 to 4.5".	
	21 Oct.		Enemy rifle on fire their were very quiet – less sniping – Major C.A. Dawson took over comd.	
	22 Oct.		Enemy again very active with rifle fire, rifle grenades Lieut. G. Challis later also as usual. W. rifle grenades Our considerable damage – Casualties Lt. Wilson and 6 men wounded and 1 man killed –	

Army Form C. 2118

WAR DIARY
or
INTELLIGENCE SUMMARY
(Erase heading not required.)

Instructions regarding War Diaries and Intelligence Summaries are contained in F. S. Regs., Part II. and the Staff Manual respectively. Title Pages will be prepared in manuscript.

Place	Date	Hour	Summary of Events and Information	Remarks and references to Appendices
Sh Flouvelin.	23rd Oct.		Our guns fired on enemy's trenches a good deal in afternoon turning of 2 BM and a few hours 23rd. – Result enemy quiet – though they sent over 9 big shells which fell between our support trenches and left company – 2 Shells were blinds – no casualties from enemy's fire – unfortunately 2 men were accidentally wounded in support trench by premature burst from own bombs. Shop men were receiving instruction as to merits of hurling it when a dummy threw it down to ground. Result one had been sent off.	
	24th Oct.		At about 10.30 am enemy opened fire with rifle grenades – 70 mm guns + HE shells on our trenches but were soon silenced by our guns – They had plenty of own quiet – Battalion relieved in night 24/25 by 9th Welch Regt. – Been very steady at it. Bullets especially A Coy who received most of the enemy fire – Battalion arrived in Billets at Locon about 1.0am 25th Oct.	
LOCON.	25 Oct.		Men cleared up after coming out of the trenches – Drew clothing for men and arranged for hot baths. Officers drew blanket leave.	
	26 Oct.		Inspection of companies by C.O. Orders received to dig trenches at W.S.C. 33. BETHUNE Sheet in accordance with "Secret" instructions received. – All leave cancelled. B.H.Q.A. Dugout at off Hulluch road in England. 40 men & 1 NCO detailed to Bomb throwing – 360 details for digging – W.S.C. 33.	
	27 Oct.		150 men detailed for digging in S.D.7 hrs support trench. – 'C' Coy 40 men for Bombing Instruction.	
	28 Oct.		380 men detailed for digging W.S.C. 33. – B.Coy 40 men instructed in Bomb throwing.	

WAR DIARY
or
INTELLIGENCE SUMMARY
(Erase heading not required.)

Army Form C. 2118

Instructions regarding War Diaries and Intelligence Summaries are contained in F. S. Regs., Part II. and the Staff Manual respectively. Title Pages will be prepared in manuscript.

Place	Date	Hour	Summary of Events and Information	Remarks and references to Appendices
LOCON	30th Oct 1915		12.0 noon Diggry at 9.30. Remained here, paraded for kit baths - received clean underclothing	
	31st Oct		3.50 p.m. Diggry at W.S.C. 33. Men cancelled the work - Revd. Scheme cancelled - Leave opened. Revd. Scheme killed - as same orders had come inforce at a later date.	

P. Cathcartwight Major Comg.
9th Bn Welsh (Anc.) Regt

56th Inf.Bde.
19th Div.

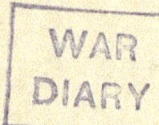

7th BATTN. THE EAST LANCASHIRE REGIMENT.

N O V E M B E R

1 9 1 5

WAR DIARY or INTELLIGENCE SUMMARY

Army Form C. 2118

November 7" "B" East Lancashire Regt.

Place	Date	Hour	Summary of Events and Information	Remarks and references to Appendices
LOCON.	1915 11th Nov.		3.40 a.m. Detailed to furnish Piquet at W.S.C.33 - men carrying 150 rds. + Intrench. tool - Intrench. tool of spade - 12.0 a.m. Piquet at 11.0.I. has gone very hot - 4 B" killed + 10 wounded -	
	2nd Nov.		Too hot for Piquet - The following extract from B" Orders has received - "On 22nd Oct. No.16493 L.Cpl. T. Smith 7 Bn. E.Lanc. Regt. went out under fire and attempted to rescue Pte. Hill of this Regt. who was lying wounded + helpless some 50 yds from the German lines - He himself was wounded before he could reach him - No.12639 P.H.A. Blue 7 Bn. E.Lanc. Regt. him was at miles long fire and succeeded in bringing Pte Hill in - Pte Hill would unfortunately have died from exposure had he not been rescued - The Brigadier before he went on leave, expressed his admiration of his conduct of these two men."	
		3.p.m	190 men Detailed for Piquet at 11.0.I. - new they went - 120 men paraded for Piquet at W.S.C.33. W.it was thought when Lt. Col. Dauberry proceeded to Kingston in Jena then Battalion Headquarters took over Command of Battalion from 2nd Nov. Leave granted to his Battalion	
		4 a.m	Piquet paraded for practice in Crabo holes - having never bombing into which our 150 men Detailed for Piquet at 11.0.I. - Got Shells but no Casualties	
	3rd Nov		150 men Detailed for Piquet at W.S.C.33 "B"	

J.C.Ellicott Major

Army Form C. 2118

WAR DIARY
or
INTELLIGENCE SUMMARY
(Erase heading not required.)

Instructions regarding War Diaries and Intelligence Summaries are contained in F. S. Regs., Part II. and the Staff Manual respectively. Title Pages will be prepared in manuscript.

Place	Date	Hour	Summary of Events and Information	Remarks and references to Appendices
LOCON	1915 7th Mar		40 men (Gurkhas) maluricks in Reserve – 3 Officers + 150 men detailed for diggers in IND I (BESTUBERT AREA) – Party escape by no Casualties.	
	8th Mar.		3 Officers + 150 men detailed for digging in IND I. – Quiet night.	
	9th Mar.		4 Officers + 280 men detailed for digging in IND I – one Company was ordered to get into bullets – others however to move to LE HAMEL in Brigade Reserve – Relieving No 10: Worcestershire –	
LE HAMEL	9th Mar.		Battalion arrived in fresh Billets at LE HAMEL – Billets – A/4 + C/600	
			9th A.A. Hart joined the Battalion from School at STOMER	
	10th Mar.		Major G.A. Dashury relieved Officer leave & returned Command of the Battalion – 20 men for Coy. practices in bombing –	
	11th Mar.		4 Officers + 300 men Detailed for digging in INDIA – very hot – trenches fell in parts – 1 man killed by stray bullet	
	12th Mar.		4 Officers + 300 men Detailed for digging in IND I A – no Casualties – orders received to relieve the N.S. Lancs in Ridges – troops rode in BESTUBERT & LE PLANTIN no local leave –	
FESTUBERT	13th Mar.		Battalion relieved 7/S. Lan in evening of 13th – Brigade on Very Extended –	

Instructions regarding War Diaries and Intelligence Summaries are contained in F. S. Regs., Part II. and the Staff Manual respectively. Title Pages will be prepared in manuscript.

WAR DIARY
or
INTELLIGENCE SUMMARY

(Erase heading not required.)

Army Form C. 2118

Place	Date	Hour	Summary of Events and Information	Remarks and references to Appendices
LE PLANTIN	14th		A few shells (90 mm) were sent over during Day. No casualties. Battalion furnished working parties at night in front line.	
	15th		Quiet — a few stray shells came over by day & night — worked working parties forward — orders received to move forward into the trenches by 16th Kings on	
	16th		the Right. Battalion to Relieving Black — 2/Lt. Craig from 10th R. Lancs. joined his Battalion — Battalion relieved the 9th Kings being in front line between 9th Position from BARNTON RD. on right to about 150 yds to right of PIONEER TRENCH. A night of 16/17: Relief took a long time. Whole battalion in line.	
	17th		Enemy Quiet except for Snipers — one man wounded in neck by R. Rifle and one man day of 17th by Snipers. Impossible to have a rest. Sent to State of trenches.	
	18th		Enemy Quiet — several Snipers and a few Shells — one man accidentally killed through digging out falling in dug-out to bed — one man wounded by Sniper.	
	19th		Enemy on white coast — Our Snipers accounted to two of the enemy — also bombs were sent over into our lines but did no damage. Water still short in trenches — our Casualties for the day being 1 killed and two wounded.	

WAR DIARY
or
INTELLIGENCE SUMMARY

(Erase heading not required.)

Army Form C. 2118

Instructions regarding War Diaries and Intelligence Summaries are contained in F.S. Regs., Part II. and the Staff Manual respectively. Title Pages will be prepared in manuscript.

Place	Date	Hour	Summary of Events and Information	Remarks and references to Appendices
Meuville	20th		Enemy very quiet – one sniper accounts for 1 German Sniper. On line were shelled at about 12 noon by 90 mm guns – one casualties 1 man wounded – weather still tiring – concussion broken at 6.15 – weather peaceful –	
	21st		Enemy were active – bombing (shelling) on line on the right – no damage to our infantry and arm – on return troops another of the enemy – on throw this hill.	
	22nd		Enemy sniping active – 1 flying post fired – two shots fired on our light company but fell short – we led to casualties – Orders received that the battalion was to proceed to MERVILLE into hot billets	
	23rd		Enemy quiet – weather foggy – Mountain Saving Carries on by 6th Coy. Battalion relieved by 6th Gordons and 22nd Surrey. – All ranks were very glad to get out of the trenches for a rest – has been a very tough time from first to last – trenches were quite impossible and all which had to be men across the open. The front line was very broken and really owing to 8th Johannes – 25 have been evacuated with chills	

1875 Wt. W593/826 1,000,000 4/15 J.B.C. & A. A.D.S.S./Forms/C. 2118.-

WAR DIARY or INTELLIGENCE SUMMARY

Army Form C. 2118

(Erase heading not required.)

Instructions regarding War Diaries and Intelligence Summaries are contained in F. S. Regs, Part II. and the Staff Manual respectively. Title Pages will be prepared in manuscript.

Place	Date	Hour	Summary of Events and Information	Remarks and references to Appendices
Gonnehem to LOCON.	1915. 24th Nov.	1.30 am	Battalion arrived in billets at LOCON — When it started until 11. am as him marched to MERVILLE who had billets — We made very slow but back at gonnehem Battalion occupied the same billets which they occupied formerly —	
MERVILLE	25th		Parade inside Bn. Boundaries — Cleared up etc — Issue of Clothing —	
"	26th		Battalion paraded for inspection by Commanding Officer — who went over — Syllabus of Company training — Companies hours of his Sunday.	
"	27th		Battalion inspected by the Brigadier in heavy order — turn out good — told the General required more attention. The Brigadier congratulated the men for the Battalion on his behaviour & this him in the trenches during the longer time in the trenches —	
"	28th		Sunday — Church Parade — 2/Lt Bearman admitted to Hospital	
"	29th		Battalion carried on Company training — 2/Lt Col Hugh took over Transport duties —	
"	30th		D. Company were Baths at MERVILLE — also the Transport — Remainder Coys — Carried on with Company training —	[signature]

56th Inf.Bde.
19th Div.

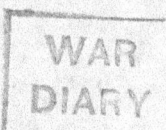

7th BATTN. THE EAST LANCASHIRE REGIMENT.

D E C E M B E R

1 9 1 5

WAR DIARY or INTELLIGENCE SUMMARY

Army Form C. 2118

7th Bn. EAST LANCASHIRE Regt.

December

Place	Date	Hour	Summary of Events and Information	Remarks and references to Appendices
MERVILLE	1915 1st Dec		Companies carried on with Company training – Officers horse carried out Bomb Throwing in the afternoon.	
	2nd Dec		Companies carried out usual training in the morning and in the evening did a Ceremonial march.	
	3rd Dec	3.30 am	Sudden orders received that the Brigade was to move back into the line – a 14th Bn. was to relieve the 6th Bn. Battalion to move at 11 am.	
			Battalion marched off at 11 am and marched into Billets at R.13.C. (Bethune ambries map), roads in a very bad state and in places flooded.	
	4th Dec		Sent to him on french north course. Battalion remained quiet in Billets which were very crowded – Orders received from RICHEBURG ST VAAST.	
	5th		Battalion moved to ST VAAST via LACOUTOUR – from where it entered into ST VAAST by platoons –	
			Billets have very bad – chiefly consisting of farm houses –	
	6th Dec		Parade with Coy arrangements – C.O. also wanted to pay inspection parade by platoons whose covers as to billets he never discovered by falling few turnip pieces.	
	7th Dec		Orders received to relieve the 2nd Kings own in the line – Billets relieved by every M.E. 15 breakfast – no other news –	

WAR DIARY
or
INTELLIGENCE SUMMARY

(Erase heading not required.)

Army Form C. 2118

Place	Date	Hour	Summary of Events and Information	Remarks and references to Appendices
Trenches	8 Dec		Battalion relieved 1st Bn King's Own — today up to the line — from COPSE St on the right to OXFORD St on the left — Sgt Smith was wounded during relief by a stray bullet	
	9 Dec		Going very quiet — shelled a my buy on about 1300 yds — finished 4 tell company fire 920 yds — Really shot not CORPSE. Hand been at fault by the Battalion — One man wounded. Our guns shelled enemy front line — there also battalion won.	
	10 Dec		Enemy quiet — our Company Bomb Sgt Lt 2/Lt left up 1st & 2nd line to A Coy to support line — On Sniper hit one hun — our Casualties — two Casualties	
	11 Dec		Enemy quiet — Enemy aeroplanes — no Casualties	
	12 Dec		On Snipers had well sight to the lines to certain — enemy very quiet only snipy — no Casualties — 9 men wounded — bullet was a good shot. Turret he Ay thrust hinself on parapet in 3 places	
	13 Dec		Battalion relieved by 9th Rifles — Battalion went into billets about CROIX BARBÉE —	
	14 Dec		Battalion found working party of 2 officers & 200 men to put huts —	
	15 Dec		Working party as above — A stagged party paraded by Colonel &c hot hin — Orders received to relieve 9th Hampshire in the line — Major E.A. Lindsay leaves now to proceed Kingstown and Khaki with Command of Battn & Major P. Ca Macbeth	

1875 Wt. W593/826 1,000,000 4/15 J.B.C. & A. A.D.S.S./Forms/C.2118.

WAR DIARY
or
INTELLIGENCE SUMMARY

(Erase heading not required.)

Army Form C. 2118

Instructions regarding War Diaries and Intelligence Summaries are contained in F.S. Regs., Part II and the Staff Manual respectively. Title Pages will be prepared in manuscript.

Place	Date 1914	Hour	Summary of Events and Information	Remarks and references to Appendices
BIYANST	Dec 18		Major & Culleton's attacks & commands the Battalion who took up trench 31 Cent 27 B 2.1. Battalion relieved the 1st Kings own in the line from COPSE 31 to right of OXFORD RD on left. Halfway house became Quart relief. — B' Coy 10th Welsh Regt attached to inclination — left halfway & R.E. dugout. Grenay Querl — Kund Sniping — Kinches very quiet — Dugouts in the line very poor — 2/Lt Duggan badly wounded — head — left eye blown out — 1 man wounded —	
		11pm	Enemy's snipers quiet — that has been Stullen Copse Street usa Battn HQ — no answer sent — Enemy's guns seen to have received a good deal of their ammunition which that 3 were RE. — Casualties 1 Killed and 1 wounded —	
		12 midt		
		4am	Enemy quiet, our snipers bigger & officers arising to return — 2 Minie tom Chinese — left Companys (A) disposed thus Until midday today — Orders received that Battn would be relieved at night by 2nd & 4th Welch Regt & 4th Lincoln Regt.	
		2pm	Enemy snipers active and trouble guns — Battalion M.O. skilled at 12 noon — no name His stullen again during relief heavily to his by H.E. — on shell landed in yard of farm — rather things kept him on release there dug-out — a marvel he was hit — Battalion arrived in Billets about 11.30 pm at LE TOURET —	
	21 Dec		Billets poor — Dugouts for huts — Coys cleaned up and then Coffee and were deserved by all of 50 men come as per train —	
	22" Dec		Inspection of Coys by CO	

D.W. Morrow Lt Col

WAR DIARY or INTELLIGENCE SUMMARY

(Erase heading not required.)

Army Form C. 2118

Place	Date	Hour	Summary of Events and Information	Remarks and references to Appendices
LE TOURET	23rd Dec		Coys paraded for Baths — then left for Baths formed under Coy arrangements —	
	24th Dec		Remaining Coys paraded for Baths — then left for Baths formed under Coy arrangements —	
	25th Dec		Church Parade — Battalion turned to take Eucharist & Confetti etc. for Xmas —	
	26th Dec		Battalion paraded as shortly as possible to be relieved by 9.00 LG 1st Bn 1st Brigade. 5th Light Road — Inspected "Moss" — then lines at Guard tahar — orders received for Battalion to go into billets — no Brigade Reserve at RICHEBOURG ST VAAST	
	29th Dec		Battalion went to RENDEZ-VOUS N.E. LACOUTRE — entered St VAAST by Platoons — march relieved through bring Old RICHEBOURG ST VAAST — no Casualties —	
	28th Dec		A Coy left our posts toward ESTAIRES — arrangements made to furnish Whole temporarily in case of Shelling — 6 him per Coy detailed for trench relief —	
	29th Dec		Parade under Coy arrangements — inter Carriers on to posts round billets	
	30th Dec		Orders received that 6 men from 9th Kings own — 2 Coys A & B not to leave billets instantly on account of Shelling —	
	31st Dec		Battalion held over line from 9th Kings own — from FARM CORNER to HILL & COPSE on the left — no Casualties —	
				D. Wilkinson Lt Col.

56/19

7th E. Lancs:
Vol: 3
January 1916

T.W.

ad. B.W.
    8 Mch

WAR DIARY or INTELLIGENCE SUMMARY

(Erase heading not required.)

Army Form C. 2118

January.

4th Bn East Lancs Regt.

Place	Date	Hour	Summary of Events and Information	Remarks and references to Appendices
Trenches	1.1.16		Enemy Quiet. Occasional machine gun fire. Enemy replied to our gun with a few bursts. Greeting of 6 shells, 3 were blind. Hostile Working Party dispersed.	
"	2.1.16		Enemy very quiet, but their Artillery active in the morning putting about 30, 4.7" shells about WINDY CORNER. Also at 15.15 HQ shelled with HE. HQ party forced to take cover but no damage done. Our Patrol went out from the left & reported 2 ditches running parallel to our front. Ground beyond fairly dry. Wind very light. Boys worked on raising parapet improving trench.	
"	3.1.16		Usual Sniping by Enemy. His Artillery again active. HQ shelled at 11.15 a.m. with HE & Shrapnel & again at 2.30 with 3 large HE. Result no one wounded. More suffering from stiff shock. One of our patrols from the left again encountered ditches. No signs of enemy leaving the. Patrol fired on while examining ground. None wore, had to retire, went on men wounded. Weather wet, & strong wind. Confirmed continued with improvement of trenches.	
"	4.1.16		Gun Trench. Battery fired 11 rounds, fired a 4" howitzer about 3.30 p.m. It for landed in Enemys front line site retaliated with 4 rounds from powerful Bomb gun. One round nearby reached GUARDS TRENCH. This gun was located approx. One of our officers patrols again examined ditch reported that it can be crossed but not easily. Usual work on trenches. Relieved by 4th R Lancs Regt at about 4.10 p.m. Moved into Rest Billets at RICHEBOURG ST VAAST for the night.	

Capt & Adjt 4th Bn
4th Bn E Lancs Regt

WAR DIARY
or
INTELLIGENCE SUMMARY

(Erase heading not required.)

Army Form C. 2118

Place	Date	Hour	Summary of Events and Information	Remarks and references to Appendices
MERVILLE	5.1.16		The Battn moved into Billets at MERVILLE. Coys left RICHEBOURG S'VAAST at 9.15am marched to by Platoons with 200 yd intervals. L'Edwards remained behind to hand over Billets to 16" R.I.S. Fusiliers. Arrived at MERVILLE at 3.15pm. Billets good. All ranks very glad to get back to rest.	
"	6.1.16		Coys cleaned equipment relotting which needed it very badly after spell in trenches. Often parade under Coy arrangements.	
"	7.1.16		Commanding Officer inspected the Battalion at Coy Billets. Turn out very good considering the conditions under which men had been living. O's inch. new clothing as possible. Issued draft of 50 arrived.	
"	8.1.16		New draft arrived yesterday evening were inspected by CO today. Standard fairly good, several of our own men from hospital with the draft. Further issue of clothing. Parade under Coy arrangements.	
"	9.1.16		Brigade Church Parade. Battalion marched to Bdg HQ where service was held.	
"	10.1.16		Battalion commenced special programme of Coy training. Today Physical Training, Arms Drill Saluting &c. Regimental Grenadiers & Coy's Bombers also started training. Very good ground for this has been secured. Ground for other training very scarce. Men clothes repaired by Bttn Tailors.	

Wattatham(?)

WAR DIARY
or
INTELLIGENCE SUMMARY

Army Form C. 2118

Place	Date	Hour	Summary of Events and Information	Remarks and references to Appendices
MERVILLE	11.1.16		Training continued. Battn. went on a Route march, about 6½ miles. Roads very bad. Medical Officer commenced inspect the Battn. D.O. Coy also Transport inspected. Bombers carried out training. Received information that we shall move to ROBECQ tomorrow.	
ROBECQ	12.1.16		Battalion moved to ROBECQ & exchanged billets with the 3rd Coldstream Guards. Paraded at 10.15 am. Brigadier received the salute of the Battn. on Route; men marched well on bad roads. Arrived at ROBECQ at 12.45. Billets not as good as those just left. 13 Coy only one room for 4 officers	
"	13.1.16		Coy training, Arms drill, Coy drill etc carried out by all Coys	
"	14.1.16		Battalion inspected by Commanding Officer. Men's turn out very much improved. Bayonet fighting carried on in afternoon. Wired for two Armourers Staff for 13 Coys Officers. Coy Bomber comm. ed course of training. Battn. tailors woburn repaired mens equipment. Some put in very bad state.	
"	15.1.16		Battn. Route march about 8 miles, through ST VENANT & ROBECQ, left marching being marked very well. L't House attend at Bde Offices for special reconnaissance work. Bombing as usual.	
"	16.1.16		Church Parade at Battn H.Q. Bqoh Tailors repaired mens clothes. Medical Officer finished inspection of Battn.	M.A. Hadking Lt.Col

WAR DIARY
or
INTELLIGENCE=SUMMARY
(Erase heading not required.)

Army Form C. 2118

Instructions regarding War Diaries and Intelligence Summaries are contained in F. S. Regs., Part II. and the Staff Manual respectively. Title Pages will be prepared in manuscript.

Place	Date	Hour	Summary of Events and Information	Remarks and references to Appendices
ROBECQ	17.1.16		Batt paraded for Batt at CALONNE. No clean underclothing was available & the boys arrived both needed bathing & had underclothing which not at Bath. Boys carried out by taking. Bombing continued training. A Coy blankets disinfected. Hay badly needed at Lieutenants. 2nd Hebron & held. Similar a special Bombing Course at RIEZ BAILLEUL.	
"	18.1.16		Continuing Programme. Batt went on a Route march, about 9 kilos, marching much better. Special Order issued re Steel Helmets.	
"	19.1.16		Programme continued. Physical Training, Bayonet fighting, Batt drill under 2ND carried out in a field at 7th NewZealand Area Bombers continued programme. Draft of 63 men arrived	
"	20.1.16		Material not being available for Engineering. Batt went on a route march of 10½ miles through ROBECQ, GARBECQUE, ST VAAST, men marched well. Numbers were inspected by Medical Officer, no repetition. Afternoon, Men paraded for arms drill under Reg Sergt Major. Bombing continued.	
"	21.1.16		Field not available for Batt drill. Batt carried out Coy drill. Arms drill etc. In the afternoon D Coy had baths at MERVILLE. Capt G.B. Type detailed President of a F.G.C.M. The party under Lt Edwards returned from Bombing Course.	
"	22.1.16		Batt carried out field Engineering at it's own billets. Construction of fascines etc. 9/1 AC 2C Coys drew boots from Bde H.Q., these were badly needed. A lecture by the Coys. Commander was delivered at Batt H.Q. all available officers attended	

WAR DIARY or INTELLIGENCE SUMMARY

Army Form C. 2118

Place	Date	Hour	Summary of Events and Information	Remarks and references to Appendices
ROBECQ	23.1.16		Batt. attended Divine Service at TB. HQ. Received notification of Base Route march for tomorrow. Received a draft of 31. 2/Lt H.M. Dibdin joined the Batt.	
"	24.1.16		Batt. paraded for Bdy Route march at 9.30 transport attached. Staff medically inspected. A B.C coys set fatigue parties to unload the transport on arrival. Left Plogsteen. Details of HQ Coy. Moors were set aside in these area for the use of NCOs only. Priest - HQCK.	
"	25.1.16		Coys carried out training in field Engineering construction work entanglement etc. B.C Coys supplied working parties to construct rifle range (1K 26.a.3.5) Two men detailed for Traffic control at St Venant 2/Lt H.M. Webb joined the Batt. Received notification of Inspection by Brigadier.	
"	26.1.16		Batt. inspected by Brigadier. Inspection was at Coy billets. The General was pleased with the general turnout. Arms drill, but thought Transport needed a little more attention. A roll of differences from last Coy was handed to Bde.	
"	27.1.16		Coys carried out Arms drill. Kit inspection etc. M.O. inspected dentition of men in the Battn. Coys drew boots from Base HQ 2/CR Carr joined the Batt.	
"	28.1.16		Baths were allotted for today but lack of clean under-clothing caused them to be cancelled knitted Coys carried out Coy rotn drill.	O.M.Halfhat

1875 Wt. W593/826 1,000,000 4/15 J.B.C. & A. A.D.S.S./Forms/C. 2118.

WAR DIARY
or
INTELLIGENCE SUMMARY

(Erase heading not required.)

Army Form C. 2118

Instructions regarding War Diaries and Intelligence Summaries are contained in F. S. Regs., Part II. and the Staff Manual respectively. Title Pages will be prepared in manuscript.

Place	Date	Hour	Summary of Events and Information	Remarks and references to Appendices
ROBECQ	29.1.16		Batt- had Batts today. Lnol. Lea obtained charge of handwriting. Team of Regt¹ Grenadiers definitely selected.	
"	30.1.16		Church Parade at Batt- HQ. Weather colder & foggy. Service shorter than usual. Settled on uniform charge for Barbers in each Coy Viz 1/- per head. Received notification of move to the training area at ESTRÉE BLANCHE tomorrow. Sorry to have to leave in middle of present training	
SERNY	31.1.16	8·40 AM	Batt- paraded at 8·40 AM marched with the Bgde to SERNY (near ESTRÉE BLANCHE). Distance 15¾ miles. Dinner served en route, men marched well only 2 or 3 fell out. Reached new Billets at 4·30 PM. They are fair, but appreciate hills again after spending over 6 months in the flat country. 2/. Copies proceeded on a Course at Brit HQ.	

$ Co ?Woodsworth ?Lt.Col Comm
?1/6 ?Glen Regt

Army Form C. 2118

WAR DIARY for February 1916
or
INTELLIGENCE SUMMARY
(Erase heading not required.)

4th B'n East Lancs Regt

Instructions regarding War Diaries and Intelligence Summaries are contained in F.S. Regs., Part II. and the Staff Manual respectively. Title Pages will be prepared in manuscript.

Place	Date	Hour	Summary of Events and Information	Remarks and references to Appendices
ESTREE BLANCHE (SERNY)	1.2.16		Received orders that the Batt will move back to form Billets at ROBECQ. Holiday for all Ranks	
"	2.2.16		The Batt Paraded at 8.20 marched back to old billets at ROBECQ. Reached Here about 2.30. No incident worth	
ROBECQ	3.2.16		The Batt carried out Field Engineering on special ground at ROBECQ. Instructed 2 lines of attack opposite one another to perform of attack drill. Drew boots from Brigade	
"	4.2.16		Continued with Field Engineering. Received intimation that the Batt will move into the trenches about the 13th Feb.	
"	5.2.16		Carried out Field Engineering in the morning & in the afternoon football. The Coy Offrs & other detailed Offrs attended Div'l Signal Exercise. An attack scheme carried out rail scheme of signalling. FULL. Very interesting day.	
"	6.2.16		Church Parade at B'n H.Q.	
"	7.2.16		Batt went on a route march. The Batt Snipers under Lt Humphrys practiced on the range at MERVILLE. Regt Grenadiers practised under	
"	8.2.16		Butts reserved for the Batt today were not available so carried out Coy + Arm drill. All officers attended a lecture by Batt major. Subject "Attack"	

WAR DIARY or INTELLIGENCE SUMMARY

Army Form C. 2118

Instructions regarding War Diaries and Intelligence Summaries are contained in F. S. Regs., Part II. and the Staff Manual respectively. Title Pages will be prepared in manuscript.

(Erase heading not required.)

Place	Date	Hour	Summary of Events and Information	Remarks and references to Appendices
ROBECQ	9.2.16		Carried out Field Engineering, i.e. the latrine scouting etc. was very successful our mounted offs: quite clear at turning People without being directed. Parties supplied for unloading coal at MERVILLE. 2/Lt BRIGGS joined the Batt.	
"	10.2.16		Batt. practised attack drill on special ground where tr. chs. had been dug.	
"	11.2.16		Attack drill as yesterday. Batts. again not available.	
"	12.2.16		Attack drill continued with parading at night. Boots drawn from Bde HQ.	
"	13.2.16		Church Parade at Batt HQ.	
"	14.2.16		Filled in trenches marked out the Coy drill. 2/Lieut Speirs rejoined the Batt. 2/ horses also joined.	
"	15.2.16		Batt. moved to Croix Barbée to Bde reserve billets. Started about 8.30 AM arrived at 1.30 pm going into the line tomorrow.	
"	16.2.16		Remained in Billets today, are going into Trenches tomorrow.	
"	17.2.16		Took over the line from PLUM STREET to OXFORD STREET from 17th ROYAL WELCH FUSILIERS. Trenches fairly dry, C Coy on the right, B in the centre, D on the left. A in reserve. We commenced 48 hr. relief, very unsatisfactory means for work, then practically doing to the men not getting settled to the line.	

WAR DIARY
or
INTELLIGENCE SUMMARY.

(Erase heading not required.)

Army Form C. 2118.

Instructions regarding War Diaries and Intelligence Summaries are contained in F. S. Regs., Part II. and the Staff Manual respectively. Title pages will be prepared in manuscript.

Place	Date	Hour	Summary of Events and Information	Remarks and references to Appendices
In the Trenches	18.2.16		Enemy very quiet, little sniping. Own M.Gs. caught hostile working parties & fired 3,000 rounds at it. Patrol sent out from own left Coy went up to Godewal in front of Hun Coy. Another patrol went out from the right along ditch in front of the right of the line, nothing seen.	
	19.2.16		Enemy not very active. Own Artillery & T.M. by bombarded hostile line with good effect. Guns replied with rifle grenades & a few T.M. & 5·9 shells. Several snipers posts located. Guns seen with black caps for coats at POPES NOSE. Built dugout. H.e. and snotty rained raised parapet. He battn is also very thin & flares. Sand deft played on our trench from hostile line. Relieved by 7th L. Regt. Voluntary ghost parade during night, etc. Casualties last 2 days 3 killed & 8 wounded, nor were very unfortunate.	
CROIX BARBEE	20.2.16		"X" Coy Royal Scots attached to the Battn for today for instruction. They arrived at 4 p.m. One platoon sent to each Coy.	
	21.2.16 ant		Relieved 9th R. Lan. Reg in the trenches 500 sub-sector.	
	21.2.16		Enemy not very active except with MG fire. One of the battn emplacements blown in by hostile artillery. Our Artillery very active. Hostile sniper post destroyed.	
	22.2.16		Enemy again quiet, just a few 77mm shells. Sent a patrol out from own right; this worked along cart road at Irpadelle except at one house. Quiet & went further out on bringing line to front of BOIS du BIEZ. Also relieved by 4 R. Lan. Reg returned to Pillets. Casualties last two days 3 wounded.	
CROIX BARBEE	23.2.16		Inspection of rifles, kit etc. Draft of 14 received. Very poor quality.	
	24.2.16		Relieved 4 R. Lan. Reg in the same subsector. Weather very bad & roads. Patrol went from left Coy & another from	

1577 Wt. W10791/1773 500,000 1/15 D. D. & L. A.D.S.S./Forms/C. 2118.

Army Form C. 2118.

WAR DIARY
or
INTELLIGENCE SUMMARY.
(Erase heading not required.)

Instructions regarding War Diaries and Intelligence Summaries are contained in F. S. Regs., Part II. and the Staff Manual respectively. Title pages will be prepared in manuscript.

Place	Date	Hour	Summary of Events and Information	Remarks and references to Appendices
In the Line	24.2.16		POPES NOSE. He hallo. Patrol reached enemy's wire. No unusual activity	
"	25.2.16		Own Artillery very active, shelled enemy's line. Yerran rifles with Rifle grenade retalliating from they shelled PORT ARTHUR with 5.9's. A strong hostile patrol approached POPE NOSE but were dispersed	
"	26.2.16		Enemy quiet. Nothing to report. Were relieved by 4th P Lancs Reg" First task 17 killed. 2 killed + 5 wounded	
(ROTY BARRES)	27.2.16		Voluntary Brevet Parade. Game both. Rifles inspected etc. 17th Royal Scots finished course dept He Batt	
In the Line	28.2.16		Relieved 4/5 Lancs Reg" in He trenches as before. Weather wet. 2 men wounded 9014 in "X" Coy 18" H.L.I joined Batt" for instruction	
"	29.2.16		We again shelled enemy's line. He replied with minenwerfen + rifle grenades. Enemy's parapet very badly damaged. Casualties last few days. 2 killed 3 wounded	

March 1916

Army Form C. 2118.

WAR DIARY
or
INTELLIGENCE SUMMARY.
(Erase heading not required.)

4th East Lancs Regt.

Instructions regarding War Diaries and Intelligence Summaries are contained in F. S. Regs., Part II. and the Staff Manual respectively. Title pages will be prepared in manuscript.

Place	Date	Hour	Summary of Events and Information	Remarks and references to Appendices
R. He TRENCHES	2.3.16		He Batt in conjunction with artillery fired bursts of rifle fire at enemy's parapet. Does not seem to have had much effect. Germans intermittently replying nearly all night. Relief appears to have taken place yesterday in their trenches tonight. He has been today more difficult than usual. Weather much warmer. He 7th R Lanc Reg relieved He Batt - thought m.g. came back into Billets. 1 man wounded	
CROIX BARBEES	3.3.16		Cleaning up. 13 Coy lad Platts. battery of interest happened	
"	4.3.16		Received information that in future this will be 4 day reliefs. Next battn system expect to have next tour work done Coys will get to know them for next battle. Relieved 7th R Lancs Regt in the line tonight	
R. He Trenches	4.3.16		Weather very cold, snowing nearly all day. Enemy very quiet as a result battery of interest supplied large working party for REs	
"	5.3.16		Quiet. Better day for observation. Good deal of perforation gained from steady of hostile fire. new OP in the Rue du Bois. Our patrols very active.	
"	6.3.16		Enemy quiet except in reply to our heavy artillery fire. A Patrol tried to cut off an enemy's listening post but found nobody in the sap 17 usually occupied. Germans are working very hard now have more wire than they have. Draft of 29 joined. Rather better than the last few drafts	

1577 Wt. W10791/1773 500,000 1/15 D. D. & L. A.D.S.S./Forms/C. 2118.

WAR DIARY or INTELLIGENCE SUMMARY

Army Form C. 2118.

(Erase heading not required.)

Instructions regarding War Diaries and Intelligence Summaries are contained in F. S. Regs., Part II. and the Staff Manual respectively. Title pages will be prepared in manuscript.

Place	Date	Hour	Summary of Events and Information	Remarks and references to Appendices
In the Trenches	7.3.16		The 18th H.L.I. moved out of the line this morning early. The weather again very bad. Heavy snow, trenches very inclement. Enemy fairly quiet. Were relieved by 4th P. Loves. Regt. Very lucky in these last few days in line only 1 casualty altogether. 2/Lt Hobson & 2/Lt Braswell went sick.	
CROIX BARBEE	8.3.16		Carried out S-o-the Helmet drill etc. Nothing to report	
" "	9.3.16		Coy's Battics at Croix Barbee Baths. Very convenient to have baths so near the line. Nothing to report.	
" "	10.3.16		Nothing to report.	
" "	11.3.16		Carried out usual drill under Coy arrangements. Relieved the 4th P. Loves Regt in the line. Enemy much less active especially with M.Gs.	
In the Trenches	12.3.16		Nothing important. The enemy still active. Received information that we shall be relieved tomorrow. Glad to be relieved after a rather long spell. Casualties last 2 days; 1 killed 1 wounded 2/Lt Boswell rejoined the Batt.	

1577 Wt W10791/1773 500,000 1/15 D. D. & L. A.D.S.S./Forms/C. 2118.

Army Form C. 2118.

WAR DIARY
or
INTELLIGENCE SUMMARY

(Erase heading not required.)

Instructions regarding War Diaries and Intelligence Summaries are contained in F. S. Regs., Part II. and the Staff Manual respectively. Title Pages will be prepared in manuscript.

Place	Date	Hour	Summary of Events and Information	Remarks and references to Appendices
In the Trenches	13.3.16		Enemy's Artillery very active today especially on S Coy Communicator. Some B' shells were fired on PORT ARTHUR no damage. Casualties. Nil. The Batt. was relieved by 9th Welsh Regt. went back to its Billets at CROIX BARBEÉ. The whole Brigade was relieved.	
MERVILLE	14.3.16		The Batt. moved back into Billets at MERVILLE for 8 day rest. Left CROIX BARBEÉ at 9.0 a.m. + arrived about 12.30 p.m. not hostel [hustled] will but roads were very bad. Billets very comfortable.	
do	15.3.16		Coys carried out arm drill etc. Very little ground for training. Bombing ground passed known	
do	16.3.16		Found coal fatigue continued drill. 2/ Cardwell rejoined the Batt. Commenced re-inoculating all ranks	
do	17.3.16		Still as usual. Bombers attend short course at RIEZ BAILLEUL	
do	18.3.16		Church Parade cancelled owing to ... of Major Edward Hunt Corps Commander will inspect Batt. to-morrow	G.W.H...

2449 Wt. W14957/M90 750,000 1/16 J.B.C. & A. Forms/C.2118/12.

WAR DIARY
or
INTELLIGENCE SUMMARY

(Erase heading not required.)

Army Form C. 2118.

Instructions regarding War Diaries and Intelligence Summaries are contained in F. S. Regs., Part II. and the Staff Manual respectively. Title Pages will be prepared in manuscript.

Place	Date	Hour	Summary of Events and Information	Remarks and references to Appendices
MERVILLE	19.3.16		The Batt. inspected by Corps Commander General Haking. Turn out was good tho' one clothing was available. It would have been much better. Inspection held in B Coy's field	
do	20.3.16		Inoculation continued. Ordinary drill rapid wiring carried on. Leave re-opened for the Batt.	
do	21.3.16		Batt. paraded as usual for Coy drill. Physical drill etc	
do	22.3.16		Ordinary drill carried on by the Batt. Received instructions to hear tomorrow into form Brigade Reserve at CROIX BARBEE.	
do	23.3.16		Batt moved off from MERVILLE at 9.15 a.m. – arrived at CROIX BARBEE at 12.30 p.m. Excellent day for a march, cold day.	
CROIX BARBEE	24.3.16		Two Coy's had Baths at CROIX BARBEE Baths. Inoculation continued nothing of interest	

WAR DIARY or INTELLIGENCE SUMMARY

Army Form C. 2118.

(Erase heading not required.)

Instructions regarding War Diaries and Intelligence Summaries are contained in F. S. Regs., Part II. and the Staff Manual respectively. Title Pages will be prepared in manuscript.

Place	Date	Hour	Summary of Events and Information	Remarks and references to Appendices
Croix Barbée	25.3.16		Baths continued. Working Parties found to revet P.E.'s, to sandbag & repair All tracks kept last. too much a good deal beaten out of the trenches this week. They are in 2/ Ragusay round Hd Bn.	
do	26.3.16		No Church Parade owing to proximity to the line. Working Parties of 200 m found.	
do	27.3.16		Small working Party found early this morning. Relieved 4th P Lancs Regt in the line tonight. Saw portion of line as before. 4th P Lancs Regt reports enemy very active indeed. 3 wounded last 3 days.	
In the trenches	28.3.16		Very quiet day. Think the Hun to have been a relief to settle down. Nothing to report.	
do	29.3.16		Weather beautiful. Enemy quiet except for a little shelling.	
do	30.3.16		Nothing of interest. This is the quietest time the Battn has ever had in the line	
do	31.3.16		Nothing to report. The 4th P Lancs Regt relieved the Battn tonight. Returned to Billets at Croix Barbée. Only 1 man wounded in the last 4 days. Also only 1 Officer & 8 Other ranks Commanding 7th = E. Lance R.	C Matheson a/ Major

WAR DIARY
or
INTELLIGENCE SUMMARY

Army Form C. 2118.

4th (S) Batt. R Lanc Reg.

XIX

No. 6

April 1916

G.W
5 wheels

Instructions regarding War Diaries and Intelligence Summaries are contained in F.S. Regs., Part II. and the Staff Manual respectively. Title Pages will be prepared in manuscript.

Place	Date	Hour	Summary of Events and Information	Remarks and references to Appendices
CROIX BARBEE	1.4.16		Nothing of Interest. Batt. bathed	
"	2.4.16		Continued baths for the Batt. Nothing of interest to report	
"	3.4.16		Parades, usual Coy arrangements. Nothing to report	
R. He Tuesdi	4.4.16		Relieved 4th P. Lan. Reg. in the Trenches tonight. Found the enemy much more active.	
"	5.4.16		Enemy fairly quiet except for some shelling. Nothing to report. 1 man wounded	
"	6.4.16		Quiet day. Port Arthur redr. heavily shelled. No damage. 1 killed. 3 wounded	
"	7.4.16		Enemy very quiet indeed. Seemingly a shot fired during the day. He appears to be working very hard on his line, probably taking advantage of fine weather. 1 man wounded	
"	8.4.16		Our Aeroplanes reported this morning that the enemy had placed planks, about 6 ft apart across all their support and reserve trench. In case they should mean an attack our relief by the 4th P Lan Reg tonight has been altered to 1.15 AM tomorrow. One man wounded	
CROIX BARBET	9.4.16		Nothing happened yesterday or early this morning. Relief by 4th P Lan. Reg. carried out	

Army Form C. 2118.

WAR DIARY
or
INTELLIGENCE SUMMARY
(Erase heading not required.)

Instructions regarding War Diaries and Intelligence Summaries are contained in F. S. Regs., Part II. and the Staff Manual respectively. Title Pages will be prepared in manuscript.

Place	Date	Hour	Summary of Events and Information	Remarks and references to Appendices
CROIX BARBEE	10.4.16		Batt- Battn today hotting of portrait	
"	11.4.16		Battn continued. Several working parties supplied to R.E.	
"	12.4.16		Parade, under Coy arrangmt- Nothing to report	
"	13.4.16		Relieved the 4th Plam Reg in the line tonight. Received notification that we shall go back into G.H.Q. Reserve near ESTREE BLANCHE. Casualties 1 killed 2 wounded	
In the trenches	14.4.16		Enemy very quiet during the day but very jumpy at night as if feared attack	
"	15.4.16		Nothing to report Hostile Artillery active	
"	16.4.16		Still very quiet. Getting nearly to snow. Improved weather has allowed a good deal of work to be done on the line. The incoming Division should be very comfortable 8 0 p.m. Were relieved by the 18" Inf. I. This is the Batt- that are to run for instruction a few months ago. We moved into Billets at LA GORGUE tonight. Weather very wet. Billets good. Casualties today 1 wounded	

WAR DIARY
or
INTELLIGENCE SUMMARY

(Erase heading not required.)

Army Form C. 2118.

Instructions regarding War Diaries and Intelligence Summaries are contained in F. S. Regs., Part II. and the Staff Manual respectively. Title Pages will be prepared in manuscript.

Place	Date	Hour	Summary of Events and Information	Remarks and references to Appendices
LA GORGUE	17.4.16		The Batt- moved into its form Billets at ROBECQ. All ranks very glad to be out of the Line, for, but for a rest, Weather has improved today, the roads will	
ROBECQ	18.4.16		Reviewing in three Billets for today to give men a rest. Transport has been cut down to 4 extra GS Wagons. Have had to take some things at MERVILLE, managed to Batt nearby all the Batt at CALONNE today.	
RELY	19.4.16		The Batt- marched for ROBECQ today. Trouble through lack of Transport. Some stores had been left behind. Will have to be brought along tomorrow. Batt- fitted out with steel helmets to wear them. Billets poor.	
	20.4.16		Commenced training through programme laid down of progressive training from Platoon to Divisional.	
	21.4.16		Platoon training continued. Very difficult to deal with sale of spirits in the village. Brandy etc. sold ½ way slept. As village is outside Army Area.	
	22.4.16		Platoon training continued. Weather very wet. 2/ Russell jounal the Batt- orders us C.O.	

WAR DIARY
or
INTELLIGENCE=SUMMARY

(Erase heading not required.)

Army Form C. 2118.

Place	Date	Hour	Summary of Events and Information	Remarks and references to Appendices
RELY	23.4.16		Batt- Outfitted Brigade Church Parade. No training today.	
	24.4.16		Commenced Coy Training. Men carried out a training run 5 miles from Billets before a good dust [ ] parading for the run. The weather is very hot. Stout helmets have to be worn.	
	25.4.16		Owing to the sudden hot weather spirits can be obtained. Ratts but drunk from the usual Special precaution laid down in Divn Transport Brigade. Coy Training continued.	
	26.4.16		Commenced Batt- Training. The Div also carried out a special area Boxing contest held in the barrier. Half of Boxers of this Batt- were on leave who entries were got in. Hooper Ratts pour refreshiter of the Batt-	
	27.4.16		Batt- Training continued	
	28.4.16		Commenced Brigade Training. Storing artcle of this training on the training area. Same tent fire caches to the ground.	

Army Form C. 2118.

WAR DIARY
or
INTELLIGENCE SUMMARY
(Erase heading not required.)

Instructions regarding War Diaries and Intelligence Summaries are contained in F. S. Regs., Part II. and the Staff Manual respectively. Title Pages will be prepared in manuscript.

Place	Date	Hour	Summary of Events and Information	Remarks and references to Appendices
RELY	29.4.16		Brigade training continued	[illegible]
"	30.4.16		Batt carried out Brigade night schm.	Reinforcement /Lt & 29 4th Gurkhas Reg

2449 Wt. W14957/M90 750,000 1/16 J.B.C. & A. Forms/C.2118/12.

WAR DIARY or INTELLIGENCE SUMMARY

Army Form C. 2118.

XIX Vol 7

4th Lancs Regt May 1916

Place	Date	Hour	Summary of Events and Information	Remarks and references to Appendices
RELY	1.5.16		Batt returned from night scheme about 4.0 am this morning. No further drills in training today	T.W Lieutenant
"	2.5.16		Batt entrained "attack" training at OUDEN	
"	3.5.16		Batt had Battle at ESTREE BLANCHE. There were 16 Bent or lame had in Lames humidity. Platoon drill also carried out	
"	4.5.16		Commenced Coy training near EUHEM. Pleased to learn that we attain to Brett's and might + do not provide transport. Comdr in Chief watched the Operation	
"	5.5.16		Rest Scheme of training continued, included Village fighting today	
"	6.5.16		Day occupied to clearing Billets, overhauling Kit etc. We are ordered that the Div proceeds to new stations by train to new area	
"	7.5.16		The Batt marched off at 9.00 am entrained at LILLERS at 12 noon. Detrained at LONGEAU near AMIENS. Marched 10½ miles to S VAST arriving at 1.30 am on 8.5.16. Troops tired after long trek. Billets very fair. Accommodation for Officers poor	

Army Form C. 2118.

WAR DIARY
or
INTELLIGENCE SUMMARY
(Erase heading not required.)

Instructions regarding War Diaries and Intelligence Summaries are contained in F. S. Regs., Part II. and the Staff Manual respectively. Title Pages will be prepared in manuscript.

Place	Date	Hour	Summary of Events and Information	Remarks and references to Appendices
GHYVAST	9.5.16		Continued training under Coy arrangements	
"	10.5.16		Training as yesterday	
"	11.5.16		Commanding Officer inspected the Batt. Men looked very much smarter for their recent tour in the trenches. Afternoon - drill under Coy arrangements	
"	12.5.16 13.5.16		Training continued under Coy arrangements	
"	14.5.16		Batt. attended Brigade Church Parade	
"	15.6.16		Training continued. Supplied a fatigue party for R.E. 2/Lt Colquhoun detailed as Brigade Liaison Officer.	
"	16.5.16		Training continued including range taking. 2/Lts Wilkie, Pfaffets (?) joined the Batt.	
"	17.5.16		Batt. paraded for Coy attack & special training area	

2449 Wt. W14957/M90 750,000 1/16 J.B.C. & A. Forms/C.2118/12.

Army Form C. 2118.

WAR DIARY
or
INTELLIGENCE SUMMARY
(Erase heading not required.)

Instructions regarding War Diaries and Intelligence Summaries are contained in F. S. Regs., Part II. and the Staff Manual respectively. Title Pages will be prepared in manuscript.

Place	Date	Hour	Summary of Events and Information	Remarks and references to Appendices
ST VAST	18.5.16 19.5.16 20.5.16		Batt continued training in training area at Billets.	
	21.5.16		Batt attended Brigade Church Parade.	
	22.5.16		Batt continued training	
	23.5.16		Batt carried out a special Scheme of proceeding to & death position of troops in the event of an advance. Signalling & telephones were practised.	
	24.5.16		Batt Training continued	
	25.5.16		Cleaning up Billets. Received notification that the Batt would have to move to FRECHENCOURT & a route for ALBERT where they will be billeted on arrival. Finally Batt confortes in Billets Spots received & 1st Phyn, & 2nd Phyn.	
	26.5.16		Batt move to FRECHENCOURT - there Billeted in billets for the night. Billets excellent.	

WAR DIARY or INTELLIGENCE SUMMARY

Army Form C. 2118.

Place	Date	Hour	Summary of Events and Information	Remarks and references to Appendices
FRECHENCOURT 27.5.16			Batt. moved to ALBERT. Men bivouaced in a valley close to ALBERT. Fortunately weather kept fine. Butts returned for first Sports meeting were satisfactory	
ALBERT	28.5.16 29.5.16 30.5.16 31.5.16		Batt. supplied digging parties each day. Digging not much liked than digging to the front of the line we have occupied previously of Thiepval toward the Bosch on the 29th inst.	

WAR DIARY
or
INTELLIGENCE SUMMARY

(Erase heading not required.)

Army Form C. 2118.

7. E. Lane 79

June VOL 8

Place	Date	Hour	Summary of Events and Information	Remarks and references to Appendices
ALBERT	1/6/16		Coys continued digging. The work is in connection with the contemplated offensive.	
"	2/6/16		Digging trenches continued. Notified that Batt will return to St VAST & CHAUSSÉE tomorrow, remaining one night en route at FRECHENCOURT	
FRECHENCOURT	3/6/16		Battalion moved away from camp at ALBERT & arrived at FRECHENCOURT at 12.0 noon Billets rather crowded. Col Goodwyn left for leave. Major OMPEN Command the Batt	
ST VAST & CHAUSSÉE	4/6/16		Battalion moved into the former billets at St VAST & CHAUSSÉE, nothing of interest	
do	5/6/16		Battalion allotted Batts at LA CHAUSSÉE - St SAEUR Road. Not a division as Batts were in the op. Received notification that rations very soft. Pte A SHEA no.12637 has been awarded 35/- for having under fire an no.16943 L/Cpl SMITH received the distinction for heroic also no.16943 L/Cpl SMITH received the distinction for bravery under fire while with the Batt.	ACFB Summary 3/4

WAR DIARY
or
INTELLIGENCE SUMMARY
(Erase heading not required.)

Army Form C. 2118.

Place	Date	Hour	Summary of Events and Information	Remarks and references to Appendices
ST VAST (L CHAUSSEE)	6.6.16		Battalion continued the Batting today.	
FLESSELLES	4.6.16		Moved into new Billets at FLESSELLES today. Bathn carried out practice attack with the 4th R Lanc. Reg. attached to this Batt. for discipline. Major ORPEN remained at ST VAST as Salvage Officer. Major TYSER commands the Batt.	
"	8.6.16		Battalion continued training today carried out practice attack with the remainder of the Brigade. This attack was similar to one the Brigade may be called upon to make in the coming offensive.	
"	9.6.16		Continued training on same lines as above.	
"	10.6.16		Continued training.	
"	11.6.16		Church Parade ordered, but cancelled.	
"	12.6.16		Route march, practice digging of trenches.	

WAR DIARY
or
INTELLIGENCE SUMMARY
(Erase heading not required.)

Army Form C. 2118.

Instructions regarding War Diaries and Intelligence Summaries are contained in F. S. Regs., Part II. and the Staff Manual respectively. Title Pages will be prepared in manuscript.

Place	Date	Hour	Summary of Events and Information	Remarks and references to Appendices
FLESSELLES	13.6.16		Training continued	
"	14.6.16		Training continued	
	15.6.16		Battalion Route March. Received notification that six staff must ride new bicycles tomorrow	
MOLLIENS au BOIS	16.6.16		Battalion marched into new billets at MOLLIENS au BOIS. Billets very bad. Officers ? have very crowded	
	17.6.16		Battalion bathed at BEHENCOURT Baths	
	18.6.16		Brigade Church Parade. Col. Goodwyn returned from leave resumed command of the Battalion. Major H.T. Jones joined the Battalion & posted 2nd in Command	
	19.6.16		Continued Training	

WAR DIARY
or
INTELLIGENCE SUMMARY

(Erase heading not required.)

Army Form C. 2118.

Instructions regarding War Diaries and Intelligence Summaries are contained in F. S. Regs., Part II. and the Staff Manual respectively. Title Pages will be prepared in manuscript.

Place	Date	Hour	Summary of Events and Information	Remarks and references to Appendices
MAILLENS au BOIS	20.6.16		Continued training	
"	21.6.16		Training continued	
"	22.6.16		Training continued	
"	23.6.16		Battalion carried out Wood fighting & Route march	
"	24.6.16		Wood fighting practice continued. Officers attended Trench mortar demonstration	
"	25.6.16		Brigade Church Parade	
"	26.6.16		Battalion prepared to move, in connection with the Grand Offensive	
BAIZEUX	27.6.16		Battalion moved into Bivouacs at BAIZEUX WOOD	
HENENCOURT	28.6.16		Battalion moved into camp at HENENCOURT WOOD	
"	29.6.16		Battalion remained at HENENCOURT WOOD Intermediate	
"	30.6.16		Battalion moved up to the USNA - TARA Line in preparation of the attack tomorrow	

Army Form C. 2118.

WAR DIARY
or
INTELLIGENCE SUMMARY

(Erase heading not required.)

Instructions regarding War Diaries and Intelligence Summaries are contained in F. S. Regs., Part II. and the Staff Manual respectively. Title Pages will be prepared in manuscript.

Place	Date	Hour	Summary of Events and Information	Remarks and references to Appendices
HENENCOURT	30.6.16		Major H.L. Jew & 50% of Batt Officers left behind. Lowth Transport. These will be used to replace casualties who may get knocked forward to the attack.	

56th Inf.Bde.
19th Div.

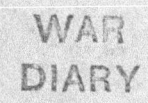

7th BATTN. THE EAST LANCASHIRE REGIMENT.

J U L Y

1 9 1 6

Attached:

Appendices I, II,
III & IV.

	Sent		Service.	Date
	At ......m.			From
	To			
	By	(Signature of "Franking Officer.")		By

TO: Hdqtrs. 56th Infy Brigade

Sender's Number.	Day of Month	In reply to Number	AAA
B61	4 8 16	SC469E	

Reference application for War Diary
attached please furnish copy for
month of July

H.Q. 19 Division.

Forwarded

4. 8. 16.   J. Norby B: Gen?
Commandg 56th Inf. Bde.

From: J. EASTLAKE Rgt
Place:
Time:

The above may be forwarded as now corrected. (Z) H. Blythe Lt
Censor.   Signature of Addresser or person authorised to telegraph in his name.
* This line should be erased if not required.

(4179) Wt. W14042—M 14. 300,000 Pads. 12/15 Sir J. C. & S

"A" Form.
MESSAGES AND SIGNALS.
INTELLIGENCE SUMMARY
(Erase heading not required.)

Army Form C. 2118.

19 5/6/19 — 7. East Leues — Vol 9

9.W
17 inst

Place	Date	Hour	Summary of Events and Information	Remarks and references to Appendices
ALBERT.	1.7.16		The Batt. remained in Intermediate Line until 7.30 A.M. (Zero Hour) when in accordance with instructions it moved forward to the UZNA TARA Line replying part of 8th Division that had attacked battle Sunday 7.30 A.M. Operations having progressed successfully the Brigade was ordered to attack but remained in reserve in the vicinity of UZNA-TARA line until 9 P.M. When it returned to Bivouacs in Railway Cutting at ALBERT	
	2.7.16		The Batt. remained in Railway Cutting all day with the exception of 2 Companies (C & D) & two Sections of Regimental Bombers who proceeded to BECOURT WOOD & assisted in the attack on LA BOISELLE in conjunction with the 101st Brigade. Captain House was in Supreme Command. Lt. LOWE Command of D Coy & Lt EDWARDES in charge of Regimental Bombers. The party made a bombing attack on HELIGOLAND REDOUBT in conjunction with the main attack. Operations were very successfully carried out with few casualties. The party was congratulated by the Brigadier of 101st Brigade and its excellent work.	Reference operations see appx 1
		3 P.M	B Coy was detailed to proceed to UZNA TARA line & act as carrying party.	See appx 11 Arthur L de Vee Lt Colonel

WAR DIARY or **INTELLIGENCE SUMMARY**

Army Form C. 2118.

Place	Date	Hour	Summary of Events and Information	Remarks and references to Appendices
ALBERT	3/7/16		The Batt. together with the remainder of the Brigade moved at 3 AM to the USNA TARA line & remained in this position in reserve to be called up.	
		all day	C, D & B Coys & section of Reginald Bombers opposed the Batt.	
	4/7/16		The Batt. still in the USNA TARA line. Moved into early captured trenches at LA BOISSELLE relieving the 7th Royal Lanc Rgt.	
	5/7/16		The Batt. examined entered German front line X15C24 – X14 D58 – X14 D38 by bombing up communication trenches (92–24, 33–58, 95–38)	Ref LA BOISSELLE Map 1/5000
			37th Brigade operated on the left, 23rd Div on the right attack was preceded by heavy bombardment & this attention operation commenced succeeded by a heavy bombardment of 1 hrs duration the left of the right being gained its objective on the left. The Batt being on the left had to fall back to its original line.	
		at 2 p.m	The Batt. Suffered severely from fire it had & but had felt no original line. Held up by heavy machine gun's fire. Casualties were as follows Officers 4 killed 6 wounded ORs 31 killed 49 wounded 7 missing.	
	6/7/16		The Batt. continued the attack with the same objective as yesterday with the addition that it was relieved & put in front with the 58th Brigade on its right. Who had relieved the 69th Brigade (23rd Div.) This was to be carried out this latter line 96–33–72–92–49 It was ordered that this line should be held at all cost.	

H. Blythe Lt. Col.
Ret. Adjt.

WAR DIARY or INTELLIGENCE SUMMARY

Army Form C. 2118.

Place	Date	Hour	Summary of Events and Information	Remarks and references to Appendices
ALBERT	6/7/16		Received an order that the contemplated general advance under the Secretly commenced formes operations commenced at nightfall and the objective occupied by 6 AM on the 7th July after very severe fighting. Casualties were as follows. Officers 1 Maury Believe killed 1 wounded. O.R.'s 6 killed 40 wounded	
	7/7/16		The Batt. was relieved by the 7th Royal West Kent Regt at 8AM & proceeded into billets at ALBERT	
	8/7/16		The Batt. remained in present billets until 6 P.M. when it moved up into the trenches recently occupied on the 6th at LA BOISSELLE. Shelling very heavy throughout the right.	
MILLENCOURT	9/7/16		Heavy throughout the right. Shelling very heavy throughout the day. Relieved at 11 P.M. by the 13th K.R.R. & moved back to billets at MILLENCOURT	
HENENCOURT WOOD	10/7/16		The Batt: moved with its former encampment at HENENCOURT WOOD at 3 P.M.	
	11/7/16		The Batt. spent the day cleaning up.	

H.B. Taylor Lt Col
Act/O.C.

Army Form C. 2118.

WAR DIARY
or
INTELLIGENCE SUMMARY

(Erase heading not required.)

Instructions regarding War Diaries and Intelligence Summaries are contained in F. S. Regs., Part II. and the Staff Manual respectively. Title Pages will be prepared in manuscript.

Place	Date	Hour	Summary of Events and Information	Remarks and references to Appendices
HENENCOURT WOOD	12/7/16		The Batt. employed in training	
	13/7/16		The Batt. was inspected by the Corps Commander who expressed his appreciation of the work of the Brigade	
	14/7/16		Major TORRIE 2nd Life Guards took over command of the Batt.	
	15/7/16		The Batt. employed in training	
	18/7/16			
	19/7/16	7pm	The Batt. moved off	
BAZENTIN-LE-PETIT WOOD	20/7/16	12.0AM	On relief of the 1st Inniskilling Regt on the Northern & Western fringes of BAZENTIN-LE-PETIT WOOD was complete	
	21/7/16		The Battalion were employed in digging a trench line in the position taken over by us on the 20th inst. 4 Enemy machine guns were found in the wood & returned to the depot. Disposition of Batt. is as shewn on attached reprints. Sketch. Orders for night attack by the 13th on the night 22/23rd were received. Battalion operation Orders issued and attached	See app. III See app. IV [signature] act adjt.

2449 Wt. W4957/M90 750,000 1/16 J.B.C. & A. Forms/C.2118/12.

WAR DIARY or INTELLIGENCE SUMMARY

Army Form C. 2118.

Place	Date	Hour	Summary of Events and Information	Remarks and references to Appendices
BAZENTIN -LE- PETIT	22/23 July 1916	11 p.m.	Instructions as to Brigade Objectives in attack altered. Hour do will effect action to be taken by the Battalion	
		2 A.M.	"A" Company was sent forward to fill gap between 7th North Lancashires and Camerons	
		2.8 A.M.	Remainder of Batt. was moved to Northern Edge of BAZENTIN-LE-PETIT Village to support attack of South Lancashires on our right. Their attack having been unsuccessful & the situation on the right of our Brigade being considerably in the air as the South Lancashires held a firm line running thrown back it was decided to withdraw again to our original Trenches North & East from BAZENTIN-LE-PETIT to withdraw being impractical any further attempt to attack being impractical	
	23/7/16 1/2 noon		"A" Company was eventually withdrawn to our own line by midday having been relieved by a similar party of the Camerons	
		8 p.m.	The Batt. moved to a position in Divisional Reserve in Sq. X.23.b.	
Sq. X 23.b.	24/7/16 July 1916		The Batt. was employed in digging in on the position in Sq. X.23.b. Various working parties [?]	

WAR DIARY
or
INTELLIGENCE SUMMARY

Army Form C. 2118.

(Erase heading not required.)

Place	Date	Hour	Summary of Events and Information	Remarks and references to Appendices
Sq X 23.6.	24/29 July 1916		Parties were detailed by Brigade during this period.	
BECOURT	30/7/16		The Battalion moved to BECOURT WOOD, attached temporarily to 38th Brigade	
FRANVILLERS	31/7/16		The Battalion marched to billets at FRANVILLERS	
			Total Casualties for period 19th – 31st July 1916 :–	
			Officers. 1 wounded	
			O R's 37 Killed	
			88 wounded	
			1 Died of wounds	
			1 Missing	
			1 Missing believed killed	
			3 Gassed	
			1 Shell Shock	

HRDoyle Lt Col adjt.
for lt col Commanding
7th Batt. East Lanc Regt

[Stamp: ORDERLY ROOM 1 AUG 1916 EAST LANC'S REGT]

APPENDICES

I, II, III & IV.

App. I

Report on the action.

"C" two Coys ("C" & "D") of Reg.t Sedans during a period of quiet from 12 noon July 3rd till 3 am July 4th 1916. Assisted by helpful Reg.t Bombers. Ref: Map 57.D. S.E.

About 12 noon July 3rd these two Coys having taken over 2600 yards to "C" Coy's right through BECOURT WOOD down communication Trenches to the old British front line to a point about X 26 B 4.7. At this point the trench ran Horses to waggons, and 2 relieving works informing this. A narrow communication trench, nearly dug, (joining up the old British & old German front line, was similar, traffic blocked in several places. At this point the enemy opened a heavy barrage of what appears to be 4.2.9 (? shrapnel at H.Q.) on the communication trench, sufficient to try his two Coys. This lasted intermittently for two hours, and eventually the trenches were clear of over half sufficient to enable his two Cos to concentrate into their trench at point X 26.B.88: this was about 6.30 p.m.

By 7 p.m. "D" Coy which was detailed to clear the German support line was in the position at X 27 A 28, "C" Coy in position at X 26 B 8.9. The Reg.t Bombers were at the front of "C" Coy – both parties numbered at 7.20 p.m.

"D" Coy commanded by Lieut. ht. Lowe, started to pt. X 21, C 3.6 without much of position being time "C" Coy moved along to 21. C. 2.1/ having driven (with no losses) [detachment and Machine Gun.

The Reg.ts Bombers were Lieut. P.E. Edwards cleared from X 20 R 7.0. to X 20 R 9.3. in which further they captured 5 prisoners & accounted for approximately the same number - relieving at the same time some wounded of the Northumberland Fusiliers and R.y. of Scots (34th Div.) who were prisoners in the deep dug out.

The Reg.ts Bombers then joined "C" Coy at 21. C. 2.6 moving with a platoon of that Coy round by

"C" Coy pushed along the old German front line, bombing most of the way, to X.20.B.43 at which point the Germans made up a somewhat line back to X.20.B.8c. Half "C" coy followed them back up at X.20.B.6, the enemy block & 2 M.G.s. The Germans Bn. contained a bomb & fire trench towards the CENTER at X.20.C.A.83 until they met a party of 9 CHESHIRE REGT. This half then returned & went up the communication trench to where the remainder of the Coy was located. Parties of this were sent out to establish communication & succeeded in their bringing out the M.G. & fairly late in were delivered to X.20.B.88. Block was established by "C" Coy M.G.76. A party was worked up German Sp.Ft. line to X.21.A.4.t where "C" Coy carried & at "R" "S" Coy where had made good along the main German support in that line to this had to be taken 17 men prisoners & accounted for will be many.

southwards to point X.20.D.7.8. and joining the remainder of "C" Coy at X.20.B.9.2. The enemy with M.G. was still located in the N.E. corner of LA BOISELLE. The party attempted to about to "the morning of "C" Coy" and about and could B Company attack X.21.C.23 & accessed by a considerable number to the dug-out. Here (X.21.C.29) they were joined by a desperate of "S" Coy who captured "X" Coy and pushed towards SCOTS REDOUBT 21 central. "X" Coy then had captured 6 prisoners & were met by with considerable opposition.

Lieut. Townsend, at X.2.C.28 sent word to Lieut. Lane [?] representatives to push on to SCOTS REDOUBT which he found taken. 12.55 P.M. Div. in SAUSAGE VALLEY.

"S" Coy temporarily blocked the main German support line about X.21.C.4.9 & set out a party to connect up with the garrison in SCOTS REDOUBT. This was done.

this position was reached by 9.30 a.m. The enemy held a [strong?] dug out that required an organised [assault?] to start [clearing?] block.

About 9 a.m. a July 30 a party was sent to [assist?] an attack by the 9th Cheshires who were seen to be in a difficulty at X.20.C.3.2 but they did not appear to need assistance.

In the course of [clearing?] dugouts X Coy captured 22 more prisoners, bringing the total to 58.

Complete connection was obtained on the flanks, in to the old German [front?] and support lines. The two Coys Coys relieved on the morning of July 4th at about 3 a.m. by 9th YORKSHIRE REGT.

The work of X Coy thus achieved the relief of SCOTS REDOUBT where the garrison had been almost cut off (?) for some 48 hours - more without food than tea.

Our total casualties were 2 Officers + 114 [wounded?].

How Howe
Capt Gen
O.C. "C" Coy, 7th Lincolns Regt

July 11/5/1916.

Appendix 11

Copy Letter sent to G.O.C. 56th Infy Bde
by G.O.C. 101st Infy Bde. July 1916.

Will you please express to the Officer Commanding the Battalion of the EAST LANCASHIRE REGIMENT whose two Companies were placed under my command last Sunday & Monday my appreciation of the Excellent work done in clearing two long lines of GERMAN trenches of all the enemy remaining in them which greatly facilitated the holding of the forward line. It was dangerous and difficult work requiring much organisation and was very ably carried out by all ranks; the energy & zeal displayed by the Officers was beyond all praise.

Appendix III
56th Infantry Brigade

D#22   2/7/6
                                                    11.25 AM
My experience on the 3rd July (Please acknowledge)

Company, holding trench in a sunken appear
West sheet from the line (S26 a1) to
BAZENTIN LE PETIT and NORTH Road (S26 b)
in touch with 20th NTLI (1st by 15th) on left
and 7th with Leicesters Regt on right.

The telephone to the telephone was cut up my
Batt + HQ would come to electrically
sought to ascertain the whereabouts
to further cases + communication.

It is reported that the company was by no
means found ... by direction of the relief to their
... to strengthen the slides.

...

...

...

2 companies ...

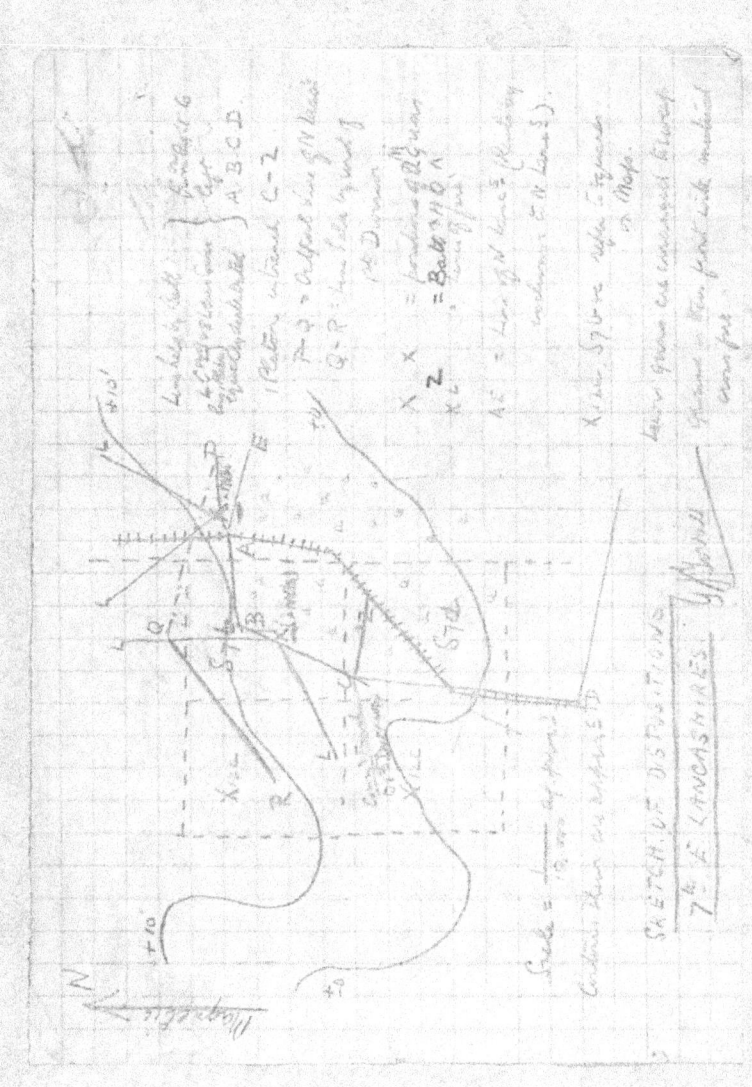

Appendix IV   Copy No.

Secret   7th East Lancashire Regt. Operation Order No 1

Reference Map: Area of MARTINPUICH 1/20,000   31.7.16

1. The Brigade attacks German Switch Line tomorrow
   (zero hour to be notified later)
   57th Brigade attacks on right of our Bn. and 1st
   Brigade on left of our Brigade.

2. Objective of our Brigade is the line
   P.26.b.9 — track at S.2.a.5.8.

   In Front Line   (Point from previous to trenches)
   ~~Right~~ 7th ~~North~~ Lancashire Regt.   S.2.b.6.9 —
   Right 7th S. Lancashire Regt. in the line   { S.2.d.8.7 — S.2.d.4.5
                                                   { S.2.d.2.4 — S.2.b.5.8
   Left 7th North Lancashire Regt. in the line   { S.2.d.4.5 (inclusive) to track S.2.c.8.8 (inclusive)
                                                   { S.2.b.5.8 (exclusive) —
                                                   { S.2.a.8.7 (exclusive)

   Support
   The Battalion is in support to above with dispositions
   as follows
   A Company field ready to move into line
   (with Lewis guns)
                   S.2.a.4.4 — S.2.a.8.7.
   as soon as this line has been vacated by a Battalion
   of 1st Brigade who will presumably occupy it temporarily previous to attack
   (B Company) latter to be prepared to fill up any gap in Brigade objective between 7th S. Lancs & 11th S. Lancashire Regt
   B Company } to remain in their present positions or ready
   C Company } to move on receipt of orders
   D Company will be relieved by a unit of the 1st Brigade
                at an hour to be notified later, & on relief
                will at once occupy present trenches now
   * see appendix [illegible] held by B Company. This Company will
   appendix to follow   then be held in readiness for further move on
   to be entered on S.S.A.14

Receipt of orders.

Reserve 2/ Royal Lancaster Regt. tonight about present Brigade Head qrs.

4. An advanced Battalion dump is being established at S S a 14. (at the present front of A Company) No stores to be drawn from this until attack has commenced.

5. Reports to present Battn H.Q.

6. Acknowledge by wire.

3. Signals D Coy when it moves into A Company's line will
(a) hand over his telephone apparatus to O.C. A Coy for installment by the latter at S S a 4 in a dugout near S S a 8 7.
(b) take over A Coys telephone.
Remaining communication will remain as at present.

Copy No 1. Bde H.Q
  2 retained
  3 A Company.
  4 B
  5 C
  6 D

War Diary August '16
7/ East Lancs Regt

Army Form C. 2118.

WAR DIARY
or
INTELLIGENCE SUMMARY
(Erase heading not required.)

Vol 10

Place	Date	Hour	Summary of Events and Information	Remarks and references to Appendices
FRANVILLERS	1.8.16		Training. Baths in the morning.	
	2.8.16		G.O.C 3rd Corps addressed the Brigade in the afternoon.	
	3.8.16		Marched in the afternoon to FRECHENCOURT and entrained. Detrained at LONGPRÉ and marched to billets at GORENFLOS.	
GORENFLOS	4.8.16		Training	
	5.8.16			
PONT REMY	6.8.16		Marched in the afternoon to PONT REMY and entrained	
BAILLEUL	7.8.16	2pm	Detrained at BAILLEUL and marched to billets on western outskirts of the town.	
	8.8.16	8am	Moved from billets, proceeded via LOCRE and halted for dinner 3/4 mile NE	
		12 midnight	LOCRE. Moved into the line in the evening. Relief of the 9th Batt: Durham Light Infantry was complete. The sector occupied being from PICCADILLY (exclusive) to the Road at N.29.B.9.6½ (inclusive) Reference map Sheet N°28 S.W. 1/10000. The 7th NORTH LANCASHIRE REGT being on our left and the 57th Bde on our right. Disposition of the battalion being as follows:— A/ Front line, 2 Coy (140 Rifles) with complement of LEWIS guns. B/ Holding STRONG POINTS SP8, SP9, SP10. 1 Coy C/ Battalion Reserve, 1 Coy less Guards of 1 N.C.O. and 3 men each at REGINA FORT, LINDENHOEK CROSS Rds and MORTUARY Rd. D/ Garrison. 1 Squad close to junction of FRONT LINE and (a) PICCADILLY (b) REGENT STREET 2 Squads with Reserve Coy (Batt)	

WAR DIARY
or
INTELLIGENCE SUMMARY

(Erase heading not required.)

Army Form C. 2118.

Place	Date	Hour	Summary of Events and Information	Remarks and references to Appendices
PICCADILLY to N.29.B.9.6½.	8.8.16		E/ Regimental Aid Post. Regent Street dugouts. F/ Batt. H.Qrs. at FORT VICTORIA.	
	9.8.16		Situation Normal. Our guard at REGINA FORT was relieved during the day by the 10th WARWICKS.	
	10.8.16		Situation Normal.	
	11.8.16		Situation Normal. Enemys Trench Mortars very active for 1 hour starting at 6 pm on our unoccupied support line. No real damage done.	
	12.8.16		Situation Normal. A patrol sent out from 15 with the object of examining the enemy wire & effecting an entry if possible found the wire from BLACK REDOUBT (N.30.A.4.4.) to a point 70 yds on the North side of REDOUBT was very strong & did not admit a penetration. Situation Normal.	
	13.8.16		Situation Normal.	
	14.8.16		An officer patrol reports enemy wire between N.30.C.19-17½ as being thick entanglements well staked 4 high, 5 to 7 yds deep, the near edge 15 yds from parapet. Our snipers claim 3 victims. The Battn was relieved by the 7th KINGS OWN REGT in the evening and then marched to billets in WAKEFIELD HUTS at LOCRE	

WAR DIARY
or
INTELLIGENCE SUMMARY

(Erase heading not required.)

Army Form C. 2118.

Place	Date	Hour	Summary of Events and Information	Remarks and references to Appendices
LOCRE	15.8.16		Situation Normal. Training	
	16.8.16		Casualties from 8/8/16 - 14/8/16 - 1 Killed, 5 Wounded	
			Training	
	17.8.16		Training. Bath at LOCRE	
	18.8.16		Training	
	19.8.16		Training. Capt A.REDGELL, N.R.N.RUSSELL, & R.B.WALKER joined the Batt.	
	20.8.16		Church Parade in the morning.	
			Moved in the evening from WAKEFIELD HUTS into the line and relieved 7th Batt. KING'S OWN REGT. reoccupying the same sector as on 8/5/16 - 14/8/16	
PICCADILLY (exclusive) to N29.T.9.6½	21.8.16		Situation Normal	
			Enemy's Trench Mortars were very active about 4pm, our parapet being breached in 2 places. Our artillery retaliation was effective.	
	22.8.16		Situation Normal	
	23.8.16		Situation Normal	
	24.8.16		Situation Normal	
			An officers patrol remained out for an hour. No hostile movement seen or heard. 2/Lt H.G. RAPHAEL, 2/Lt M.O. EVANS joined the battalion	

WAR DIARY
or
INTELLIGENCE SUMMARY

Army Form C. 2118.

(Erase heading not required.)

Place	Date	Hour	Summary of Events and Information	Remarks and references to Appendices
PICCADILLY (reserve)	25.8.16		Situation normal. Enemy shelled our Reserve Trenches & Dump at REGENT STREET Dugouts between 11.45 a.m. & 12.15 pm. Very little damage & no casualties were caused.	
NRQ 13.9.64.	26.8.16		Enemy machine guns active all last night. Situation normal. A & B Coys, O.C. Coy, Adjutant & Battalion Signallers & (Battalion Bombers?) & Battalion Snipers of the 72nd Cdn. Canadian Infantry (1st Coy of Bde) were attached to the Battalion in the trenches for instructional purposes. The Batt. was relieved by the 7th Kings Own Regt & marched to KEMMEL SHELTERS in Brigade Reserve. Casualties between 20th & 26th August 2 killed 9 wounded.	
KEMMEL SHELTERS	27.8.16		Working Parties of 195 men employed in and about Trench line. Baths in the afternoon at WESTOUTRE.	
	28.8.16		Working Parties of 200 men.	
	29.8.16		Working Parties of 220 men.	
	30.8.16		Bathing Parties of 170 men.	
	31.8.16		Working Parties. Church Parade in the morning.	

WAR DIARY
or
INTELLIGENCE SUMMARY

Army Form C. 2118.

Sept 1916
1st E Lanc Regt
Vol II

Place	Date	Hour	Summary of Events and Information	Remarks and references to Appendices
TRENCHES PICCADILLY N29 B 9.4	1/9/16		In evening relieved 7th Kings Own Regt in the trenches. Taking over line from Piccadilly - N.29.B. 9.4. ½ Bat'n 38th Canadian Inf'y attached for instruction	MAPSHEET No 28 SW/27
	2/9/16		Situation normal. Working parties 20 men	
LE ROMARIN	3/9/16		Relieved in afternoon by 72nd Bat'n Canadian Inf'y and marched to Billets at Rue Du Sac, LE ROMARIN	
PLOEGSTEERT WOOD	4/9/16		Relieved 9th Yorks in trenches at Ploegsteert Wood in afternoon. Taking over line from U28.A.29 - U.15.D.5¾.0	
	5/9/16		Situation normal. Very quiet. Capt Hunt joined the Batt'n	
	6/9/16		Situation normal. Artillery active on both sides between 12 noon and 2.30 pm	
	7/9/16		Situation normal. Our trench mortars active.	
	8/9/16		Relieved by 7th Kings Own Regt in afternoon and proceeded to occupy line of reserve trenches about PLOEGSTEERT WOOD	
	9/9/16		Baths. Working parties of 230 men supplied to R.E.	
		3 pm	75 NCOs and men under Capt Hunt attended presentation of Medal Ribbons by the Corps Commander at NIEPPE. The following men of the Battalion received ribbon Sgt Neary, Pte Sullivan, Sgt Hooper, Pte Fairchild, L/Cpl Bairn Capt Palmer, 2/Lt Mitray, 2/Lt Gouldens and 2/Lt Brown joined the Battalion	11 sheets

Army Form C. 2118.

WAR DIARY
or
INTELLIGENCE SUMMARY
(Erase heading not required.)

Instructions regarding War Diaries and Intelligence Summaries are contained in F. S. Regs., Part II. and the Staff Manual respectively. Title Pages will be prepared in manuscript.

Place	Date	Hour	Summary of Events and Information	Remarks and references to Appendices
PLOEGSTEERT WOOD	10/9/16		Working parties 220 men	
	11/9/16		Working parties 220 men	
	12/9/16		Working parties 180 men. Draft of 4+3 other Ranks arrived	
	13/9/16		Working parties 210 men	
	14/9/16		Relieved the 9th Bn KINGS OWN REGT in trenches taking over same line as before	
	15/9/16		Situation normal. Enemy quiet. In the evening Lt EDWARDS with 32 O.Rs raided enemy trenches at junction of LA BASSÉE VILLE – LE GHEER ROAD and their front line, securing 5 prisoners and killing about 30 Germans. Our casualties were one other rank slightly wounded. Detailed reports (one by OC the other by LIEUT EDWARDS) are attached.	10 R prisoners 20 R wounded 10 R killed
	16/9/16		Situation unchanged	
	17/9/16		Situation quiet	
	18/9/16		Situation normal. All Companies inspected. Their arms, entanglements which were found to be in good condition. Heavy rain in the day damaged trenches.	
	19/9/16		Situation normal	
	20/9/16		Situation normal. Two patrols were sent out by D Coy. Reports attached. Enemy trench lines between 10 PM and 3 AM	

Army Form C. 2118.

WAR DIARY
or
INTELLIGENCE SUMMARY
(Erase heading not required.)

Instructions regarding War Diaries and Intelligence Summaries are contained in F. S. Regs., Part II. and the Staff Manual respectively. Title Pages will be prepared in manuscript.

Place	Date	Hour	Summary of Events and Information	Remarks and references to Appendices
PLOEGSTEERT WOOD	21/9/16		Relieved in the trenches by 2nd Bn Royal Warwickshire Regt and moved into billets in RUE DU SAC, LE ROMARIN. Operation orders attached. Lieut J.S. Spicer rejoined Battn.	Casualties Nil
	22/9/16		Moved to Billets in OUTTERSTEENE area. Operation Order attached. 2/Lt Duggan rejoined Battn.	
	23/9/16		In reserve billets - Capt Cheney, 2/Lt Mitchell, Knock and Parton joined the Battn	
	24/9/16		In reserve billets - Battalion commenced training	
	25/9/16		In reserve billets - Training carried out. 2/Lt Ridden joined the Battalion	
	26/9/16		In reserve billets - Training carried out - Draft of 81 joined Battalion	
	27/9/16		In reserve billets - Training carried out - Draft of 14 joined Battalion	
	28/9/16		In reserve billets - Training carried out	
	29/9/16		In reserve billets - Training carried out. 2/Lt H. Potter accidentally wounded. PTE PICKENS 13827 awarded Military Medal	
	30/9/16		In reserve billets - Training carried out.	

Yours H. Cott
Comdg 2/R Warwickshire Regt

1.10.16

SECRET. — 56th Infantry Bgde.   16-9-16

1. I forward herewith Report on Raid effected by a party of this Battalion under Lieut. EDWARDES.

2. DETAILS.
                                                    PAGES.
   General Impressions   1
   Cooperation with other arms.   1-2
   Narrative of Raid   3
   Points of Interest noted }
   by Lieut. EDWARDES.   }   4-5
   Rough Sketch   6.

3. I would mention that we are much indebted to the guns and Trench Mortars for their invaluable assistance.

                        (SGD) T. S. TORRIE. Lt Col.
                        Comdg. 7th East Lanc Regt.

Report on Raid expected night 15/16 9-16.

Reference to sketch attached.

1. **General Impression noted from our Front Line**

PM
8.20. Party started to get clear of our line taking advantage of:
   (a) ditches existing either side of LAGNICOURT – LA BASSÉVILLE Road to within 50 yds of enemy line.
   (b) two shell holes (marked "X" & "Y")

8.45. Leaders of party getting on to enemy parapet.

8.50. Enemy sent up 2 Red Lights (evidently S.O.S. signal from point G)

8.55. Enemy opened heavy rifle fire on our frontage P–Q (no damage to us)

9–0. Enemy established light barrage of shrapnel & H.E. between our front & support lines on frontage P–Q (no damage to us)
   We consequently increased rate of our field guns to "battery fire" and shortened range on to the enemy's front line on front F–T for 10 minutes.
   Raiding party's return reported by Lieut EDWARDES.

9–15. Situation practically normal.

2. **Weather conditions** Dry, very bright till 8.5 PM when a dark cloud coming over considerably improved conditions for raiders.

3. **Co-operation other arms.**

   Howitzer Battery.
   (Commenced to shoot 8.45 PM) (TARGETS) (a) QUADRILATERAL
   (b) LOOPHOLE FARM.
   (c) ENEMY LINE A–B IN ENFILADE.

   Field Battery
   (Commenced – – – –) ENEMY SUPPORT LINES & COMMUNICATION TRENCHES, BEHIND THE FRONT. F–T.

   Medium Trench Mortars
   (Commenced – – –) (TARGET) QUADRILATERAL.

   Stokes Mortars
   (Commenced – – –) ESTABLISHING A BARRAGE OF 3 MORTARS EACH PERPENDICULAR TO ENEMY LINE. ONE 10 NORTH OF D THE OTHER TO NORTH OF F

2. <u>Vickers Machine Guns.</u> (commenced to fire 8-45 p.m.) from left Battalion front overhead fire on enemy's support line with direction (LOOPHOLE FARM)

<u>LEWIS GUNS.</u>
(COMMENCED. 8-15 PM)

1 gun to neutralise enemy machine gun at G

2 guns to sweep front F-T. till 8.30 PM. after that to concentrate on and about QUADRILATERAL

2 guns to sweep with intermittent bursts the front D-C.

<u>Cooperation</u> worked admirably with one slight exception (the southern Stokes mortar barrage switching too much to our left).

Synchronization of times, a noticeable factor.

Narrative of Raid

The front portion of the enemy wire close to the SAP had been cut but more wire existed buried in a borrow pit with yet more loose coils of barbed wire at the bottom of the enemy parapet. The wire in the borrowed pit was "jumpable" but the loose coils caused a slight delay. The leaders of the party gaining the top of the SAP parapet found several Huns bolting back to the enemy front line, Lieut Edwardes hitting two with revolver fire.

By this time the remainder of the party was up and getting into the Hun front line divided as follows:-

- 2 men remained on the parapet in observation and to direct the party on its return

- 4 men acted as a stop about II to prevent Hun interference from the NORTH

The remainder divided into two equal parties
one under LIEUT EDWARDES working SOUTH along enemy front line trench.
the other under Sergt NEARY passed along the communication trench leading from T alongside the LE GHEER – LA BASSEVILLE Road

Lieut EDWARDES' party after working down 5 bays encountered our Stokes Mortar barrage (which had swung too much to the left of what was intended) having previously accounted for 4 Huns dead. Lieut Edwardes then left 4 men in observation taking the rest of his party to join SERGT NEARY'S which had taken full advantage of a long straight trench full of cowed Germans not recovered from their surprise. Cudgels were applied and bombs thrown on the demoralized crowd until the stock of bombs ran out when the party having passed back five prisoners Lieut EDWARDES' ordered its return.

Lieut. EDWARDES reports:-

(1) At least 20 Germans killed and an equal number wounded by his party; also at least ten more caught in our Artillery barrage when flying back eastwards over the top across the open

(2) that
 (a) either a relief was in progress
 or (b) a strong fatigue party was on the move

His reasons for the former assumption is that the trenches were filled with Huns quite unprepared for attack, also several firesteps had German packs fully equipped laid out on the fire steps in their front line trench.

(3) No machine guns were detected nor did any fire on the raiders

(4) No German Officer was seen but somebody was directing from the southern flank in front line trench until the voice suddenly ceased

(5) Enemy demoralized by the raiders movements offering practically no resistance to our Raiders bombing + "cudgel drawing"
His observation posts seemed undoubtedly slack

(6) <u>Enemy trenches</u> Front line parapet 20 feet thick inside revetting also floors of trenches (breastworks) made of wood, flooring not duckboards like ours   drainage very good.

(7) Dimensions of trenches.
  (a) <u>FRONT LINE</u> width of trench {at bottom 2 ft 6 inches wide / top 8 feet}
  Fire steps 18 inches above flooring
  Top of parapet 5 feet above fire steps
  At least 2 Rifle loopholes in each fire bay
  Bays appeared fairly regular in shape and are well traversed

  (b) Communication trench just South of and parallel to LE GHEER — LA BASSEVILLE ROAD
  Depth much the same as the front line though much more narrow and it ran perfectly straight for a distance of 50 yards.

· 8 <u>Dugouts</u> Only two actually seen, these were in the front line, of no appreciable depth capacity three men lying down entrance towards front line proof against light howitzer fire
No dugouts in the Communication trench

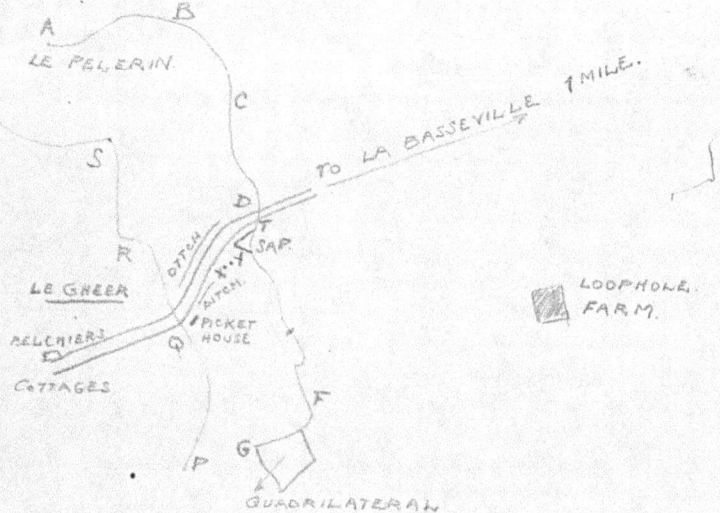

SECRET.   Copy No 7

7th East Lancashire Regiment.
OPERATION ORDER No 2.   21-9-16

1. <u>Move</u> The Battalion will move to OUTTERSTEENE (3 MILES S.W. OF BAILLEUL) tomorrow at 8-25 AM. STARTING POINT Road Junction B.3.C.5½.2½.—
   ORDER OF MARCH — HOURS. (Battalion Bombers included), A Coy; B Coy; C Coy; D Coy; LEWIS GUN DETACHMENT; TRANSPORT.

2. <u>ROUTE</u>. Road Junction B1 central — NIEPPE — BAILLEUL road, Road Junction in S.20.d.8.5. — BAILLEUL Railway Station — thence NORTH via Road Junction S.20-a.5.2. — S.19 b 7.9.

3. All movements EAST of BAILLEUL by half Companies at intervals of 100 yards. At the first halt after BAILLEUL the Battalion will close to column of route.

4. <u>Officers Kits</u>. Officers kit to be packed and ready for loading outside their billets by 7-0 am.
   The Transport Officer will arrange to collect these kits

5. <u>Officers Chargers</u>. Grooms will report with Officers Chargers at Billets at 8-0 am.

6. <u>Billeting Parties</u> orders will be issued on receipt of instructions from Brigade Headquarters.

7. <u>Rear Party</u>. A rear party of two other ranks per Company and Headquarters will remain behind to go round the Billets after evacuation and to ensure

1.

2.

they are left perfectly clean. Second Lieut. H. H. Johnson will be in charge of this party and will march them to OUTTERSTEENE rejoining the Battalion on completion of duty.

8. <u>Cleanliness of Billets</u>. Order No 8 does not relieve Company Commanders of their responsibility that billets are left clean.

9. <u>Drums</u>. The Drums will load packs and rifles on the transport at 7.0 am.

10. <u>Tents &c</u>. All tents, tent shelters and huts of all kinds are to be left standing in the Divisional area for the use of the incoming Division.

    Lists of tent & camp equipment handed over to be sent to this office by 6-0 pm. 21st inst.

(SGD) R.W. PALMER
Capt & B/Ady.
7th East Lancashire Regt.

Copy No 1   Hdqrs
— 2   A Coy
— 3   B -
— 4   C -
— 5   D -
— 6   Depot
— 7   File

WAR DIARY or INTELLIGENCE SUMMARY

Army Form C. 2118.

7th E. LANCS REGT.

Vol 12

Instructions regarding War Diaries and Intelligence Summaries are contained in F.S. Regs., Part II. and the Staff Manual respectively. Title Pages will be prepared in manuscript.

1916.

Place	Date	Hour	Summary of Events and Information	Remarks and references to Appendices
DOULIEU	Oct 1		In reserve billets. Training carried out	
	2		In reserve billets — do —	
	3		In reserve billets — do —	
	4		In reserve billets — do —	
	5		Battalion marched to BAILLEUL and entrained for DOULLENS leaving BAILLEUL at 1.18 pm and arriving at DOULLENS at 8.45 pm. Battalion then detrained and marched to billets at "A" Camp COUIN arriving there at 4 AM (6/10/16)	
COUIN	6		In billets. Battalion had Baths at COUIN	
	7		" billets. Training carried on	
	8		" billets — " —	
	9		" billets — " —	
	10		" billets — " —	
SAILLY AU BOIS	11		Battalion moved by march route to Bivouacs near SAILLY AU BOIS	
	12		In Bivouacs. Working parties found	
HEBUTERNE	13		Working parties found. Battalion moved into trenches relieving 7th North Lancs	12 W 16 wounded
	14		In trenches. Casualties 5 other ranks wounded	
	15		In trenches. 1 killed 1 died of wounds 2 wounded (Other Ranks)	

WAR DIARY
or
INTELLIGENCE SUMMARY

Army Form C. 2118.

Instructions regarding War Diaries and Intelligence Summaries are contained in F. S. Regs., Part II. and the Staff Manual respectively. Title Pages will be prepared in manuscript.

(Erase heading not required.)

Place	Date Oct	Hour	Summary of Events and Information	Remarks and references to Appendices
ROSSIGNOL FME	16th		In Trenches relieved by 2 Companies 12th East Yorks & 1 Coy 13th East Yorks. The Battalion moved to ROSSIGNOL FARM. Casualties 1 died of wounds 2 wounded (other ranks)	
VADENCOURT WOOD	17th		Battalion moved to VADENCOURT WOOD a mean CONTAY	
	18th		In huts at VADENCOURT WOOD. Brigade Training carried out	
	19th		Battalion ordered to move but cancelled when on the move and returned to above wood.	
	20th		Carried on Brigade Training	
	21st		The Battalion moved to Bivouacs in BRICKFIELDS W20.a.9.4	
BIVOUACS at W20.a.9.4 LEIPZIG REDOUBT	22nd		Battalion moved to WOOD POST and LEIPZIG REDOUBT	
WOOD POST	23rd		In Brigade Support	
STUFF TRENCH	24th		The Battalion moved into the front line C & D Coys in STUFF TRENCH relieving the 7th Kings Own Regt. A Coy in Battalion reserve in SCHWABEN TRENCH. B — in Battalion support in BAINBRIDGE. 1 other rank killed	(a) Orders re Patrol A/9 (c) Report on Patrol B/732
	25		2 killed 5 wounded. Os Cmdg C & D Coys ordered to carry out patrol work. Oders and result attached. R. Russell +20 other ranks of C Coy and J. Nyllis and 15 other ranks of D Coy were sent out on this work	

J. McDian Capt & Adjt
7 East Lanc Regt

Army Form C. 2118.

WAR DIARY
or
INTELLIGENCE SUMMARY

(Erase heading not required.)

Instructions regarding War Diaries and Intelligence Summaries are contained in F. S. Regs., Part II. and the Staff Manual respectively. Title Pages will be prepared in manuscript.

Place	Date Oct	Hour	Summary of Events and Information	Remarks and references to Appendices
STUFF TRENCH	26th		1 Officer killed (Lt. H.N. WYLLIE) 2 other ranks killed 9 other ranks wounded 1 Officer (Lt Rumbold) and 6 other ranks missing. The enemy attacked the Battalion front line at about 5 am but were effectively repulsed. Parties attached. The Battalion was relieved by the 9th Cheshire Regt and proceeded to DONNET POST	(a) 1st Report A (b) Full Report B (c) Further Report C (d) Further Report D
DONNET POST	27"		At DONNET POST. The day was spent in cleaning up. Lt Russell and 3 other ranks previously reported missing returned after having been out in No Man's Land for 30 hours. He brought back useful information	
	28"		At DONNET POST Training carried out.	
	29		At DONNET POST Training carried out	
	30		The Battalion went into Brigade Reserve at AVELUY	
AVELUY	31		In Brigade Reserve	

J. W. Dina Capt & Adjt
1/4th East Lancashire Regt

WAR DIARY
INTELLIGENCE SUMMARY

Army Form C. 2118.

56/19 7 E Lanc Regt

Sept 1916

Place	Date	Hour	Summary of Events and Information	Remarks and references to Appendices
ANCRE	1.11.16		Moved into front line (STUFF TRENCH) relieving 7th Kings Own. Trenches in a very bad state - Casualties. 3 other ranks killed 6 wounded	
J. Mattipthie	2.10.16		Trenches heavily shelled - Casualties 2 died of wounds 17 wounded Relieved by 9th Chesh'rs and proceeded to DONNET POST Tents	
DONNET POST	3.11.16		Parade and general cleaning up performed	
" "	4.11.16		Parade and general training carried on	
" "	5.11.16		Battalion moved into front line (STUFF & REGINA trenches) relieving 8th Wilts - Trenches very bad state - Relief had to be carried out by night	
In the trenches	6.11.16		Casualties - 2 Wounded Headquarters dugout in STUFF REDOUBT heavily shelled	
" "	7.11.16		Casualties - 1 killed 5 wounded 1 missing	
" "	8.11.16		Casualties - 1 killed 1 died of wounds 1 wounded	
" "	9.11.16		Casualties 1 wounded 1 missing - The Battalion was relieved by the 5th North Staffords proceeded to the old German front line trenches - battalion in reserve. Nothing particular found - Many men suffered from bad feet owing to state of trenches	
Battalion in front line	10.11.16		Nothing particular found - The Battalion was relieved by the 9th Welch & proceeded to OVILLERS POST HUTS relieving the 7th King's Own Regt.	
" "	11.11.16			
OVILLERS POST	12.11.16		The Battalion was busy preparing for projected attack and moved into STUFF TRENCH preparatory to the attack relieving the 7th Yorkshires	

J. Moorhouse Lt/Col
7 East Lanc Regt

WAR DIARY
INTELLIGENCE SUMMARY

Army Form C. 2118.

Place	Date	Hour	Summary of Events and Information	Remarks and references to Appendices
Stuff Trench	13th	5.45 AM	At 5.45 AM (Zero Hour) the Battalion was attacked as follows:- C Coy on left, B Coy in centre and D Coy on right were lying well in front of the parapet and A Coy was occupying STUFF TRENCH. Four Machine Guns were held in front ready to cover the advance. The objectives allotted to the Battalion were all gained. Casualties - 2/Lt T.A. DUGGAN + 2/Lt P.W. MAY killed 13th 2/Lt T.B. WRACK + 2/Lt S.W.T. RISELEY wounded 13th 2/Lt T. BROWN missing 13th Capt. E.G. EDWARDES M.C. + 2/Lt L.G. KITCHIN wounded duty 13th. Other ranks 18 killed 66 wounded 12 missing 13th/14th. Attached (1) Operation Orders (2) Narrative of Operations	
" "	15th		The Battalion marched in the trenches by the 6th Wilts and returned to MARLBOROUGH HUTS	
MARLBOROUGH HUTS - AVELUY	16th		The Battalion remained in HUTS	
" "	17th		The Battalion moved into the trenches in HANSA LINE	
HANSA LINE	18th	3.30 AM	At 3.30 AM orders were received that the Battalion was to take part in the operations for the capture of GRANDCOURT. They had allotted to the Battalion being the capture of BAILLESCOURT FARM. Owing to the first stage of the attack not being successful the Battalion was not able to gain the objectives allotted to it	Capt & Adjt [signature]

WAR DIARY or INTELLIGENCE SUMMARY

Army Form C. 2118.

Place	Date	Hour	Summary of Events and Information	Remarks and references to Appendices
HANSA LINE CONTD	18th 11-18		(A) Operation Orders attached. (B) NARRATIVE attached. Casualties — Lt Col T.G.J. TORRIE killed. 2/Lt W.L. HARKER attached T.M.B. wounded — 3 other ranks killed 12 wounded to Division	
ENGELBELMER of GRANDCOURT	19th		The Battalion remained during the day in the positions gained on the 18th and in the early hours of the morning (20th) was ordered to withdraw into Reserve dugouts near (ST. PIERRE DIVION) Casualties 1 Died of Wounds 12 wounded.	
RESERVE DUG-OUTS	20th		The Battalion remained in Reserve. Capt H.W. House rejoined the Battalion from England	
"	21st		The Battalion was relieved by 9th Sherwood Foresters moved into dugouts about ATHUILLE	
ATHUILLE	22nd		The Battalion moved by bus motor lorries to WARLOY 2/Lt G. ALLEN joined on first appointment	
WARLOY	23rd		Battalion moved to HARPONVILLE. Major H.K. Jones appointed to temporary Command	
HARPONVILLE	24th		The Battalion moved into billets at LONGUEVILLETTE	
LONGUEVILLETTE	25th		The Battalion moved to its rest area in FIENVILLERS	
FIENVILLERS	26th		In rest billets. The Battalion was busy cleaning up.	

J. Hunt Lt/Col
7 Royal Warwick Reg

WAR DIARY

INTELLIGENCE SUMMARY

(Erase heading not required.)

Army Form C. 2118.

Place	Date	Hour	Summary of Events and Information	Remarks and references to Appendices
FONVILLERS	27/11/16	In rest billets	Training carried out.	
" "	28/11/16	In rest billets	Training carried out	
" "	29th	In rest billets arrived	Training carried out. A draft of 120 other ranks	
" "	30th	In rest billets	Training carried out.	

J. C. Newhurst. Capt & Adjt
9th Bn. East Lancashire Regiment

A.

Account of Operations carried out by
1/ East Lancashire Regt on 13th & 14th
November 1916

Battalion Operation Order No 5 attached

At 5.20 am under cover of a thick mist the
Battalion was disposed as follows - C & D Coys as first
wave on left & right respectively were lying out well
in front of our parapet. B Coy as second wave
was lying out in rear of C Coy. - A Coy remained
in STUFF TRENCH

At 5.45 AM the barrage commenced and the
waves advanced well under the barrage. A few
casualties were sustained from our own barrage but did
not deter the waves from keeping well up.

At 6.5 AM D Coy reported by runner that their
objective had been gained and that they were digging
themselves in. The mist was still thick and considerably
aided this operation.

At 6.15 AM prisoners commenced to be passed to the
rear and were all of the 144th R.I.R.

There was very little hostile machine gun or rifle fire
until 6.23 AM when a heavy fire was opened from
about R.15.c.6.5. Our own machine guns in
O.G.1 opened a heavy fire in reply

The enemy now commenced to send up a large
number of red flares.

More prisoners now came in and the escort reported
that the left objective had been taken, but this was
regarded as unreliable

At 6.45 AM a VICKERS gun was established at
point R20.b.8.6½ in O.G.1 in the strong point which
was being constructed there. This gun was later
knocked out but was at once replaced.

At 6.47 AM the enemy opened shrapnel fire on B
& C Coys and the rifle fire slackened

At 6.54 AM communication by telephone was
obtained with D Coy

Up to now no information had been received
from B & C Coys. Two platoons from A Coy under 1 Officer
were sent out to find and fill the gap that existed
between the right and left companies. The Officer
was killed and the platoons lost their way and
eventually returned to STUFF TRENCH

A message was sent to B Coy to gain
touch with the right company but was never
delivered

Two platoons of A Coy were sent up O.G.1 as
a reinforcement to D Coy.

1.

2

At 7.40 am a message was sent to Bde Hqrs asking for one Company as a reinforcement.

This Coy (Kings Own) arrived at 9.15 AM and took up position in STUFF TRENCH

The situation remained obscure until 6.15 pm when B Coy's Commander reported personally that he had gained his objective.

He reported that C Coy had gone too much to the WEST (this Coy had been ordered to keep close touch with the Battalion on its left [E.N. LANCS REGT]) owing to the fact that the left Battalion had closed rather too much to the left B'Coy had followed but on crossing LUCKY WAY at about R.20.b.2.8 he realised that he had lost direction so he immediately attempted to get to the real objective, it Communication trench from R 20.b.4.9 – trench junction at R 20.b.5.9 which he did and linked up with D Coy. C Coy were unable to get forward on the left owing to machine gun fire but were ultimately able to do so at about 4.30 AM on the morning of the 14th instant.

The line thus reached was as follows Right on R.21.a.0.8 thence West to LUCKY WAY at about R.20.b.4.8 and thence across LUCKY WAY to Communication trench from R 20.b.4.9 to R.20.b.5.9 where they were in touch with the Kings Own

This line was consolidated with the aid of the S.W. B.

The situation remained quiet throughout the 14th and the Battalion was relieved by the 6th Wilts about 11 pm

A2

7th EAST LANCASHIRE REGIMENT.
OPERATION ORDER NO 5.   12/11/16

REF. GRANDCOURT MAP 1/5,000. EDITION 4.

1. INFORMATION. (a) The original programmes issued with Operation Order No 4 of 31-10-16 will now be undertaken in stages.
(b) The first stage will take place on Zero Day. Zero hour to be notified later.
(c) In the event of a decisive success as regards operations by V Corps on our left it is possible that this success may be exploited by further action on that day.

11. OBJECTIVES. (a) In the first stage the Brigade viz 7th KINGS. OWN v 7th S. LANCS. objective is (RIGHT) (R.21.a.5.8). (LEFT) R.14.c.2.1. (off the map)
7th EAST LANCS ON THE RIGHT
7th NORTH LANCS ON THE LEFT.
(b) The Battalion objective being (right) R.21.a.0.5. — (left) back junction R.20.b.1/2.9. both inclusive with advance posts. along O.G.1. and LUCKY WAY.
(c) 6th Wilts Regt. cooperates with rifle & Lewis Gun action on our right from STUFF TRENCH
(d) The attack will be carried out by D Coy & B Coy. A Coy will remain in STUFF TRENCH between R.21.a.0.8. and R.20.b.1.2/2.(both inclusive)

111. DISPOSITIONS. D. Coy to attack in one line disposed in queues of platoons; each platoon extended to one pace. Right platoon with its right on O.G.1. to reach about R.20. b.8.9. (200 yds NORTH OF STUFF TRENCH) Two centre platoons to occupy incomplete trench which extends from (roughly) R.20. b. 7.8. to R.20. b.5.7/2. (175-200 YDS NORTH OF STUFF TRENCH.)
Left platoon with its left on LUCKY. WAY. to reach junction of LUCKY. WAY. and C.T. R.20. b. 4.9. inclusive.

'C' Coy to pass over LUCKY WAY and occupy Communication Trench from R.20.b.4.9 — track junction (probably not recognisable on the ground) R.20.b.2.7 both inclusive; and to be extended on this frontage (ie 200 yds)

'B' Coy in rear of 'C' Coy at a distance of 30 y. will advance with its right directly behind that of C Coy and its left approximately behind the centre of that Coy. (frontage 100 yds roughly)

Then dropping into LUCKY WAY it will clear that sunken road from R.20.b.2.7 North eastwards whilst taking due precautions to clear it also to the south west.

NOTE In all cases any unknown dugouts or trenches not hitherto detected must be dealt with on the initiative of Company or other Commanders

REGIMENTAL BOMBERS 2 squads will advance astride 'C' Coy with head immediately behind the right flank of B Coy clearing that C.T en route and making it their object to gain the trench junction with LUCKY WAY at R.14.d.8.2

2 squads to advance extended at one yard interval simultaneously with and on the immediate right of B Coy and on arrival in LUCKY WAY to precede that Coy whilst clearing up LUCKY WAY North eastward to trench junction R.14.d.8.2 (ie joining hands there with the other two squads

Blocks will be at once established in either case at the furthest point gained but no advance should be made beyond that junction

LEWIS GUNS of
A Coy one about R.21.a.0.8 the other about R.20.b.1.2½

B Coy one immediately in rear of and to co-operate with Regimental Bombers along O.G.1 one with 2 centre platoons and one at disposal of O.C. Coy

'C' Coy guns to be equally distributed along the Company front.

B Coy be on right of Company to co-operate with Regimental Bombers up LUCKY WAY the other being left at disposal of O.C Coy

CO-OPERATION OTHER ARMS

(a) Artillery Barrage will be notified late
(b) Machine Guns will be pushed out in advance of STUFF TRENCH prior to ZERO hour and thence will move at first opportunity, one to O.G. R20.b.8.5½ where it is intended to establish a strong point. The other to drop into LUCKY WAY at R20.b.2.7 and later to gain the trench junction R20.b.4.9 where another strong point will be established
(c) R.E section prior to ZERO hour will be accommodated in STUFF TRENCH in immediate vicinity of Battalion H.Qr dugout R20.b.12.5 in order to establish after dark strong points in O.G. at R20.b.8.7½ and in LUCKY WAY R20.b.4.9
(d) PIONEERS. 1 Coy S.W.B. pioneers will immediately after be assist D Coy in digging a trench across the gap between R21.a.0.8 and LUCKY WAY

CONSOLIDATION

(a) The captured line is to be consolidated as far as feasible during hours of daylight
(b) All consolidation will be protected by covering parties thrown forward a distance of at least 30 yards.

(i) On night Y/Z the Battalion will take over trench line from R21.a.3.7 to R20.b.1.2½ in order from Right to Left A.D.C.B. Movements immediately prior to ZERO hour will be notified later

(ii) Capt Palmer and 2 runners from "A" Coy will report to O.C 1/North Lancs Regt tomorrow for instructions by 12 noon.

(iii) TIME Watches will be synchronized at 12 midnight Y/Z days and 3 A.M Z morning

4.

(IX) Flares — Flares will be shown at the following times only (ZERO + 35 minutes) and (ZERO + 1 hour)

They will **not** be shown on reaching the objective

(X) REPORT CENTRE — Reports to Battalion H.Q in dug out off STUFF TRENCH at R.20.b.5½.5

(XI) ACKNOWLEDGE

(Sd) T. G. J. TORRIE Lt Colonel
CMDG. 4th EAST LANC REGT

Issued at 8AM to
(1) 56th Infantry Bde
(2) 6th Welch (Thro 58th Infy Bde)
(3) 7th North Lancs R91
(4) 5th South Wales Bdrs
(5) 56th M.G. Coy   } Thro 56th
(6) 81st Field Coy R.E. } Infy Bde
(7) Captain Palmer
(8) A Coy
(9) B Coy
(10) C Coy
(11) D Coy
(12) Bombing Officer
(13) Headquarters
(14) WAR DIARY

B.1.

NARRATIVE of OPERATIONS during 18th November
7th East Lancashire Regt

The Battalion took over the HANSA LINE from the 7th Kings Own Regt at 11pm 17th November. At 3.15 AM 18/11/16. Operation Order No 132 of the 56th Infy Bde was amended and it was the role of the 7th East Lancs Regt to attack and capture BAILLESCOURT FARM after the 1st and 2nd objectives had been gained.

Owing to small numbers the Battalion was at this time organised into 2 Coys and the Commanding Officer at once sent for the Coy Commanders and explained verbally about the plan of attack was — Operation orders were also issued (attached)

At 6.10 AM the barrage commenced and about 7.45 AM Battalion Headquarters were moved into the HANSA TRENCH.

No news being received of the success or otherwise of the attacks on the first and second objectives, the Commanding Officer determined to carry out the orders given him with the object of

(1) attacking BAILLESCOURT FARM if the previous operations had been successful

(2) of helping the 7/South Lancashire Regt had they been unsuccessful

At 8.20 AM No 1 Coy with ½ Bombers & Lewis guns moved from the HANSA LINE crossed the R. ANCRE to the Railway embankment and proceeded along the embankment. Progress was good to point R.8.c.9.7 where the Company was held up by machine gun fire about 9.50 AM. During this time our own artillery barrage was playing on the embankment & hindered progress.

Efforts were made to push forward but it was recognised that GRANDCOURT had not fallen. At this time Colonel Youll was dangerously wounded (10 AM)

Owing to the machine gun fire from direction of O.G.1, PUISIEUX Trench and along the embankment orders were given to this Company to dig in which they finished doing about 1p.m. Meanwhile, at 8.30 am No II Coy had left the HANSA LINE and proceeded down HANSA Road.

No messages were received from this Company until 11.53 am when the OC the Coy reported that he had been held up by machine gun fire just outside the village and was now digging in about point R.8.d.3.5.

The situation remained unchanged when MAJOR H. L. Jones arrived to take command about 5 pm. He at once ascertained personally the situation and reported at 6.25 pm that the Battalion now held the following line; Right on R.8.d.1.3 thence north along northern along northern bank of railway embankment to about R.8.d.1.7. Right Coy Commander was ordered to get into touch with troops in O.G.1 and left Company with troops in PUISIEUX trench. This they both proceeded in doing. The left Company Commander getting into touch with the 4th Middlesex Regt who were holding the southern end of PUISEUX Trench and were holding a line of posts from there through the Bois D' Hollande to ARTILLERY LANE. At 9 pm the left Coy Commander was ordered to make a strong point at R.8.d.3.8 on the north side of the Railway embankment. This was done and garrisoned by 1 Vickers gun, 1 Lewis gun & 25 N.C.Os & men.

At 12.40 AM on 19/9/16 the right Coy was withdrawn to the support line in rear of HANSA TRENCH.

3

At 8.50 pm on 18/11/16 orders were received to withdraw the left Coy and its strong posts on the completion of the new trench.

The method being as soon as the 7/ South Lancashire Regt on the right had withdrawn their strong post at R.8.d.5.4½ the 7/ East Lancashire strong post would then withdraw. An Officer patrol was sent to the 7/ South Lancashire Regt strong post for the purpose of notifying their withdrawal.

The withdrawal was completed about 3.30 am and was effected without a casualty.

(B 2)

BATTALION EAST LANCASHIRE OPERATION
ORDER. NO 3.   REF. 1/1000 OPERATION TRENCH MAP.
                                                           15-11-16.

1. The 19th Division is to capture the western & major position of GRANDCOURT.

2. OBJECTIVE: (a) 57th Brigade with South Lancashire Regt on their left are to take the line of the road running from R.9.a.9½ - O.R.9.b.20.25 dividing line between above units will be the main road through the village working eastwards.
   (b) after capture of 1st objective the 4th East Lancashire Regt will attack BAILLESCOURT FARM.

3. ACTION. With above intention the battalion will leave the NORTHERN END HANSA LINE as follows.
   No. I Coys (A & B) at 8.40 A.M. moving thence to BEAUCOURT MILL across the river to the southern side of the RAILWAY EMBANKMENT under cover of which they will move, finally halting and facing North with their left just south of junction of road and railway embankment R.9.a.6.4. their right on railway embankment about 9.a.y.y.
   No. 2 Coys (C & D) at 9.30 a.m. moving thence via the HANSA ROAD under the cover of R.9.a.7.1 to the railway embankment where they will form up facing North with their left about R.9.a. 7.2. and their right about R.9.a.20.4.2. Both Coys will reorganise in readiness to push northwards for the assault on BAILLESCOURT FARM.

4. POSITIONS as far as Railway Embankment (position of assembly) companies will move by Platoons at distances of 50 yards between Platoons which will move in file.

5. The intention then is to cross the river at bridges. No.1 company by the bridge at R.9.a.y.8. No.2 Coy. at R.9.b.9.6. whence both will proceed under the Artillery barrage direct on BAILLESCOURT FARM. both leaving the railway embankment at 9.40 a.m.
   Horn Barrage lifts off BAILLESCOURT FARM at 10.20 a.m. Lewis open at 10.40 a.m.

6. REPORTS: To Headquarters with No.I Coy along Railway Embankment.
   (a) up to position of Railway Embankment Bombers will move half with No.1 & half with No. II Coy. In the movement northwards from the Railway Embankment they will be half & half as a Regimental Reserve.
   (b) one VICKERS Gun will move with & in rear of each Coy up to position of assembly on Railway Embankment. Afterwards they also will be employed on Railway Embankment as a Regimental reserve.

WAR DIARY
INTELLIGENCE SUMMARY

Army Form C. 2118.

ORDERLY ROOM - 7th BN. EAST LANCS REGT - 4 JAN 1917

Vol 14

Place	Date	Hour	Summary of Events and Information	Remarks and references to Appendices
FIENVILLERS	1916 DEC 1st		In Billets	
	2nd		do	Training carried out
	3rd		do	do
	4th		do	The Battalion furnished for Brigade Service Instruction party of 200 N.C.Os and men. Remainder worked at Camouflage under R.E.
	5th		do	Training carried out
	6th		do	do
	7th		do	do
	8th		do	Escort of 30 O.R.s furnished. Training carried out. Working party of 30 N.C.Os and men found for whole or half of ripple range.
	9th		do	Route march of 8 miles. Escort of 9 O.R.s found. Battalion furnished for Brigade Service.
	10th		do	Working party of 200 N.C.Os and men found for Ripple Range at Candas under R.E.
	11th		do	
	12th		do	Battalion found fatigue parties for Ripple Range.
	13th		do	Training carried out, and working party on Ripple Range found. Major W. Manning's Brigade Staff dinner. Lieutenan posted to Battn. Training carried out.
	14th		do	Training parties furnished for R.E.

WAR DIARY or INTELLIGENCE SUMMARY

Army Form C. 2118.

(Erase heading not required.)

Instructions regarding War Diaries and Intelligence Summaries are contained in F. S. Regs., Part II. and the Staff Manual respectively. Title Pages will be prepared in manuscript.

ORDERLY ROOM – 4 JAN 1917 – 4th M. EAST LANCS REGT.

Place: FIENVILLERS

Date	Hour	Summary of Events and Information	Remarks and references to Appendices
1916 DEC 15th	.	Working party of 20 O.R's found for working under R.E. at Candas, also working party on Rifle Range. During carried out.	
16th	.	do — Baton Range for Evening Service Baths at Candas.	
17th	.	do — During carried out. 2nd Lt B.E. Freeame rejoined the Batn.	
18th	.	do — Draining carried out	
19th	.	do — do —	
20th	.	do — Inspection by Bn'de Commander	
21st	.	do — Training carried out on Rifle Range	
22nd	.	do — Drafts practised on Rifle Range. Bathing party at 20 A.R.S. Kinema	
23rd	.	do — Lu range at Candas. G.O.C. 56th Brigade inspected drafts newly received.	
24th	.	do — Baselim learned for Divine Service.	
25th	.	do — do —	
26th	.	do — During on Range for Drafts and working parties found. Entertainment Section under 2nd Lt Tait formed	
27th	.	do — During carried out	

2449 Wt. W14957/M90 750,000 1/16 J.B.C. & A. Forms/C.2118/12.

Army Form C. 2118.

WAR DIARY
or
INTELLIGENCE SUMMARY
(Erase heading not required.)

Instructions regarding War Diaries and Intelligence Summaries are contained in F. S. Regs., Part II. and the Staff Manual respectively. Title Pages will be prepared in manuscript.

Place	Date	Hour	Summary of Events and Information	Remarks and references to Appendices
FIENVILLERS	DEC 1916 28th		In Billets. Training carried out	
	29th		—do— Running, carrying out Bayonet Fighting on Rifle Range. 2nd Lt. J. Bevir and 2nd Lt. R. Ashton joined. Baths at Candas.	
	30		—do— Working party found for work on Range. Baths at Candas.	
	31		—do— Battalion paraded for Divine Service	

[Stamp: ORDERLY ROOM – 4 JAN 1917 – 7th BN. THE LONDON REGT.]

Army Form C. 2118.

WAR DIARY
or
INTELLIGENCE SUMMARY
(Erase heading not required.)

7th East York Regt
Vol 5

Instructions regarding War Diaries and Intelligence Summaries are contained in F. S. Regs., Part II. and the Staff Manual respectively. Title Pages will be prepared in manuscript.

Place	Date	Hour	Summary of Events and Information	Remarks and references to Appendices
FIENVILLERS	2-7-17		Training carried out. Work of entraining fatigue however gave a charging party of 160 other ranks and rendered near the ridge.	
	3-7-17		Training carried out. Entraining party of 1 officer and 50 other ranks employed on ongoing trains.	
		2 p.m.	Game. Capt P.L. Shern and Lieut Coe reported on to Divnl training school of CANDAS. One officer and 25 other ranks ongoing funds.	(small 8) 60 ORKS absent
	4-7-17		Training. Parties of 50 other ranks dug trenches.	
	5-7-17		Training. 150 other ranks dug trenches.	
	6-7-17		A lecture to reinforcements put up by 2/Lieut Hartman (Bombing officer) was witnessed by Brig. General Commander and officers of Brigade.	
	7-7-17		Lieut Banks to Divnl School. Entraining Command had a return to available officers, NCOs and men of Bn, 187th Bn marched off for reconnection for garrison. Command had him assisted in reconnections for garrison and arrangements made on the plan. Major in charge NCO and men to attend to training of men. Training officer: CAPT. R. Parkinson. I/C. 3 O.R. MILITARY CROSS. CAPT E. G. EDWARDS 13.30 Left by motor 13.30 Fell in parties 13.30 by 1	
			Battalion moved out by march route bundling parties at Brigade Ground to RAINCHEVAL	
	8-7-17		Route via COIGNEUX ACH 37 at Ingers Counterpoint known attack.	
RAINCHEVAL	9-7-17		Reinforcement joined from York Regt Dep. 37 2nd Lieut T.H. EAST.	

2449 Wt. W4957/M90 750,000 1/16 J.B.C. & A. Forms/C.2118/12.

WAR DIARY or INTELLIGENCE SUMMARY

Army Form C. 2118.

Instructions regarding War Diaries and Intelligence Summaries are contained in F. S. Regs., Part II. and the Staff Manual respectively. Title Pages will be prepared in manuscript.

(Erase heading not required.)

Place	Date	Hour	Summary of Events and Information	Remarks and references to Appendices
COIGNEUX	11/1/17		Working parties of Cpls. Palmer and 200 other ranks employed by the Divisional of B Coy 6th Lakes Bn. Remainder of Bn. Battalion employed in cleaning up the camp. Guinsby.	
"	12/1/17		A Coy and 2 pts. now of B Coy sent on the trek and with B Coy 6th Lakes Regt. sent north on the railway improving the camp. Remainder of Battalion employed in carrying out Company training & at rate training. C Coy and Res. B Coy went up to Russell trench under 2nd Lieut. 6th Lakes Battalion.	
"	13/1/17		CHURCH PARADES. C.E. at Y.M.C.A. hut COIGNEUX. R.C. at COURN CHURCH. NONCONFORMIST AT Y.M.C.A. hut COIGNEUX.	
"	14/1/17		Cpl. aspt. working party of Battn. Lieut. Breeze at pm 15-1-17. Drums band and B Coy and 2 A Coy under Capt. Johnson marched out 2/Coy 6th Lakes Battalion.	
"	15/1/17			
"	16/1/17		During the quiet working parties as on the 15th inst were found. The 6th Lakes Battalion (Lieut. Johnson D Coy training and two working parties of R.E. dumps. Two Coys. by D Coy improving the camp.	Bands as the other morning
"	17/1/17		B.C. and 2 platoons of A Coy on working parties. Remainder of Bn. taken training.	
"	18/1/17		A and B Coys trenching to reach. C and D on marching & firing	
"	19/1/17		C and D Coys trenches to reach. A & B on marching & firing.	
"	20/1/17		All parades the same as on 19th inst.	
"	21/1/17		C & E and NONCONFORMIST SERVICES in Y.M.C.A. HUT. COIGNEUX. C and B Coy on marching parties.	

WAR DIARY
or
INTELLIGENCE SUMMARY

Army Form C. 2118.

Place	Date	Hour	Summary of Events and Information	Remarks and references to Appendices
COIGNEUX	25/1/17		Route march taken over by the Lieut. Colonel. Training from 8th North Staffordshire Regt. Regimental training in Warfare under Lieut. Hann & Section Commanders from the Brigade in the Trenches at BAYENCOURT. Two Coys A and B Relieving them K 16.6.5.1/2. – K 16.6.5.6. Relieving posts Nos 1.2.3.4.5.6.7.8.9. Two Coys C and D in support in trenches in HEBUTERNE. Band and two Corps attd. to us for the meanwhile.	
	26/1/17		MAP SHEET HEBUTERNE 1/10,000	
	27/1/17		General Routine carried out	
	28/1/17		" " " "	
	29/1/17		Relieved in the line by 1/4 Kings Own R Regt and Kings Own 1st & 6th other ranks swimming at BAYENCOURT. Available from 10.25am to 2.25pm. Company inspections carried out and Company inspections. Bank held-up made by Brigadier in the morning.	
BAYENCOURT	29/1/17		C of E SERVICE at Y.M.C.A. hut. BAYENCOURT. R.C. MASS in BAYENCOURT CHURCH. Battalion to be ready to take over the line from 1/4 Kings Own R Regt in the trenches 26 to 39 & 32 by subsection 1/6 West Yorkshire Regt 62nd Division are about to carry out a raid midway 26 in trench K and 2/6 KO in front- aud Battalion 2/6 West Yorkshire Regt. 24 hours notice carried out two Kensham at 2/6 West Yorkshire Regt. Awaited for 24 hour inspection. Brigadier to change-over and become as further.	
	30/1/17		No. 1 Coy. 3 platoons 1/4 Kens R Regt from K 16.6.5.1/2 – K 16.6.5.6. Relieving Posts No 1.2.3.4.5. 1 Keuchain in KENSINGTON HOUSE who and to "G" in POSISIER. Bn HDQRS in the "R" line.	
	30/1/17		No. 2 Coy. 3 platoons [?] K 16.6.5.6 – K 10.d.4.0. Keuchain from posts No 6.7. 8. 9. Bn HDQRS and two platoons in Kensington House S.E. sent to on Yellow line (POSISIER)	

WAR DIARY or INTELLIGENCE SUMMARY

Army Form C. 2118.

(Erase heading not required.)

Instructions regarding War Diaries and Intelligence Summaries are contained in F. S. Regs., Part II. and the Staff Manual respectively. Title Pages will be prepared in manuscript.

Place	Date	Hour	Summary of Events and Information	Remarks and references to Appendices
	29/1/17 (contd)		No. 3 Coy. Relieving posts for "R" line from K.10 d. 4.0 – K.10 d. S.3. Relieving posts at K.9 d. S.2. Coy HQRS and two platoons in support at K.9 d. S.2. "Jumps" to WHISKEY STREET and WHISKEY STREET.	
			No. 4 Coy. Coy HQRS and two platoons from K.10 d. 3/2 – K.10 d. I.8. Relieving posts No. 8 and 9. 2 platoons in support at K.9 d. S.2. "Jump to" on YELLOW LINE between WOOD STREET and WOMAN STREET. MAPSHEET HEBUTERNE 1/10,000	
	30/1/17		Front Line Posture. Two platoons of 2/5th WEST YORKSHIRE REGT. 62nd DIVISION attached for 24 hours instruction.	
	31/1/17		Relieved by 4th Hunts. Own Royal Lancaster Regt. A and B Coys went to HEBUTERNE KEEP. C and D Coys to SAILLY. 2 platoons of 2/5 WEST YORKSHIRE REGIMENT attached. Casualties 28th to 31st. 6 other ranks wounded.	

WAR DIARY or INTELLIGENCE SUMMARY

Army Form C. 2118.

7 E Lanc Regt
Vol 20/16

Place	Date	Hour	Summary of Events and Information	Remarks and references to Appendices
SAILLY	4/2/17		Battalion in Brigade Support. A and B Companies in HEBUTERNE KEEP. C and D companies with Battalion Hqrs in SAILLY. One Platoon employed on trench tramway pushing. Following officers attached to 12th HEAVY ARTILLERY GROUP for two days. 2/Lieut N.J. JONES D.S.O. Sgt R.E. EDWARDS M.C. 2/Lt R.H. RUSSELL 2/Lt I.E. HART.	
	2/2/17		Capt P. DIXON and 2/Lt EPR Encaring attached to 56th Heavy Artillery Group.	
			Baths at RED DELH. SAILLY for 280 men. Fine platoons employed on trench tramway pushing.	
TRENCHES	3/2/17		Battalion moved into the line and takes over from 8th BN KINGS OWN REGT.	
			Lecture by 2/5th DUKE OF WELLINGTON'S X.L. INFANTRY as arranged for instruction in Lewis Gun matériel.	
			2/LT R.D. ALLSOPP from O.W.B. 3rd BN attached to the Regiment.	
	4/2/17		Usual trench routine. Situation normal.	
	5/2/17		Usual trench routine. 1 O.R. killed 2 wounded 2/Lt Bentley 7th DUKE OF WELLINGTON'S REGT and 2 O.Rs reporting ordered on ration.	
	6/2/17		Each Coy relieved in turn and moved by 7th ROYAL LANC. REGT. Battalion moved into BRIGADE RESERVE at SAILLENCOURT. 2 O.Rs. wounded.	
SAILLENCOURT	7/2/17		Battalion arrived in Battn. Adjt N.C.Os received instruction in musketry under Serj Duncan 9th (R) BATT ROYAL SCOTS.	
	8/2/17		Platoon training carried out.	
	9/2/17		Training carried out. Battalion moved into trenches at HEBUTERNE and relieved 2nd ROYAL LANCASTER REGT. MAJOR W MORRISON took over command until 2/Lt Coxe on leave. 1 O.R killed and 1 wounded.	

2449 Wt. W14957/M90 750,000 1/16 J.B.C. & A. Forms/C.2118/12.

WAR DIARY or INTELLIGENCE SUMMARY

Army Form C. 2118.

Instructions regarding War Diaries and Intelligence Summaries are contained in F.S. Regs., Part II and the Staff Manual respectively. Title Pages will be prepared in manuscript.

(Erase heading not required.)

Place	Date	Hour	Summary of Events and Information	Remarks and references to Appendices
TRENCHES	10/3/17		Sniping Parties carried out. R.R.O. Messing Corp. and Parties of A/ADJT 5TH K.O. Parties and OR's Establishment Batteries.	
"	11/3/17		1 O.R. killed and 1 wounded. Sniper Parties carried out.	
"	12/3/17		Sniper Parties carried out. 2 O.R. wounded, 1 Killed.	
"	13/3/17		Sniper Parties carried out. Relieved in trenches by 2ND KINGS OWN REGT and moved into BRIGADE SUPPORT, A and B COYS. 5TH BN HQRS at SAILLY AU BOIS C and D Coys in HEBUTERNE KEEP. Employed digging an infantry trench. 3 OR's wounded.	
SAILLY	14/3/17		Parties on Brigade Gothic Running Trench and by A and B Coys. C and D Coys staying Trench at the Deep, SAILLY. Battalion also	
"	15/3/17		Wiring and trenching trenches carried out.	
"	16/3/17		Wiring and improving trenches carried out.	
"	17/3/17		Wiring and working parties carried out. Battalion moved into trenches and relieved 2ND KINGS OWN REGT at HEBUTERNE. Dispositions RIGHT TO LEFT - A.B.C.D Coys.	
TRENCHES	18/3/17		Sniper Parties carried out. 1 OR wounded.	
"	19/3/17		Sniper Parties carried out.	
"	20/3/17		Sniper Parties carried out. 1 O.R. wounded.	
"	21/3/17		Battalion relieved in the trenches by the 16TH WEST YORKS REGT and moved into huts at BUS LES ARTOIS.	
BUS	22/3/17		Battalion enjoying generally cleaning up kits kinging.	
"	23/3/17		Battalion cooking and training, including general interior economy & organising N.C.O's and baths.	
"	24/3/17		Training carried out. Battalion had baths. R.S.M. R.B. NUGENT granted a commission in Battalion	

2449 Wt. W4957/M90 750,000 1/16 J.B.C. & A. Forms/C.2118/12.

Army Form C. 2118.

WAR DIARY
or
INTELLIGENCE SUMMARY
(Erase heading not required.)

Instructions regarding War Diaries and Intelligence Summaries are contained in F. S. Regs., Part II. and the Staff Manual respectively. Title Pages will be prepared in manuscript.

Place	Date	Hour	Summary of Events and Information	Remarks and references to Appendices
BUS	27/3/17		Church Parade cancelled. Battalion ordered to "stand to" ready to move at 1 hours notice owing to General Retirement of enemy.	
BUS. COURCELLES	2/4/17		Battalion ordered to move to COURCELLES-AU-BOIS in reserve. Move completed by 10 AM. Battalion in Reserve and Rest.	
—	2/4/17		Working parties and Covering party by Battery Battalion received orders to move to LEALVILLERS for eight days retirement from Reserve and took over Command.	
HENUILLERS	3/4/17		Whole Battalion engaged on railway working.	

R. Rudolph Lt/Col/A/M
7th East Lanc. Regt.

WAR DIARY or INTELLIGENCE SUMMARY

Army Form C. 2118.

7 Etrucis Vol 17

Place	Date	Hour	Summary of Events and Information	Remarks and references to Appendices
LEALVILLERS	1/3/17		Battalion carried out training. 300 men (not including officers and N.C.O's) engaged on VARENNES NEW SIDINGS.	
	2/3/17		Battalion carried out training. 300 men (not including officers and N.C.O's) engaged on VARENNES NEW SIDINGS.	
	3/3/17		Battalion carried out training.	
	4/3/17		Battalion harnessed for Divine Service.	
BERTRANCOURT	5/3/17		Battalion moved to BERTRANCOURT.	
	6/3/17		Battalion engaged on work at EUSTON under R.E.	
	7/3/17		Battalion engaged on work at EUSTON under R.E.	
	8/3/17		Battalion carried out training. Cleaning up &c generally. Preparing for a new movement.	
BERTRANCOURT / AUTHIE	9/3/17		Battalion moved to AUTHIE.	
LONGUEVILLETTE	10/3/17		Battalion moved into billets at LONGUEVILLETTE.	
NEUVILLETTE	11/3/17		Battalion moved into billets at NEUVILLETTE.	
	12/3/17		Battalion carried out training.	
	13/3/17		Battalion march to billets in HERICOURT and GUINECOURT. B and HDQRS billeted at HERICOURT, A+C Coys at GUINECOURT.	
HERICOURT AND GUINECOURT	14/3/17		Battalion moved to billets at MONCHY CAYEUX.	
MONCHY-CAYEUX	15/3/17		Battalion carried out training.	
LAIRES	16/3/17		Battalion march to LAIRES.	

Army Form C. 2118.

WAR DIARY
or
INTELLIGENCE SUMMARY

(Erase heading not required.)

Instructions regarding War Diaries and Intelligence Summaries are contained in F.S. Regs., Part II. and the Staff Manual respectively. Title Pages will be prepared in manuscript.

Place	Date	Hour	Summary of Events and Information	Remarks and references to Appendices
LAIRES	17/3/17		Battalion carried out training	
LAMBRES	18/3/17		Battalion moved to LAMBRES	
LAMBRES	19/3/17		Battalion moved to EBBLINGHEM	
EBBLINGHEM	20/3/17		Battalion moved to ZOUAFQUES	
ZOUAFQUES	21/3/17		Battalion carried out training, musketry and signal Platoon training	
"	22/3/17		Battalion carried out training	
"	23/3/17		Battalion carried out training	
"	24/3/17		Battalion carried out training	
"	25/3/17		Battalion carried out training, and handed in kits and Divine Service (voluntary)	
"	26/3/17		Battalion carried out training	
"	27/3/17		Battalion carried out training 2nd Lt L.C. Tomlin rejoined	
"	28/3/17		Battalion carried out training	
"	29/3/17		Brigade tactical scheme carried out	
"	30/3/17		Battalion carried out training	
"	31/3/17		Brigade tactical scheme carried out in conjunction with 2nd KINGS OWN ROYAL LANCASTER REGT.	

Brampton
Lt and Adjt.
2nd East Lanc Regt

WAR DIARY
INTELLIGENCE SUMMARY
(Erase heading not required.)

Army Form C. 2118.

7 E Lanc Rgt
Vol 18

Place	Date	Hour	Summary of Events and Information	Remarks and references to Appendices
ZOUAFQUES	1/4/17		Strength in France. Officers 36. Other ranks 1245.	
— do —	1/4/17		Battalion Billets at ZOUAFQUES and carried out Training, also parade for Divine Service.	
ZOUAFQUES	2/4/17		Battn moved into billets at LONGUENESS W. ST OMER and was billeted there one night.	
LONGUENESS	3/4/17		" " " HAZEBROUCK and was billeted there one night. 2/Lt F.V. Lewish joined.	
HAZEBROUCK	4/4/17		" " " ROUGE CROIX near CAESTRE.	
CAESTRE	5/4/17		Battn carried out Training.	
— do —	6/4/17		Battn moved into Canvas Camp called WESTON CAMP nr. SCHERPENBERG	
WESTON CAMP	7/4/17		" carried out Training.	
— do —	8/4/17		" " " "	
			" moved into tents at Murrumbidgee Camp near to CLYTTE and carried out working parties as follows:– 200 men on VIERSTRAAT SWITCH and 100 men carrying party to emplacement. 2/Lt H.B. Nelson joined Battalion.	
MURRUMBIDGEE CAMP	9/4/17		Major W. Duckworth took over command of Bn vice Lt Col Innes to course. Battn carried out training and working parties as yesterday.	O.O.1.
— do —	10/4/17		" paraded for baths at WESTOUTRE. Other changes were available.	
— do —	11/4/17		" carried out training and working parties as before. No working parties	
— do —	12/4/17		" carried out training	
			Battn moved into line and relieved 9th Cheshire Regiment in Left subsector of DISPENDAAL SECTOR (Belgium) Sheet 28) Dispositions – C. Coy on right, D Coy on left of Subsector, A Coy in Support at BOIS CARRE and B Coy in Reserve	
TRENCHES (DISPENDAAL SECTOR)	13/4/17		Battn carried out ordinary Trench Routine. Enemy Artillery shelled Bois Carre with 5.9's. Casualties. 3 Other ranks wounded.	
— do —	14/4/17		Battn carried out ordinary Trench Routine. Casualties 3 men killed, 1 died of wounds and 6 wounded.	
— do —	15/4/17		Battn carried out ordinary Trench Routine. Casualties – 1 killed.	

Army Form C. 2118.

WAR DIARY
INTELLIGENCE SUMMARY
(Erase heading not required.)

Instructions regarding War Diaries and Intelligence Summaries are contained in F. S. Regs., Part II. and the Staff Manual respectively. Title Pages will be prepared in manuscript.

Place	Date	Hour	Summary of Events and Information	Remarks and references to Appendices
TRENCHES (DIEPENDAAL SECTOR)	16/4/17		Battn. relieved in the trenches by 7th King's Own Royal Lancaster Regiment and on relief moved into RIDGE WOOD in support. Shortly after Battn. had settled in RIDGE WOOD about 12 noon, the enemy shelled and caused casualties, one killed and four wounded. Lt Col Jones returned from Course and took over command. Captain H.O. Paint took over duties of 2nd i/c via Captn. R. S. F. Warlock.	O.O. 2.
RIDGE WOOD	17/4/17		At night Battn. carried out working parties.	
— do —	18/4/17		Battn. in Ridge Wood. Enemy again shelled Wood about 5 p.m. causing Casualties. - 2 killed and 1 wounded. Battn. found working parties.	
— do —	19/4/17		Battn. still in Bde Support. Found working parties for line and improving dugouts.	
— do —	20/4/17		Battn. still in Bde Support. Found working parties for line and improving dugouts. Battn. carried out working parties. Orders to relieve at night starting at 8.45 p.m. Enemy shelled line with shells of all calibre; relief postponed for hour. Relief afterwards carried out without casualties. Battn. now situad in Right Subsector of DIEPENDAAL SECTOR. Dispositions - A Coy on right. B Coy on left. D Coy in Support and C Coy in Reserve with 1 Platoon in VIERSTRAAT.	O.O. 3.
RIGHT SUB-SECTOR	21/4/17		Trench Routine carried out. No casualties. Enemy planes active.	
— do —	22/4/17		— do —	
— do —	23/4/17		— do —	
— do —	24/4/17		— do —	
— do —	24/4/17		Battalion relieved by 7th King's Own Regiment and moved into MURRUMBIDGEE CAMP. Relief completed without casualties.	
MURRUMBIDGEE CAMP	25/4/17		Battn. in Murrumbidgee Camp in Bde Reserve. Carried out training. C.O. and A Companies had baths in the Camp. 80 men attended Anti-Gas Course.	
— do —	26/4/17		Battn. carried out training. 20 men attended Anti-Gas Course. B Coy and other details attended baths.	

REFERENCE MAP
WYTSCHAETE 28
S.W.2. 1/10.000.
D.O.H.

WAR DIARY

INTELLIGENCE SUMMARY

Army Form C. 2118.

Instructions regarding War Diaries and Intelligence Summaries are contained in F. S. Regs., Part II. and the Staff Manual respectively. Title Pages will be prepared in manuscript.

(Erase heading not required.)

Place	Date	Hour	Summary of Events and Information	Remarks and references to Appendices
MURRUMBIDGE CAMP	27/4/17		Training carried out. Bath. found 2 officers and 150 other ranks for working party in front line, filling gaps at midnight. 80 men attended Anti-Gas Course. Gas Course	
—do—	28/4/17		Training carried out. 80 men attended Anti-Gas Course. 1 Officer and 50 other ranks working party at 9-30 p.m on support line.	
—do—	29/4/17		Battalion paraded for Divine service. Working party of 60 other ranks found for work on DICKEBUSCH SECTOR.	
—do—	30/4/17		Battalion carried out training.	
			Strength of Battalion in France. Officers 36 - other ranks 1148.	

RELIEF ORDERS No 1.

By MAJOR W. MORRISON, M.C.
Comdg 7th East Lancashire Regiment.
11 - 4 - 17.

REVEILLE . . . . . . 3-30 a.m.
BREAKFAST. . . . . . 4- 0 a.m.
SICK PARADE . . . . 4-30 a.m.

MOVE 1.   The Battalion will move into the line tomorrow morning and relieve 9th CHESHIRE REGIMENT.
Companies will relieve the corresponding Companies of that Regiment and will move off in the following order :-
C. D. A. B. and HDQRS Companies at the following times :-
C Company   5-15 a.m.
D   "   5-45 a.m.
A   "   6-15 a.m.
B   "   6-45 a.m.
HEADQUARTERS 7-15 a.m.

Route :- Via D I C K E B U S C H.

All movements to be by platoons at 100 yards interval to DICKEBUSCH and then by sections at 100 yards interval EAST of that place.
GUIDES for Companies will be at the BRASSERIE at 6-30 a.m.
Cooks will take up Camp Kettles and rations and move off in advance of Battalion and prepare dinners for men.
Two limbers will report to the Master Cook at 5 a.m. who will see them loaded and then move off to the Tramway Junction on the HALLEBAST ROAD, load trollies there and take them to BATTALION HEADQUARTERS.
Maltese Cart, Mess Cart, 2 limbers for Lewis Guns and pack animals for Company Officers' Mess Stores will report at HDQRS with one limber for HDQRS STORES at 6 a.m.
These will proceed to Tramway Junction and take Stores to the BRASSERIE.
Officers Servants will accompany pack animals. All trucks to be returned to junction after use.
B Company will find all carrying parties from Battalion Headquarters to C and D Companies.
Headquarters will find carrying parties from Tramway Junction to Battalion Headquarters.
5 Scouts per Company will report to R.S.M. at 6-30 a.m. tomorrow and will be rationed and attached to Battalion Headqrs while in the line.
C.Q.M.Ss and Company Clerks will proceed to DEPOT tomorrow.
L'Cpl Fairburn will act temporarily as Hdqrs C.Q.M.S.
DRUMMERS will be left behind and be billeted in 2 huts near Farm close to D Company's huts.
Instructional Staff will be billeted in a barn in this Farm.
Sergt Stevens will be in charge of all men and stores left in this Camp and will move men into new quarters by 7-15 a.m.
BLANKETS, Officers Kits and Company Stores will be dumped in this Barn by 5-0 a.m.
Receipts for trench stores taken over will be carefully checked and forwarded to ORDERLY ROOM by 6 p.m.
As little smoke as possible will be visible while in this Sector.
On completion of relief, Companies will wire the words "RED ROSE".

(Sgd)
R. D. ALLSOPP,
Lt and Adjutant,
7th East Lancashire Regiment.

SECRET.   Copy No

7th EAST LANCASHIRE REGIMENT.

OPERATION ORDER No 2.   15 - 4 - 17.

1. **RELIEF**   The Battalion will be relieved in the LEFT SUB-SECTOR tomorrow by the 7TH BATTALION KINGS OWN ROYAL LANCASTER REGIMENT and on being relieved will move into RIDGE WOOD.

2. **GUIDES**   Two Guides per platoon and one for Battalion Headquarters will be at the BRASSERIE at 5-0 a.m. and report to C. S. M. HEYS.

3. **ADVANCE PARTY.**   1 Sergeant and 1 man per Company will report to Captain HOUSE at Battalion Hdqrs at 5-30 a.m. to take over Stores and to guide Companies in.

4. **ORDER OF RELIEF.**

	KINGS OWN									
D Coy 7th	"	"	"	"	will relieve	D Coy 7th	East Lanc Regt			
C "	"	"	"	"	"	C "	"	"	"	"
A "	"	"	"	"	"	A "	"	"	"	"
B "	"	"	"	"	"	B "	"	"	"	"
HDQRS	"	"	"	"	"	HDQRS	"	"	"	"

5. **COMMUNICATION TRENCHES.**   P. & O. Communication Trench will not be used,   All Companies will be relieved via CHICORY LANE Communication Trench.

6. **MOVEMENTS.** All movements in trenches and all the way to RIDGE WOOD will be in parties of 3 at 50 paces interval.
   While moving down CHICORY LANE TRENCH arms must be carried at the trail.

7. **LEWIS GUNS** will be carried all the way to RIDGE WOOD.

8. **COMPANY MESS STORES** Cooking Utensils &c will be at the BRASSERIE at 5-15 a.m.   These will be placed direct on the trollies and sent to RIDGE WOOD.
   Trollies will then be sent to TRAMWAY JUNCTION for use of 7th KINGS OWN REGIMENT.

9. **TRENCH STORE RECEIPTS** will be forwarded to ORDERLY ROOM by 6 p.m.

10. **ON** completion of Relief, Companies will wire the word "MERCI".

                    (Sgd)
                        R. D. ALLSOPP.
                        Lt and Adjutant,
                        7th Bn East Lancashire Regiment.

Issued at 2 p.m.
                Copy No 1   O. C. A Company
                        2   O. C. B   "
                        3   O. C. C   "
                        4   O. C. D   "
                        5   Commanding Officer.
                        6   Captain House.
                        7   Signalling Officer.
                        8   Lewis Gun Officer.
                        9   Q'Mr & Transport Officer.
                       10   R. S. M.
                       11   56th Infantry Brigade.
                       12   58th   "   "
                       13   7th King's Own Regiment.
                       14   War Diary.
                       15   File.

SECRET.   Copy No

EAST LANCASHIRE REGIMENT.

OPERATION ORDER No 3.

                                              19th April 1917.

REFERENCE   1/10,000 WYTSCHAETE TRENCH MAP.

1. RELIEF.   The Battalion will move into the trenches (Right Sub-sector) tomorrow evening, relieving Loyal North Lancashire Regiment.

2. ORDER OF RELIEF   Companies will relieve corresponding Companies of Loyal North Lancashire Regiment.
   B Company (less two platoons) A C and D Companies will move via Cross Roads N. 5. b. 2. 2. along Cheapside to duckboards at N. 11. a. 1½. 8. thence to Poppy Lane Communication Trench. Head of B Company to pass N. 5. b. 2. 2. at 8-45 p. m.
   Two platoons B Company will move via BRASSERIE N. 6. a. 1½. 1½. and Chicory Communication Trench; Head of B Company to pass N. 5. b. 2. 2. at 8 p. m.

3. MOVEMENTS.   B (less 2 platoons) A C and D Companies will move by platoons at 200 yards distance.

4. GUIDES.   Guides (1 per platoon) for B (less two platoons) A C and D Companies will be on Cheapside Road N. 11. a. 1½. 2. at 9 p. m.
   Guides for two platoons of B Company will be at new Reserve Line N. 12. b. 9. 8. at 8-15 p.m.

5. STORES   Officers Mess Kits etc will be at Tramway Junction N. 4. c. 5. 0. at 7-30 p. m.

6. TRENCH STORE RECEIPTS will be carefully checked and copies sent to Orderly Room by 9 a. m. on 21st instant.

7. COMPLETION   On completion of relief, Companies will wire the word "AUTHIE".

                 (Sgd)
                          R. D. ALLSOPP.
                             Lt and Adjutant,
                          7th East Lancashire Regiment.

Issued at 9 p.m.

            Copy No 1 to 56th Infantry Brigade.
                 2 " L. N. Lanc. Regiment.
                 3 " Commanding Officer.
                 4 " O.C. A Company.
                 5 " O.C. B Company.
                 6 " O.C. C Company.
                 7 " O.C. D Company.
                 8 " Lewis Gun Officer.
                 9 " Signalling Officer.
                10 " Transport Officer.
                11 " Quartermaster.
                12 " R. S. M.
                13 " War Diary.
                14 " File.
                15 " Adjutant.

SECRET.   EAST LANCASHIRE REGIMENT.   Copy No.

OPERATION ORDER No 4.

23rd April 1917.

REFERENCE TRENCH MAP WYTSCHAETE 1/10,000.

1. **RELIEF.** The Battalion will be relieved in the Right Sub-sector tomorrow by the KINGS OWN ROYAL LANCASTER REGIMENT and on relief will move into MURRUMBIDGEE CAMP.
    Route :- Via HALLEBAST CORNER N. 3. a. 2. 6. - La CLYTTE.

2. **ORDER OF RELIEF.** Companies will be relieved by the corresponding letter Companies of the King's Own Regiment in the following order :-
    A Coy King's Own Regiment will relieve A Coy East Lanc. Regiment.
    B "   "   "   "   "   "   B "   "   "   "
    D "   "   "   "   "   "   D "   "   "   "
    C "   "   "   "   "   "   C "   "   "   "

3. **GUIDES.** One guide per platoon will be at Advance Dressing Station N. 10. b. 1. 9. at 7-45 p.m. and will report to C.S.M. HEYS.
    Two guides for B Company's two front line platoons to be at BRASSERIE at 7-30 p.m.

4. **ADVANCE PARTY** 1 Sergeant and 1 man per Company will report at Battalion Headquarters at 2-30 p.m. to take over huts at Murrumbidgee Camp; also 1 N. C. O. for Headquarters.
    Major Morrison will meet this party at the Camp at 3-30 p.m.

5. **COMMUNICATION TRENCHES** 2 platoons B Coy and A C and D Companies will be relieved by Poppy Lane Communication Trench and front line platoons of B Company via Chicory Communication Trench.

6. **MOVEMENTS.** All movements by platoons at 200 yards interval.

7. **COMPANY MESS STORES.** Cooking Utensils etc will be dumped at Batln Headquarters at 6 p.m. The Transport Officer will arrange for the Mess Cart, Maltese Cart and 2 limbers for stores to be at Headquarters at 6 p.m. also 2 limbers for Lewis Guns at 10 p.m.
    Officers Chargers to be at Headquarters at 9 p.m.

8. **TRENCH STORE RECEIPTS** will be sent to Orderly Room by 10 a.m. on 25th instant.

9. **COMPLETION.** On completion of relief, Companies will wire the word "LEALVILLERS".

(Sgd)
R. D. ALLSOPP.
Lt and Adjutant,
7th East Lancashire Regiment.

Issued at 9-45 p.m.

1. 56th Infantry Brigade.
2. King's Own Regiment.
3. Commanding Officer.
4. Major W. Morrison.
5. O.C. A Company.
6. O.C. B   "
7. O.C. C   "
8. O.C. D   "
9. Lewis Gun Officer.
10. Signalling Officer.
11. Transport Officer.
12. Quartermaster.
13. R. S. M.
14. War Diary.
15. File.

1/E Lan R

WAR DIARY
INTELLIGENCE SUMMARY
(Erase heading not required.)

Army Form C. 2118.

Vol 19

Instructions regarding War Diaries and Intelligence Summaries are contained in F. S. Regs., Part II. and the Staff Manual respectively. Title Pages will be prepared in manuscript.

Place	Date	Hour	Summary of Events and Information	Remarks and references to Appendices
MOERENBRIDGE CAMP Nº 14 CITTE BELGIUM	1/5/17		Battalion moved from MOERENBRIDGE Camp (Brigade Reserve) into Camp at CARNARVON Camp Nº 10 & S.9 and rested there one night.	MAP SHEET 28 1/40,000 O.O.Nº 5 App.1
CARNARVON CAMP	2/5/17		Battalion moved to ST LAWRENCE Camp G.H.C. Sheet 28 1/40,000	O.O.Nº 6 App. 2
ST LAWRENCE CAMP	3/5/17		Usual Training carried out	
— do —	4/5/17		— ditto —	
— do —	5/5/17		— ditto — Battalion had Baths at POPERINGHE and WINNIPEG Camp	
— do —	6/5/17		Battalion paraded for Divine Service.	
— do —	7/5/17		Battalion training carried out	
— do —	8/5/17		— ditto —	
— do —	9/5/17		Battalion moved to CARPAGH Camp M.17.C.9.8. and rested there during day. In the evening moved into the trenches Right Subsector DIEPENDAAL Sector relieving ½ Royal Inniskilling Fusiliers. Dispositions are D Coy Left Front. C Right Front. A Right Support with one platoon in CONATO TRENCH and B Coy Left Support in new Reserve Line. Enemy quiet front to Relief fairly heavy, trenches and several casualties to ½ Royal Inniskilling Fusiliers who were being relieved. Our relief carried out without a casualty	O.O.7 Ap.3 Sh.3 ½ O.O.8 App.4
TRENCHES RIGHT SUBSECTOR DIEPENDAAL SECTOR	10/5/17		Trench Reliefs carried out	

[signature]

Army Form C. 2118.

WAR DIARY
INTELLIGENCE SUMMARY
(Erase heading not required.)

Instructions regarding War Diaries and Intelligence Summaries are contained in F. S. Regs., Part II. and the Staff Manual respectively. Title Pages will be prepared in manuscript.

Place	Date	Hour	Summary of Events and Information	Remarks and references to Appendices
TRENCHES RIGHT SUBSECTOR DICKEBUSCH SECTOR	11/5/17		Trench Routine carried out. No Casualties	
—do—	12/5/17		— ditto — No Casualties	
—do—	13/5/17		— ditto — 1 wounded 2 shell shock	
			Battalion relieved in line by 1/K.O.R.L.R and moved into Brigade Support at RIDGE WOOD (Sheet 28.S.W. 1/20000)	O.O.9? App. 3
RIDGE WOOD	14/5/17		In Brigade support. Working parties found for front line and improving Camp.	
—do—	15/5/17		— ditto —	
—do—	16/5/17		— ditto —	
—do—	17/5/17		— ditto — Battalion relieved in Ridge Wood and moved into line RIGHT SUB-SECTOR DICKEBUSCH SECTOR relieving 7/K.O.R.L.R.	O.O.10? App.1.2?
TRENCHES	18/5/17		Trench Routine carried out	
—do—	19/5/17		Trench Routine carried out. Battalion attempted to raid German trench but failed owing to many obstacles. Casualties 2 men slightly wounded and 1 missing	REPORT
			2 Lewis guns lost, report attached.	
—do—	20/5/17		Trench Routine carried out. Battalion relieved in Right Subsector by 10th Worcestershire Regiment and move into WESTON CAMP, Nr SCHERPENBERG.	O.O.11? App.7?
WESTON CAMP	21/5/17		(Battalion moved from WESTON CAMP to new Camp near WESTOUTRE called KEMPTON CAMP at M.17 c 55 (Sheet 28 S.W. 1/20000)	O.O.12? App.6,9?
KEMPTON CAMP	22/5/17		Battalion carried out Platoon Training	
—do—	23/5/17		" " " "	
—do—	24/5/17		" " " "	

WAR DIARY
INTELLIGENCE SUMMARY

(Erase heading not required.)

Army Form C. 2118.

Place	Date	Hour	Summary of Events and Information	Remarks and references to Appendices
KEMPTON CAMP	25/5/17		The Battalion was inspected by the Divisional Commander and the inspection was followed by a practice attack. The following Officers and N.C.Os of this Battalion were noted in Gazette as having been MENTIONED IN DESPATCHES. Capt C. G. Edwards, 2/Lt J. School, 2/Lt J. G. Kitchen. 8865 C.R.M.S A. G. Ballery and 13648 f/Sgt J. W. Place.	
-do-	26/5/17		The Battn was inspected by Army Commander and the inspection was followed by a practice attack.	
-do-	27/5/17		Battalion carried out Brigade Practice Attack.	
-do-	28/5/17		Battalion carried out training.	
-do-	29/5/17		Battalion moved from KEMPTON CAMP to RIDGE WOOD into Brigade Support.	
-do-	30/5/17		Battalion in Brigade Support. Working parties found. RIDGE WOOD heavily shelled. Casualties 1/3 wounded.	
-do-	31/5/17		Battalion moved into Camp near La LYTTE M.12.a. 9.5 (Sheet 28 S.W. 1/20000) Casualties 1 killed 5 wounded.	

APPENDIX 1.

SECRET

EAST LANCASHIRE REGIMENT
OPERATION ORDER No 5

Reference Sheet 28   1/40,000

1. MOVE   The Battalion will move into CARNARVON CAMP M 10.b.5.9 via ZEVECOTEN tomorrow.

2. PARADE Companies will parade at 12.30 p.m and march off by Platoons, at an interval of 400 yards distance, in the following order
   Hdqrs, "A" "B" "C" and "D" Coys

3. ADVANCE PARTY 2nd Lieut. G.P.K.Goulding, 1 N.C.O per Company 1 man per platoon and 1 N.C.O for Hdqrs will report at Battn Hdqrs at 12.30 p.m and proceed to CARNARVON CAMP to take over the Hutments etc.

4. STORES Blankets (rolled in bundles of ten) and Officers Kits to be dumped on road North of Camp by 10 a.m and Officers Mess Cooking Utensils by 1.0 p.m
   Cookers will proceed with the Transport
   Transport Officer will arrange for Officers Chargers

5. SALVAGE PARTY 1 Officer and 6 men per Company will be left behind as Salvage Party to ensure that their huts and the vicinity are left in a thoroughly clean condition.

6. There will be no Training Parades but Companies will devote the morning to cleaning up etc.

                Sgd   R.B.Allsopp 2nd Lt & A/Adjt
                      EAST LANCASHIRE REGIMENT

Issued at 9.15 p.m

              Copy No 1   56th Infantry Brigade
                      2   Commanding Officer
                      3   Major W.Morrison
                      4   O.C A Coy
                      5   O.C B Coy
                      6   O.C C Coy
                      7   O.C D Coy
                      8   O.C Lewis Gun Sec.
                      9.   Signalling Officer
                     10.   Transport Officer
                     11.   Quartermaster
                     12   R.S.M
                     13   War Diary
                     14.   File

APPENDIX 2

SECRET   EAST LANCASHIRE REGIMENT
         OPERATION ORDER NO 6
         ....   1/5/1917

         Reference Sheet 28 BELGIUM & FRANCE 1/40,000
         ....

1. The Battalion will move to ST LAWRENCE CAMP G 11 c tomorrow via WESTOUTRE - HEKSKEN - RENENGHELST.

2. Starting Point Road Junction M.17.c.4.6

3. The following distances will be maintained :- ½ Mile between Battalions. 100 yards between Companies, 300 yards between other Units.

4. The Battalion will parade and march off in the following order B,C,D and Hdqrs   The first named Company to leave the Camp at 4 p.m

5. A Motor Lorry will report to the Transport Officer at 10 a.m and will if necessary be available for a second journey

6. Advance Party will proceed by the first lorry trip
   2nd Lt Goulding, 1 N.C.O per Company and 1 man per platoon and 1 N.C.O for Hdqrs will report at Battn Hdqrs at 9.30 a.m tomorrow.

7. Blankets (rolled in bundles of ten) and Officers Kits to be dumped on Ground opposite Orderly Room by 9 a.m and Officers Cooking Utensils by 3 p.m

8. Companies to detail 2 men as loaders to parade outside Orderly Room xxxxxxx xxxxxxx under Sergt Mattison at 9 a.m

9. A return to be rendered by Companies to Orderly Room by 12 noon shewing in detail Camp equipment Stores etc handing over.

10. Watches to be synchronised by the Adjutants by 3.30 p.m

11. Cookers proceed in rear of Companies and Maltese Cart in rear of Hdqr Coy.

12. Transport Officer to arrange for the Officers Chargers

13. Drums will move at the Head of B Coy.

                         Sgd R.B.Hoggett 2nd Lt & A/Adjt
                              East Lancashire Regiment
         Issued at 8.15 p.m

                    Copy No 1   56th Infantry Brigade
                          2   Commanding Officer
                          3   Major Morrison
                          4.   O.C A Coy
                          5   O.C B Coy
                          6.   O.C C Coy
                          7   O.C D Coy
                          8.   Lewis Gun Officer
                          9.   Signalling Officer
                         10.   Transport Officer
                         11.   Quartermaster
                         12.   R. S. M
                         13.   War Diary
                         14.   File

APPENDIX 3

SECRET

EAST LANCASHIRE REGIMENT
OPERATION ORDER NO.7
....   8, 5, 1917.

Reference Sheet BELGIUM & FRANCE 28   1/40,000
Sheet 28 S.W

1. The Battalion will move to CURRAGH CAMP (M.17.c.9.8) tomorrow Transport Lines will move to M.17.b.1.0 (North West of the LA CLYTTE-LOCRE Road) and will remain in them while the Battalion is in the DIEPENDAAL Sector.

2. Reveille 5.30 a.m Breakfast 6.30 a.m Sick Parade 6.45 a.m

3. Starting Point Road Junction G.23 c 7.5. ROUTE:- RENINGHELST -CANADA CORNER.

4. The following distances will be maintained. ½ mile between Battalions and 100 yards between Companies. The Battalion will parade and march off in the following order:-
    Drums C,D,Hdqrs.A,B Coys
    First named Company to leave the Camp at 8 a.m
    Transport will move in rear of Battalion.

5. 2nd Lt Goulding,1 N.C.O per Company and 1 for Hdqrs will proceed to CURRAGH CAMP as Advance Party They will rendezvous at Orderly Room at 7.30 a.m

6. Blankets (rolled in bundles of 10) will be dumped on ground opposite sentry box by 6.30 a.m. Officers Mess Stores,Cooking Utensils&c and other stores by 7.30 a.m

7. Companies will detail 2 men to act as loaders. They will parade at dump at 7.30 a.m

8. Transport Officer will detail Mess Cart,Maltese Cart,2 limbers for Orderly Room and Hdqrs,and 1 for A & B Coys and 1 for C & D Coys to report at 7.15 a.m to carry Stores, He will arrange for Conveyance of Blankets etc.

9. Officers Chargers to be at Battn Hdqrs at 7.45 a.m

10. Watches to be synchronised by the Adjutants by 7.45 a.m

11. Until further arrangements can be made the Training Reserve and Officers attending the Platoon Commanders Class will be accommodated in Battalion Transport Lines.

12. O.C Companies will see that the Camp is left in a thoroughly clean and sanitary condition. 2nd Lt Hoggett and 1 N.C.O per Company will remain behind to hand over stores and obtain certificate of Cleanliness They will then rejoin Battalion.

13. Battalion will move into the trenches Right Subsector, DIEPENDAAL SECTOR tomorrow evening. Details later.

                          Sd.. R.B.Allsopp Lieut & Adjt
                              11x EAST LANCASHIRE REGIMENT

Issued at 11.15 p.m

        Copy No 1   56th Infantry Brigade
             2.   Commanding Officer
             3.   Major Morrison
             4.   O.C A. Coy
             5.   O.C B Coy
             6.   O.C C Coy
             7.   O.C D Coy
             8.   O.C Lewis Gun Sec.
             9.   Capt House
            10.   2nd Lt Hoggett
            11.   Quartermaster

APPENDIX 4

EAST LANCASHIRE REGIMENT
OPERATION ORDER NO 8
....
9.5.1917

Reference Map Sheet 28 1/40,000
Map Sheet 28 S.W

1. Relief The Battalion will move into the Right Subsector, DIEPENDAAL Sector this evening relieving ROYAL INNISKILLING FUSILIERS.

2. Order of Relief Companies will relieve and move off in the following order:- D,C,B,A Coys.
   D Coy E.Lan R will relieve D Coy R.Innis.Fus in the left of subsector
   C Coy E.Lan R will relieve C Coy R.Innis.Fus in right of subsector
   B Coy E.Lan R will relieve B Coy R.Innis.Fus and will be in left support.
   A Coy E.Lan R will relieve A Coy R.Innis.Fus and will be in right support & reserve
   First named Company will leave Curragh Camp at 8 p.m

3. Route. SCHERPENBERG - LA CLYTTE - HALLEBAST - VIERSTRAAT - POPPY LANE.

4. Movements. All movements by platoons at 200 yards distance

5. Guides. One per platoon will be at Right Battalion Hdqrs at 10 p.m

6. STORES, COOKING Utensils etc will be dumped on ground near entrance to Camp by 8 p.m

7. Pack animals for Company Mess Stores. Maltese Cart and Mess Cart 2 limbers for Hdqrs and 2 for Lewis Guns will be at CURRAGH CAMP at 8 p.m to carry stores to line.

8. Rations. will be dumped at Right Battalion Hdqrs and Companies will pick them up on the way to the line.

9. Trench Stores will be carefully checked and copies of lists sent to Orderly Room by 12 noon 10th inst.

10. On completion of relief Companies will wire the word "Crump"

                    Sd... R.D.Allsopp Lieut & Adjt
                        EAST LANCASHIRE REGIMENT

Issued at 5.30 p.m

        Copy No 1   56th Infantry Brigade
             2.   7th Inniskilling Fusiliers
             3.   Commanding Officer
             4.   Major Morrison
             5.   O.C A Coy
             6.   O.C B Coy
             7.   O.C C Coy
             8.   O.C D Coy
             9.   Lewis Gun Officer
            10.   Quartermaster
            11.   Capt House
            12.   2nd Lt Hoggett
            13.   M.O
            14.   War Diary
            15.   File

SECRET EAST LANCASHIRE REGIMENT
        OPERATION ORDER No.9   12. 5. 1917
        ....

REFERENCE Map Sheet WYTSCHAETE 28. S.W 2   1/10,000
          Map Sheet 28 S.W   1/20,000

1. Relief. The Battalion will be relieved in the line by the
   Kings Own Royal Lancaster Regt. tomorrow the 13th inst and on
   relief will move into RIDGE WOOD.
        Route via Poppy Lane- Cheapside- Ridge Wood.

2. Order of Relief. Companies will be relieved as follows:-
        D Coy R.Lan. R will relieve D Coy East Lan. R
        C Coy R.Lan. R will relieve C Coy East Lan. R
        B Coy R.Lan. R will relieve B Coy East Lan. R
        A Coy R.Lan. R will relieve A Coy East Lan. R

3. Movement   All movement by platoons at 200 yards distance.

4. Guides 1 guide per platoon will report to Sergt Hart at POPPY
   LANE R.E Dump at 9.15 p.m.   1 guide for platoon in COCKATOO
   Trench to be at point where duckboards cross CHEAPSIDE
   N.11.a.2.6 at 9.30 p.m.

5. Officers Mess Stores.Kits and Cooking Utensils will be dumped
   at Railhead near 1st Aid Post at 9 p.m

6. Trench Store lists will be forwarded to Orderly Room by 12 noon
   14th inst.

7. Advance Party 1 N.C.O per Company,1 man per platoon and 1 N.CO
   for Hdqrs will report to 2nd Lt Hoggett at Battalion Hdqrs at
   5 p.m. They will take over Billets in RIDGE WOOD and and
   draw rations of their respective Companies.

8. Completion On Completion of relief Companies will wire the
   word "EXTRAS"

                Sgd.   R.D.Allsopp Lieut & Adjt
                       East Lancashire Regt

        Copy No 1   56th Infantry Brigade
                 2. Commanding Officer
                 3. Major Morrison
                 4. O.C A Coy
                 5. O.C B Coy
                 6. O.C C Coy
                 7. O.C D Coy
                 8. Lewis Gun Officer
                 9. 2nd Lt Hoggett
                10. M.O
                11. Lt & Qr Mr
                12. R.S.M
                13. War Diary
                14. File.

Appendix 6

SECRET   EAST LANCASHIRE REGIMENT   Copy No. 14

OPERATION ORDER No 10

Reference Sheet 28 S.W   1/20,000   17.5.17

1. The Battalion will relieve the KINGS OWN ROYAL LANCASTER REGIMENT in the Right Subsector, DIEPENDAAL SECTOR tonight.

2. Distribution in the line will be as follows:-

    A Coy   3 Platoons in Right Front Line relieving whole of C Coy Kings Own.
             1 Platoon in Right Support relieving 1 Platoon A Coy Kings Own.
    B Coy   2 Platoons in Left front line relieving whole of D Coy Kings Own.
             2 Platoons in New Reserve Line relieving left two platoons of B Coy Kings Own.
    C Coy   3 Platoons in New Reserve Line relieving 4 Platoons of A Coy Kings Own.
             1 Platoon in Cockatoo Trench relieving 1 platoon A Coy Kings Own.
    D Coy   in New Reserve line relieving right two platoons of B Coy Kings Own.
    Hdqrs relieving Hdqrs in Right Subsector Hdqrs.

3. Companies will move off in the following order B,A,D,C Coys at 200 yards interval between platoons. B Coys first platoon to move off at 9.10 p.m
    Route via CHEAPSIDE - POPPY LANE
    Hdqrs via Tramline to Hdqrs Right Subsector moving off at 9.10 p.m

4. Guides will meet platoons at POPPY LANE R.E Dump.

5. Officers Kits &c Camp Kettles etc will be stacked at Hdqrs by 8.30 p.m. Party of 1 N.C.O and 3 men will be sent from each Company to trolley them round to new Bn Hdqrs.

6. Rations will be delivered at New Bn Hdqrs at 9.45 p.m Coys will detail a ration party to proceed to Ration Dump on their way up to the line. This party will take up rations after completion of relief.

7. Trench Stores will be carefully checked when taking over and lists sent to Orderly Room by 9 a.m on 18th inst.

8. On completion of relief reports will be sent to Bn Hdqrs by wiring = "6564".

                                     Lieut & Adjt
                            EAST LANCASHIRE REGIMENT

Issued at 2 p.m

             Copy No 1.   56th Infantry Brigade
                   2.   Kings Own(R.L) Rgt
                   3.   Commanding Officer
                   4.   O.C A Coy
                   5.   O.C B Coy
                   6.   O.C C Coy
                   7.   O.C D Coy
                   8.   Lewis Gun Officer
                   9.   Quartermaster
                  10.   Transport Officer
                  11.   2nd Lt Hoggett
                  12.   R.S.M
                  13.   War Diary
                  14.   File. ✓

APPENDIX 7

SECRET

EAST LANCASHIRE REGIMENT
OPERATION ORDER No.11

30/5/1917.

Reference Sheet 28 S.W 1/20.000

1. The Battalion will be relieved in the Right Subsector tonight by the WORCESTERSHIRE REGIMENT and on relief will move into WESTON CAMP
Route:- via HALLEBAST CORNER N.3.a.2.6 - LA CLYTTE - SCHERPERBERG - WESTON CAMP

2. Companies will be relieved by the corresponding companies of WORCESTERSHIRE REGIMENT who on relief will be disposed as follows:-

A Coy   3 Platoons in Right Front Line
         1 Platoon in Right Support

B Coy   2 Platoons in Left Front Line
         2 Platoons in New Reserve Line

C Coy   3 Platoons in New Reserve Line
         1 Platoon in COCKATOO TRENCH

D Coy   In New Reserve Line

Hdqrs   In Right Subsector Hdqrs

3. Platoon Guides will be at Battalion Hdqrs by 9.15 p.m

4. An Advance Party of 1 N.C.O per Company, 1 man per platoon and 1 N.C.O for Hdqrs will report at Battalion Hdqrs at 3.0 p.m to 2nd Lt R.B.Hoggett and will take over WESTON CAMP from 8th North Staffordshire Regt allotting tents to Companies

5. All Companies will be relieved via Poppy Lane C.T and on relief will march out by Platoons at 100 yards interval.

6. Company Mess Stores, Cooking Utensils &c will be dumped at Battalion Headquarters by 9.15 p.m   Transport Officer will arrange for Maltese Cart, Mess Cart 3 Limbers for Hdqrs and 2 for Coy Stores to report at Battn Hdqrs at 9.30 p.m
2 Limbers for Lewis Guns will report at 11 p.m and Officers Chargers at 12 Midnight.

7. Trench Store Lists to be forwarded to Orderly Room by 12 noon on 31st inst.

8. On relief being completed Company Commanders will report at Battn Hdqrs on their way out.

Sgd R.D.Allsopp Lieut & Adjt
XIth East Lancashire Regt.

Copy No 1. 58th Infantry Brigade
        2. Worcestershire Regt
        3. Commanding Officer
        4. O.C A Coy
        5. O.C B Coy
        6. O.C C Coy
        7. O.C D Coy
        8. Lewis Gun Officer
        9. Quartermaster
       10. Transport Officer
       11. 2nd Lt Hoggett
       12. R.S.M
       13. War Diary
       14. File

APPENDIX 8

Secret

EAST LANCASHIRE REGIMENT
OPERATION ORDER No.13

31.5.1917

Reference Map Sheet 28 S.W 1/20.000

1. The Battalion will move into New Camp at M.14.b.9.8. tomorrow

2. Route via Cross Roads M.17.c.5.5 X - WESTOUTRE

3. Companies will move off in the following order Hdqr Coy,B,C & D Coys at intervals of 100 yards between Companies. Hdqr Coy to leave present Camp at 11.30 a.m.

4. A Company and Party of B Coy detailed for Baths will move off independently and rejoin Battalion in new Camp.

5. All Stores Blankets and Officers valises will be dumped on ground near Cookers and Officers cooking utensils by 10.30 a.m

6. The Transport Officer will arrange to Transport all Stores etc

7. All tents to be left in a clean and sanitary condition and certificates rendered to O.C.Coys by Orderly Room ½ hour before their parade to this effect.

      Sgd.. R.D.Allsopp Lt & Adjt
      EAST LANCASHIRE REGT

Issued at 3.30 a.m

    Copy No. 1   56th Infantry Brigade
       2. Commanding Officer
       3. O.C A Coy
       4. O.C B Coy
       5. O.C C Coy
       6. O.C D Coy
       7. Lewis Gun Officer
       8. 2nd Lt. Hoggett
       9. Transport Officer
      10. Quartermaster
      11. R.S.M
      12. War Diary
      13. File

APPENDIX 9

Secret

EAST LANCASHIRE REGIMENT
OPERATION ORDER No.13   29/5/1917

Reference Map Sheet 28 S.W   1/30,000

1. The Battalion will move into RIDGE WOOD today relieving R.War.R

2. Companies will move off in the following order Hdqrs.D.C.B.A Coys
   First named to leave camp at 2.30 p.m
       Companies which are alloted baths will bathe at times stated
   and then move into RIDGE WOOD.
       Transport will not move
       Drummers will proceed to Depot
       Dress   Full Marching Order.

3. ROUTE via WESTOUTRE - MILLEKRUISSE then via W Route to Ridge Wood

4. All movements by platoons at 100 yards distance. East of SWAN &
   EDGAR (N.3.d.5.0) by Sections at 100 yards distance

5. Blankets and Officers Valises will be stacked on ground near
   Canteen by Companies by 11 a.m
   Officers Mess Stores Cooking Utensils etc for Ridge Wood will be
   dumped at same place by 1.30 p.m
       Transport Officer will arrange to have these loaded by 1.45 pm

6. Advance Party of 1 N.C.O per Company and 1 man per Platoon will
   report to 2nd Lt Hoggett at Orderly Room at 1 p.m They will
   proceed to Ridge Wood and take over dugouts shelters etc.

7. Trench Stores will be carefully checked and receipts sent to
   Orderly Room by 9 a.m on 30th inst.

8. On completion of relief Companies will report to Battn Hdqrs

                    Sgd R.D.Allsopp Lieut & Adjt
                         East Lancashire Regiment
       Issued at 9.40 a.m

          Copy No 1   55th Infantry Brigade
                  2. C.O
                  3. Major Morrison
                  4. O.C.A.Coy
                  5. O.C.B.Coy
                  6. O.C.C.Coy
                  7. O.C D Coy
                  8. Lewis Gun Officer
                  9. 2nd Lt Hoggett
                 10. Transport Officer
                 11. Quartermaster
                 12. Adjutant
                 13. R.S.M
                 14. M.O
                 15. War Diary
                 16. File

REPORT 1

Report on Raid on Nags Support Trench on Morning of 19th. May, 1917.

This raiding party consisted of 3 officers and 31 other ranks and was split into parties as follows:-

Right Party. under Lt. Bracewell who commanded the whole party. A party of one N.C.O, one Bomber and one bayonet man with a Lewis Gun to go with Lt. Bracewell until they reached Nags Trench which they had to follow down to the junction with Nags Nose and there form a protection to the Raiding Party's right flank. The remainder of the right party 2 N.C.O.s and 8 men were to crawl forward and lie in front of Nags Support from N.13.b.68. to N. 13.b.4.5. and there await the signal to rush the trench.

Centre Party. This party under 2nd. Lt Bliss had one Lewis Gun which had to be dropped at Hollandeschur Farm to cover the withdrawal of the whole raiding party.
The remainder of the centre party had to crawl forward and lie close to Nags Support from N. 13.b.4½.8. and on the signal being given to rush the enemy trench and work along to join up with the right party.

Left Party. The left party under Sergt Wilkinson had 1 Lewis Gun which had to be posted at N. 13.d.5½.1 to protect the left flank of the Raiding Party. The remainder of this party had to crawl forward and lie down as close as possible to Nags Support from N.13.b.4½.8. to N.13.b.d.9. and rush the trench on the signal being given, working to their left.

Note. The ground had been gone over the previous night by the majority of the centre and left parties.

The Officer on the right had also been over the ground.
The whole raiding party left our front line trench at N. 13. d. 4. 2. at 12 midnight and extended to about one pace and moved towards the Nags Nose.
The ground is very broken indeed and became so bad at Nags Nose that the whole party had to get into groups in single file to cross the trench, and shell holes behind it.
The Lewis Guns were in rear of their respective parties.
2nd Lt Bliss had sent two men off to his left front to reconnoitre the crater at N. 13. d. 4. 1.
When the party had almost crossed the bad ground a shower of bombs landed amongst them from the direction of the crater in N.13. d. 4. 1. then lights were fired amongst the party, one light in particular which burned about a minute, every one dived into the shell holes which were full of water and made their way back towards our own line. 2nd Lt Bliss ' party halted and lay still in No Mans Land but had to come back as the enemy were firing rifle grenades amongst his party.
The two men who were sent to reconnoitre the crater got into grips with the enemy but managed to get clear and return to our own line.
The Company Commander in the front line (Captn Palmer) on the right, hearing the bombing and one of our men shouting, decided to give the signal for the artillery to open fire which he did. After 10 minutes firing the artillery fire was stopped by Captain Palmer as the raiding party had returned to our trench. The roll was called and it was reported that 4 men and 2 lewis guns were missing. Lt Bracewell and 2nd Lt Bliss immediately went out to search for same. 2nd Lt Bliss got 3 of the men but neither Lieut Bracewell or 2nd Lt Bliss could find the guns and when they went back to where their party was bombed they themselves were bombed again. It is thought the guns were lost when the men rushed into the shell holes and it is hoped the guns will be recovered to-night.

The party was unable, owing to the difficult nature of the ground to rush the crater and were forced to return.

Total losses were 1 man missing, 3 wounded, 3 lewis guns lost and the raid a failure.

. . . .

56/19
Vol 20

On His Majesty's Service.

1st East Lancashire Regt

WARDIARY
INTELLIGENCE SUMMARY

Army Form C. 2118.

Instructions regarding War Diaries and Intelligence Summaries are contained in F. S. Regs., Part II. and the Staff Manual respectively. Title Pages will be prepared in manuscript.

Place	Date	Hour	Summary of Events and Information	Remarks and references to Appendices
NR La CLYTTE M.12.a.9.5. Sheet 28 SW	1/8/17		Battalion in Brigade Support working parties for Forward Area found.	
do -	2/6/17		Battalion moved into Brigade Reserve at CURRAGH CAMP. M.14.C.98. O.O. attached.	(1)
CURRAGH CAMP	3/6/17		Battalion in Brigade Reserve	
do -	4/6/17		do	
do -	5/6/17		do	
do -	6/6/17		Final Inspection	
		8.15 PM	Moved off for Assembly. Companies at 100 yds interval in single file. Assembly complete by midnight without any losses by enemy fire. When in place dispositions were A and B Coys in the Support Line with A Coy on the right. C and D Coys in Assembly trenches 50 yds further back. C Coy on the right. Headquarters in S.P.7. Casualties 2 O.Ranks killed. Instructions for the Offensive attached.	(2) (3)
NR CARRÉ BOIS (PLAN ATTACHED)	7/6/17	3.10 AM	Mines in neighbourhood fired. Artillery and Machine Gun Barrage opened simultaneously. Kings Own went ahead. The 4 Coys followed at 3.30 a.m. It was still dark and with the	(4)

WAR DIARY
INTELLIGENCE SUMMARY
(Erase heading not required.)

Army Form C 2118.

Place	Date	Hour	Summary of Events and Information	Remarks and references to Appendices
Nr CARRÉ BOIS	7/6/17 (cont'd)		vast clouds of dust and the smoke from the shells keeping direction was difficult. The Red line was reached simultaneously with the King's Own and the advance was continued to the Blue line. There was little opposition to the barrage was too slow for the men, some of whom were hit in attempting to pass through our barrage to follow up the retiring enemy. On the Blue Line a gap in the ranks had developed on the right. During the 2 hours wait this was rectified. Connection between A and B Coys was difficult at this stage as a 4.5 Howitzer was persistently firing short and the Artillery Liaison officers were powerless to stop it for two reasons. 1. Difficulty of communication to the rear. 2. Difficulty in locating the offending Battery. The green line was attained and the 4 Coys dug in. The position of this line, which had to be sighted by a German dump in ONRAET WOOD and EVANS FARM was excellently taken up by the Company Commanders. A narrow irregular trench was dug and wire was put up. Great quantities of material were at hand from the German dump and Consolidation proceeded apace.	
		3.10 P.M.	Took over the Black Line from 8th NORTH STAFFORDS. Consolidated BLACK LINE. All quiet. CASUALTIES. Capt. H. REDDEN. M.C. and 2/Lt. H.E. RIDGWAY. KILLED. 2/Lt. H.R. HOLNESS – 2/Lt. G. ALLEN and 2/Lt. L.G. KITCHEN. WOUNDED.	

Army Form C. 2118.

WAR DIARY
INTELLIGENCE SUMMARY
(Erase heading not required.)

Instructions regarding War Diaries and Intelligence Summaries are contained in F. S. Regs., Part II. and the Staff Manual respectively. Title Pages will be prepared in manuscript.

Place	Date	Hour	Summary of Events and Information	Remarks and references to Appendices
	8/6/17	6 P.M.	Took over MAUVE LINE from 10TH WORCESTERS. S.O.S. went up from Front Line and we were intermittently shelled. Consolidated.	
	9/6/17		Consolidated MAUVE LINE.	
	10/6/17	10 P.M.	Moved back. A and B Coys to Green Line. C and D Coys to Blue Line. Headquarters in ONRAET FARM. S.O.S. from Front Line then all quiet.	
	11/6/17		All quiet.	
	12/6/17	11 P.M.	Took over Front Line from King's Own. D Coy in front line. C Coy in immediate support and A and B Coys in support. Lt. J.I. SPICER. WOUNDED.	
	13/6/17		Enemy shell fire heavy.	
	14/6/17		Enemy shell fire heavy. Raid by 6 platoons under Lt Col. Bracewell — VERHAEGE FARM Cleared.	
	15/6/17	11 P.M.	Relieved by 10TH WORCESTERS and Battalion moved to BIRR BARRACKS Nr. LOCRE.	
			FULL CASUALTIES during these operations. Officers 2 killed 4 wounded. O.Ranks 25 killed 10 died of wounds 159 wounded 3 missing.	
BIRR BARRACKS	16/6/17		In Reserve at BIRR BARRACKS.	
	17/6/17		ditto	

WAR DIARY
INTELLIGENCE SUMMARY
(Erase heading not required.)

Army Form C. 2118.

Instructions regarding War Diaries and Intelligence Summaries are contained in F.S. Regs., Part II. and the Staff Manual respectively. Title Pages will be prepared in manuscript.

Place	Date	Hour	Summary of Events and Information	Remarks and references to Appendices
BIRR BARRACKS	18/6/17		Battalion moved into RED LINE and relieved 8TH GLOUCESTERS.	(6)
RED LINE	19/6/17		Battalion moved out of RED LINE to Bivouacs on Western slopes of KEMMEL HILL.	
KEMMEL HILL	20/6/17		Battalion in Reserve. Working parties found for 1st Australian Tunnelling Coy repairing roads around WYTSCHAETE. Training carried out. Casualties O. Ranks 3 killed 2 wounded.	
do	21/6/17		do — working parties found as before.	
do	22/6/17		do —	
do	23/6/17		do —	
do	24/6/17		do —	
do	25/6/17		do — Casualties 2 O.Ranks wounded	
do	26/6/17		do — Training carried out	
do	27/6/17		do — Battalion had preliminary contest for Brigade sports. 5th Brigade held their sports.	
do	28/6/17		do — Training Carried out. Working parties as before	
do	29/6/17		do —	
do	30/6/17		Divisional Sports cancelled owing to wet weather.	

R.Allnutt
Lt/Capt
1/6th East Lancs Regiment

SECRET Copy No ....

EAST LANCASHIRE REGIMENT
OPERATION ORDER No. 14

1/6/17

Reference Sheet 28 S.W 1/20,000

1. The Battalion will move tomorrow into CURRAGH Camp M.17.c.9.8

2. Companies will parade and move off in the following order at the following times :-
   D Coy 3 p.m; C Coy 3.10 p.m; B Coy 3.20 p.m; A Coy 3.30 p.m
   Hdqrs Coy 3.40 p.m

   Dress Full Marching Order

3. Movements by platoons at 200 yards interval

4. Route will be ~~notified later~~. 'W' 'Y' + 'Z' TRACKS

5. Officers Valises, Mess Stores, Cooking Utensils and all other Stores to be dumped behind Guard Tent by 2 p.m. Transport Officer will arrange all Transport and also for attendance of Officers Chargers.

6. Usual Advance Party will report to 2nd Lt R.B.Hoggett at Guard Tent at 1 p.m

7. O.C Coys will see that the Camp is left in a clean and sanitary conditions.

Roulson Lieut & Adjt
East Lancashire Regiment

Issued at   p.m

Copy No 1. 56th Infantry Brigade
        2. Commanding Officer
        3. Major Morrison
        4. O.C A Coy
        5. O.C B Coy
        6. O.C C Coy
        7. O.C D Coy
        8. O.C Lewis Gun Sec.
        9. Transport Officer
       10. Quartermaster
       11. Medical Officer
       12. 2nd Lt. Hoggett
       13. R.S.M
       14. File
       15. War Diary.

SECRET   EAST LANCASHIRE REGIMENT   Copy No. 14

OPERATION ORDER No.15

6/6/1917

Reference Map Sheet 28 S.W   1/20.000

1. The Battalion will move into Assembly positions already notified to Company Commanders.

2. Companies will parade and move off in the following order and at the following times:-

         H.Q   8. 5 p.m
         A Coy   8.10 p.m
         B Coy   8.20 p.m
         C Coy   8.30 p.m
         D Coy   8.40 p.m

3. DRESS BATTLE ORDER

4. Movements before 10 p.m by sections at 50 yards distance. After 10 P.m by Companies at 200 yards distance.
    Troops will move in file and not in fours.

5. Route via W Track, track S side of RIDGE WOOD and "K" Track to position.

6. Reports to Battalion Hdqrs at S.P 7 when movement is complete Number of casualties, if any, to be stated.

7. 2nd Lieuts Rentoul and Ashton will act as assembly Officers.

8. No transport will accompany troops marching to assembly. Procedure on Roads and tracks will be given to infantry marching to assembly after 9.30 p.m. Each Unit will be preceded by an Officer to ensure that the roads are cleared in time to avoid checking.

                                     Bradburn   Lieut & Adjt
                                       2nd East Lancashire Regt.

Issued at 11 a.m

     Copy No. 1.   86th Infantry Bde.
               2.   Commanding Officer
               3.   Major Morrison
               4.   O.C A Coy
               5.   O.C B Coy
               6.   O.C C Coy
               7.   O.C D Coy
               8.   Lewis Gun Officer
               9.   Transport Officer
             10.   Quartermaster
             11.   M.O
             12.   R.S.M
             13.   2nd Lt Hoggett
             14.   War Diary
             15.   File

7th EAST LANCASHIRE REGIMENT

INSTRUCTIONS FOR THE OFFENSIVE

1. **GENERAL PLAN OF ATTACK**
   (a) The IX Corps is to take part in an offensive which has for its object the capture of the MESSINES - WYTSCHAETE Ridge.
   The attack will be carried out in four bounds marked in colours on the Maps issued to Company Commanders

First Bound	RED
Second Bound	BLUE
Third Bound	GREEN
Fourth Bound	BLACK

   (b) The 19th Division is to be the left of the three attacking Divisions of the IX Corps.
   The 56th Infantry Brigade is the left Brigade of the 19th Division and will assault the RED, BLUE and GREEN Lines. The 56th Infantry Brigade is to be on the right. 104th Infantry Brigade on the left of the 56th Infantry Brigade. 57th Infantry Brigade is in Divisional Reserve and is to pass through 56th and 58th Infantry Brigades after the capture of the GREEN line and assault the BLACK Line subsequently throwing out an outpost line beyond.

   (c) The front of attack of the 56th Infantry Brigade is approximately 990 yards.

   RIGHT BOUNDARY Trench Junction P.7.c.6.4 point where trench tramway cuts OBJECT ALLEY
   Point where trench tramway cuts OBSTRUCTION SUPPORT O.13.b.65.80.
   OTRAET FARM
   3 Kilometre Stone on WYTSCHAETE - St.ELOI Road
   All inclusive to the 56th Infantry Brigade.

   LEFT BOUNDARY German Line O.8.b.9.8
   House   O.8.a.90.95

   Martens Farm O.8.d.80.95

   Bondulle Farm O.13.a.1.5
   All inclusive to the 104th Infantry Brigade

2. **PLAN OF ATTACK by 56th INFANTRY BRIGADE**
   (1) The successive bounds and time at which the Artillery Barrage will lift off each are as follows:-

First Bound	Zero plus 35 minutes
Second Bound	Zero plus 1 hour 40 minutes
Third Bound	Zero plus 4 hours 10 minutes

   (2) (a) The advance from the RED Line will take place at Zero plus 1.35 and the BLUE Line is to be reached at Zero plus 1 hour 40 minutes The Right flank of the Battalion on the BLUE Line will rest at O.13.b.65.50 the left Flank at O.14.a.50.95

   (b) The Advance from the BLUE Line will be made at Zero plus 3 hours 40 minutes after a halt of two hours.

   The GREEN Line is to be reached at Zero plus 4 hours 10 minutes.

The Right flank of the Battalion on the GREEN Line will rest at O.14.c.65.60 (3 Kilometre Stone on WYTSCHAETE - ST ELOI Road the left flank at O.14.b.30.15.

(c) The 87th Infantry Brigade is to Advance from its assembly position and pass over the GREEN Line at Zero plus 4.40 reaching the BLACK Line at ZERO plus 8.00

(3) The RED BLUE and GREEN Lines are to be consolidated . In consolidating the right of the BLUE Line a new trench will be dug from 100 to 150 yards on the S.E edge of the GRAND BOIS

(4) The 56th Infantry Brigade will attack the successive objects allotted to it as under

    RED LINE   On the Right 7/R.Lan. R
                 On the Left   7/N.Lan. R

    BLUE & GREEN LINES On the right 7/E.Lan R
                              On the left   7/S.Lan R

(5) The Dividing Line between the respective right and left Battalions during the Advance will be

    BRITISH FRONT LINE - O.7.a.8.6
    RED LINE   - O.7.d.75.50
    BLUE LINE   - O.14.a.50.65
    GREEN LINE   - O.14.b.30.15

The 7/E.Lan R will assault the BLUE and GREEN Lines as follows:-
    On the Right   "A" Coy
    On the Left   "B" Coy
The assault will be carried out in two single rank waves each Company having two platoons in the first wave and two platoons in the second wave.

3rd Wave "D" Coy in a single rank wave. This Company will
            find the Moppers Up.

4th Wave "C" Coy in a single rank wave.

    The dividing line between Companies will be

    GERMAN FRONT LINE   O.7.c.75.45
    RED LINE   O.7.d.45.15
    BLUE LINE   O.14.a.13.60
    GREEN LINE   O.14.central.

The Battalion will cross the British front line at Zero plus *NOT LATER THAN* 25 minutes.

(6) (a) The attack of the 56th Infantry Brigade will not be carried out on the "leap frog" system except as regards battalions i.e 7/E.Lan R and 7/S.Lan R will leap frog 7/R.Lan R and 7/N.Lan R respectively on the RED Line but the leading Companies of each battalion will go through to the furthest objective allotted to that battalion.

(b) RED LINE 7/R.Lan R and 7/N.Lan R will advance at Zero hour and will carry out the assault as far as the RED line inclusive.

(c) BLUE LINE 7/E.Lan R and 7/S.Lan R will advance from their assembly trenches and cross the BRITISH front line at ~~Zero plus~~ *NOT LATER THAN ZERO plus 25 MINUTES*
    The leading Companies will cross the RED Line at Zero plus 1.05 and assault the BLUE Line at Zero plus 1.40.

3.

There will be a halt of 2 hours on the BLUE LINE

(d) GREEN LINE

    7/E.Lan R and 7/S.Lan R. The leading Companies will continue their advance at Zero plus 3.40 and will assault the GREEN Line at Zero plus 4.10.

    D Coy (Moppers) will detail parties to deal with trenches, dugouts etc between RED and BLUE Lines

    1 Squad for dugouts near OBSTRUCTION ROW same men to mop up OBSTRUCTION ROW Trench and Branch

    4 Squads to mop up OBSTRUCTION AVENUE

    2 Squads to mop up LOUHAGE Farm.

as soon as the mopping up has been done thoroughly these squads will rejoin their Company in the BLUE Line and will assist in the Mopping up from the BLUE to the GREEN Line.

"D" Coy will also detail the following to mop up between BLUE and GREEN Lines
    3 Squads to move up OATEN DRIVE to OBTUSE TRENCH acting as follows

    1 Squad to mop to right of OATEN DRIVE
    2 Squads to mop to left of OATEN DRIVE

    3 squads to mop up OBTUSE KEEP
    1 squad for ZERO House
    1 Squad for OBTUSE CRESCENT (that part of which is in the Battalion area)

C Coy will follow D Coy (but will close up on A & B Coys when the moppers up have dropped out) and add extra weight to the assault on the GREEN Line. Unless actually required C Coy will not assault the BLUE Line but will halt in rear of it taking advantage of all available cover This Company must however close up to the BLUE Line in time to go forward behind the second assaulting wave.

7. The 97th Infantry Brigade is to advance from its assembly position at Zero plus 3.00 so as to assault the BLACK Line under the Barrage at Zero plus 4.40

8. The 88th Infantry Brigade advance and assault the various objectives at the same hours as those laid down for the 86th Infantry Brigade.

a. The Battalion on the left of the 88th Infantry Brigade from RED to GREEN Lines will be 9/Cheshire Regt.
    O.C A Coy 7/E.Lan R will detail one section to intermingle with the left section of the 9/Cheshire Regt.
    The Right hand man of this section will march along OBJECT ALLEY.

9. The 14th Infantry Brigade is to advance and assault similar objectives at the same hours as those laid down for the 86th Infantry Brigade

4.

3. POSITION of H.Q) HEADQUARTERS
& ASSEMBLY)
ARRANGEMENTS) DIVISION   SCHERPENBERG

BRIGADE   BOIS CARRE Dugouts (N.1..b.9.8)

7/R.Lan R) double Battn Hdqrs at head of CHICORY
7/N.Lan R) LANE (O.7.a.3.5)

After the capture of the RED Line Advanced Hdqrs
of these Battalions will be established in the German
front line system.

7/E.Lan R   - S.P 7 (O.7.a.15.05)

7/S.Lan R   - Shelter at junction of P & O trenches
                and WYTSCHAETE BEEK (O.1.c.7.6)

When these two Battalions move forward to the RED Line
for assault Battalion Hdqrs will be established
temporarily in the RED Line subsequently moving forward
to a point between the BLUE and the GREEN Lines exact
position of Battalion H.Q as soon as established
will be notified to all concerned by runner

ASSEMBLY AREAS

The 56th Infantry Brigade area of assembly is
bounded on the S.W by a line drawn from O.7.c.98.85
to N.1..b.88.36 on the N.E by P.& O Trench
The dividing line between Battalions is O.7.a.3.5
- O.7.a.09.86 - O.7.a.98.65

Areas within the Brigade are allotted as under:-
ON RIGHT OF DIVIDING LINE

7/R.Lan R Front Line and area in rear up to
            but exclusive of Support Line.
7/E.Lan R Support of Line and area in rear up to
            but exclusive of the WYTSCHAETE BEEK

ON LEFT OF DIVIDING LINE

7/N.Lan R   same as for 7/R.Lan R
7/S.Lan R   same as for 7/E.Lan R

Further orders for the assembly will be issued
later.

4. MACHINE GUNS No 1 Section 56th M.G.C will operate in the Sector to
be covered by the advance of 7/R.Lan R and 7/E.Lan R

On the capture of the GREEN LINE
No 1 Section will be disposed as under:-
No.1 GUN at the trench junction O.14.b.10.15 firing
S.W to ONRAET WOOD
No.2 GUN near No 1 Gun about O.14.b.10.15 firing
east to INDESTINES CABARET
No.3 GUN & No 4 GUN to the S.P to be constructed about
O.14.b.5.3 firing S.E and S.W to cover the crest
of the Ridge in front of the Green Line.

The details contained above are only meant to indicate
the lines on which the section should operate if the
operations are carried out according to programme.
In any case the Officer Commanding the section
will keep in touch with the Senior Infantry Officer on
the spot in order to cooperate with fire as may be
necessary.

5.

| 5. TRENCH MORTAR BATTERY | Two Stokes Mortars will be allotted to the Battalion. They will advance with and in the centre of C Coy and will deal with any situation that may arise. Company Commanders should send for these guns if they need them. |

6. STRONG POINTS

A Strong Point will be constructed as soon as the GREEN Line has been gained. The actual point can only be decided on the ground after reconnaissance but it will be sited about the following locality
GREEN LINE O.14.b.2.2 B Coy will garrison this S.P with not less than one platoon.

7. DUMPS

GRENADE and S.A.A at
(a) N.19.b.0.7
(b) N.19.b.3.7

WATER N.19.b.6.0

R.E.MATERIAL 6
N.19.b.E.0 (Infantry only)

BRIGADE FORWARD DUMP

Formed by Brigade Carrying Party behind BLUE and GREEN Line only.
(marked by a white flag with D in Centre)

8. COMMUNICATION TRENCHES

From Zero hour onwards BOIS CARRE and CHICORY Communication Trenches will be reserved as IN Trenches - P & O Communication Trench as an OUT Trench.

9. ARTILLERY

An Artillery LIAISON OFFICER will be with Battalion Headquarters
(i) The creeping barrage covering the assault of the 50th Infantry Brigade will consist of 30 18 Pounder Guns.

It will open on the German Front Line OBLIGE TRENCH -OBJECT TRENCH-OBJECT SUPPORT -ONIT TRENCH at ZERO plus 4 minutes
It will lift uniformly throughout the Advance (100 yards every 4 minutes) until it reaches each successive objective (RED,BLUE,GREEN,BLACK Lines)
As it arrives on each objective it will "pile up" and remain until the hour fixed for it to lift off (viz RED 0-36 -BLUE 1-40 GREEN 4-10 BLACK 5) so as to let the Infantry into the objective simultaneously along the whole line.

(ii) After lifting off the objectives RED,BLUE and BLACK Lines (on which halts are to be made) it will form a protective barrage as follows:-
The first halt will be the normal 100 yards where it will remain for two minutes,after which a portion of the barrage will be placed on those points in the enemy trench system from which fire can be directed against troops halted on the objective.
The remaining portion will lift another 50 yards and form a barrage 150 yards beyond the objective.

(iii) At the hour the Infantry are due to advance from each line (RED BLUE GREEN) the barrage will reform on the line of the protective barrage (i.e 150 yards in front of the RED BLUE or GREEN Lines)
After reforming it will rest for the normal 4 minutes before lifting. During the first two minutes the rate of fire will be moderate for the last two intense.

6.

The reforming of the creeping barrage at 150 yards ahead of the trench will be the signal to the infantry to move out to the barrage and form for the next advance.

e.g The creeping barrage recalled from more distant targets reforms at 3.40 on the line of the protective barrage 150 yds beyond the BLUE Line and fire is delivered at a moderate rate until 3.42
From 3.42 to 3.44 the fire is intense. At 3.44 the Barrge lifts 100 yards every 4 minutes. The Infantry on seeing the barrage reform at 3.40 will move close up to it so as to follow it forward when it lifts at 3.44.

All Commanders down to platoon commanders will keep in touch throughout with the Commanders of the similar formations on his flanks.

Commanders will impress on all ranks the importance of keeping the formation above them constantly informed of the state of affairs.

Units will push forward to their respective objects regardless of the progress of units on either flank.
All ranks will be instructed as to this and reminded that care of the wounded is not in their province special personnel being detailed for that purpose.

Men will be warned against enemy ruses. Misuse of white flags and other signs of surrender.

10. S. O. S) The S.O.S Signal will remain RED Signal Cartridge as at
    Signal)   present.

11. PREPARATION) Trench Board Bridges will be placed over the front
    FOR ADVANCE) and support lines after dark on Y/Z night by 61st
    FROM TRENCHES) Field Coy R.E

    Companies in the support line will construct ramps
    and pull down gaps so as to enable troops to pass
    these lines. Work to be done after dark Y/Z night.

S I T U A T I O N   M A P.

THIS MAP TO BE USED FOR SENDING BACK REPORTS OF WHEREABOUTS OF TROOPS. RECIPIENTS CAN MARK BOUNDARIES, ETC. AS REQUIRED.

※※※※※※※※

Mark your position with a ✗ on the map.

Thus:- "My platoon has reached ✗ etc. (any written matter required can be put on this side).

Date _____

Time ....

ADDITIONS TO INSTRUCTIONS FOR THE OFFENSIVE

Particulars of Carrying Party between Brigade Dump and Forward Dump.

Line.	Time carrying party leaves Bgde Dump.	Grenade boxes.	S.A.A. boxes.	Smoke candles.	Wire and Pickets.	Petrol tins of water.	No. of men
BLUE. Rt.Bn.	Z+1 hour.	13	4	15	10 man loads.	15	40
GREEN Rt.Bn.	Z+4½ hours.	13	5	-	10 man loads.	12	32

WATER.

(a) A Divisional Reserve of water will be established at the BRASSERIE.
Empty petrol tins may be exchanged for full ones at this place.

(b) 36 tins will be issued to the Battalion on Y/Z Night and all ranks must start the attack with water bottles full.
The tins will be distributed as follows:-
A Coy. 7
B Coy. 7
C Coy. 8
D Coy. 7
Hdqrs.Coy. 7

O.C. Companies will ensure that these tins, whether empty or full are returned to the Brigade Water Dump N.13.b.6.6. before Zero Hour.

Lieut & Adjt
7th East Lancashire Regt

COPY

Secret.   19th. Division.
                                                           No. G.136/24/57

Para.25. CONTACT PATROLS.

 Aeroplanes for contact patrols will be R. E. 8 type and will be specially marked by a black flap attached to the rear of each lower plane.
 Two contact aeroplanes will be in the air at the same time. One watching the area South of WYTSCHAETE and the other WYTSCHAETE AND THE AREA North of the village.
 Contact patrols will fly over the line and call for flares at the following hours, and any time subsequent to these hours at which special aeroplanes may be ordered:-
   Zero plus 0.45
   Zero plus 2 hours
   Zero plus 4.30
   Zero plus 6.30
   Zero plus 8.30
   Zero plus 11 hours

Troops will also be prepared to put out flares at any other time if the aeroplane calls for them.
 Aeroplanes will call for flares and WATSON FANS by sounding a Klaxon Horn or firing a 'Very' white light, or both.
 Green flares will be used. They should be lit in bunches of three each about 30 yards apart.
 WATSON FANS will be used in conjunction with flares. The fans should be turned over every two seconds and not quicker, that is, the white side will be exposed to the aeroplane for two seconds then the dark side for two seconds and so on.
 Fans will be issued as they become available.
 In order to obtain as early intimation as possible from our own aeroplanes of hostile counter attacks, the following procedure will be adopted.
 On the hostile Infantry being seen to quit their trenches and advance, the observer will send down by wireless 'S.O.S.' followed by the Zone call- no map co-ordinates will be given. This will constitute a request to our artillery to put up a barrage on their 'S.O.S.' lines in that particular zone.
 A machine for this purpose will be up from Zero.
 No aeroplanes will be in the air before Zero.
 A Schedule of Code Calls for aeroplanes to be used by Divisions is given below:-

Division.	Infantry Brigade.	Code Letters.
19th.	56th.	L.G.
	57th.	L.H.
	58th.	L.I.
16th.	47th.	S.
	48th.	T.
	49th.	U.
36th.	107th.	L.D.
	108th.	L.E.
	109th.	L.F.
11th.	32nd.	N.E.
	33rd.	N.F.
	34th.	N.G.

 The addition of W,X,Y or Z to the Brigade Code Letter will give the particular Battalion of the Brigade according to the "Order of Battle"

Increase in Aircraft. A large increase of aeroplanes of all types will shortly take place on this front; many of these will be entirely new to the troops in the area, whilst some of them will closely resemble enemy machines. It is essential that these facts be made known to all Artillery and Infantry Units, otherwise the enemy will be falsely credited with largely increased forces and an aerial supremacy over our own aircraft.

SECRET.   EAST LANCASHIRE REGIMENT.   Copy No 13
                 OPERATION ORDER No 16.
                 ——————————————   19-6-17

1. Battalion will move into Bivouacs, Western Slopes of KEMMEL N. 25. b and d and will take over working parties.
   Companies will move off in the following order :-
   2nd Lt Goulding's Section, D. C. B. and A Companies.

2. All movements to be by route the platoon Guides are conversant with. Units to march by platoons at 100 yards distance to the old British Front line. After this point by Companies at 200 yards distance.

3. Battalion Headquarters will be at (not yet known)

4. Officers Mess Stores and Cooking Utensils will be dumped at 8-30 p.m. A and B Companies at junction of Butterfly Track and forward edge of GRAND BOIS. C and D Companies and Headquarters near Battalion Headquarters.

5. Transport Officer will arrange for all transport and Officers Chargers to be at their respective places at 8-30 p.m

6. Rations will be issued at the new billets.

7. 4 Cookers and 1 Water Cart will be at Bivouacs N. 25. b and d and 1 Water Cart at Battalion Headquarters.

8. Transport lines will be accommodated at DEVIZES CAMP for the present.

9. The Officers valises of A, B, C and D Companies and 2nd Lt Goulding to be conveyed to Bivouacs N.25 b and d.

10. Transport for Lewis Guns to report to Company Commanders by 10-30 p.m.

11. On receipt of code word "SPRING TIME" Companies will move off.

12. Acknowledge.
                    (Sd)   R. B. Hoggett, 2nd Lt & A/Adjt
                            East Lancashire Regiment.
Issued at 6-30 p.m.

                Copy No 1 Commanding Officer.
                         2 Major W. Morrison
                         3 Adjutant.
                         4 Medical Officer.
                         5 2nd Lt Goulding.
                         6 O.C. A Company
                         7 O.C. B   -
                         8 O.C. C   -
                         9 O.C. D   -
                        10 Lt & Quartermaster.
                        11 Transport Officer.
                        12 File.
                    ✓   13 War Diary.
                        14 R. S. M.

SECRET.   EAST LANCASHIRE REGIMENT.x   Copy No 13

OPERATION ORDERS   No 16.

19-6-17.

13. Companies and 2nd Lt Goulding's Section will rendezvous at SHELL FARM N. N̶X̶ 36. C. 1. 6. at 7-30 a.m. tomorrow.

14. ROUTE.- LENDENHOEK - SPUD ROAD -.

15. Companies will march to their work at 200 yards interval.

16. Guides will meet the Companies tonight at POLKA CABT N. 21 d. 35. 40.

17. Battalion Headquarters will be at DONCASTER HUTS M. 29. a. 3. 9.

18. Medical Officer will proceed to Bivouacs N. 25. b and d.

(Sd) R. B. Hoggett, 2nd Lt A/Adjt.
East Lancashire Regiment.

Issued at 7-0 p.m.

Copy No 1 Commanding Officer.
2 Major W. Morrison.
3 Adjutant.
4 Medical Officer.
5 2nd Lt Goulding.
6 O. C. A Company.
7 O. C. B   -
8 O. C. C   -
9 O. C. D   -
10 Lt & Quartermaster.
11 Transport Officer.
12 File.
13 War Diary.
14 R. S. M.

Army Form C. 2118.

1/4B East Lancashire Regt
Vol 21

WAR DIARY
INTELLIGENCE SUMMARY
(Erase heading not required.)

Instructions regarding War Diaries and Intelligence Summaries are contained in F. S. Regs., Part II. and the Staff Manual respectively. Title Pages will be prepared in manuscript.

Place	Date	Hour	Summary of Events and Information	Remarks and references to Appendices
DONCASTER HUTS and KEMMEL BIVOUAC SLOPES	1/7/17		Battalion moved from Bivouacs on KEMMEL SLOPES and Headquarters from DONCASTER HUTS to BIRR BARRACKS near LOCRE. Nothing Further found.	
BIRR BARRACKS LOCRE	2/7/17		Battalion carried out Training. Following men awarded Military Medal: 13828 L/Cpl J Sutton, 6798 Sgt L Lambert, 11698 Cpl J Millman, 11811 Pte W Hughes, 23493 Pte W Fitzpatrick, 6413 Pte E Robertson, 13037 Pte J Todd.	Sheet 28 S.W. 1/20.000
"	3/7/17		Battalion carried out Training	
"	4/7/17		ditto	
"	5/7/17		2 Coys Baths at LOCRE. Battalion was inspected by Divisional Commander. Inspection followed by short tactical exercise. Following men awarded Military Medal - 8100 Sgt McGinty T, + 36941 Pte J Shurrock.	
"	6/7/17		Battalion practised attack on training area N.14.c.1.	
"	7/7/17		Battalion carried out Training. In the afternoon the Battalion Recd. Regimental sports. Prizes distributed by Brigadier General E Craig Brown S.S.O.	
"	8/7/17		Battalion paraded for Divine Service.	
"	9/7/17		Battalion carried out Practice attack and musketry on RANGE near HOSPICE, LOCRE. 12798 C.S.M. O'FARRELL B Coy. awarded Military Medal.	
"	10/7/17		Battalion paraded for Practice attack and musketry on RANGE.	

WAR DIARY or INTELLIGENCE SUMMARY

Army Form C. 2118.

Place	Date	Hour	Summary of Events and Information	Remarks and references to Appendices
BIRR BARRACKS LOCRE.	11/7/17		Demonstration by specially selected Platoon on Training Ground. In the afternoon Battalion paraded for Rapid touring and practical marching on Tanks. Working parties found for work on Officer Club-Locre and for work under 250th Australian Tunneling Coy R.E.	
	12/7/17		Battalion carried out Platoon and Company training on Company Training Grounds. Musketry on RANGE	
	13/7/17		Battalion carried out Practice Attack and Consolidation.	
	14/7/17		—ditto—	
	15/7/17		Battalion paraded for Divine Service.	
	16/7/17		Battalion carried out Practice Attack and Consolidation and training generally.	
	17/7/17		—ditto—	
	18/7/17		Parades under Company arrangements. Battalion under orders to move.	
BLUE and RED LINES.	19/7/17		Battalion moved to BLUE and RED LINES near WYTSCHAETE RIDGE preparatory to moving into Line. Battalion moved into line relieving 9/R.W. Fusiliers in CENTRE SUBSECTOR O.17 a & c. Battalion disposed D Coy Left Front Line. C Coy Right Front Line. B Coy Support on ROSE WOOD. A Coy in support at GODEZEONE Fm/El. Casualties O. Ranks 1 killed 3 wounded. Trench Routine carried out.	SHEET 28.S.W. 1/20.000
—do—	20/7/17		—ditto—	
TRENCHES O.17 a & c	21/7/17		—ditto—	
	22/7/17		Battalion relieved in line by 10th Worcesters and moved to Camp at N.16 & 9.3 into Reserve. Capt E.G. Edwardes, 2/Lt H.W. Osborn 2/Lt C.H. Jeffryes wounded. 2 O Ranks killed and 11 wounded.	

WAR DIARY or INTELLIGENCE SUMMARY

Army Form C. 2118.

Place	Date	Hour	Summary of Events and Information	Remarks and references to Appendices
CAMP N.16.b.9.3	23/7/17		Battalion in Reserve. Enemy shelled Camp. Result - 2/L F.S. Lawrick killed. 2/L O'Kelly wounded at duty. 1 other rank killed.	
CAMP N.15.c.9.9	24/7/17		Camp moved to N.15.c.9.9. 2/L F.S. Lawrick buried at Kewie Brickland Cemetery. Heavy rain. Officers of his Company attended funeral.	
"	25/7/17		Parades carried out under Company arrangements.	
"	26/7/17		Practice Attack carried out at 3 a.m. Rest of day paraded under Company arrangements.	
"	27/7/17		Training carried out	
"	28/7/17		— ditto —	
"	29/7/17		Battalion carried out night training. Practice Attack at 2 a.m. Battalion paraded for Divine Service.	
"	29/7/17		— moved into line at night and relieved 10th Worcesters. Disposition: same trenches and order as on 19th instant. Trench Routine carried out. Battalion preparing for the offensive.	
In the Line	30/7/17		All days in battle positions just N of GREEN WOOD. Instructions for the offensive attached. NIGHT of 30/31st	
"	3/1/17		ZERO HOUR 3.50 a.m. Battalion attacked. 7/King's Own R.L. Regt on the right. 7/N. Lan R. on left. 1/5 Lan R. in support. All objectives taken. Position of objectives shown in attached MAP. Casualties: Officers 2/L H.S. Rayhue & 2/L.R. Tancott killed. 2/L R.H. Gould wounded and missing. 2/L H.S. Snape wounded. Other Ranks about 135 killed, wounded and missing. Battalion strength on relief 535 other ranks.	

EAST LANCASHIRE REGIMENT.

OPERATION ORDER NO. 17.

Appendix I

Reference Sheet 28 S.W. 1/20090.

1. The Battalion will move into BIRR BARRACKS, LOCRE tomorrow 1st. July, less men employed on afternoon and evening working parties.

2. Work in accordance with B.M. 1332 dated 17th. July 1917 will be carried out on 1st. July.

3. Order of march C,A,B,D and Headquarter Section at 300 yards distance Head of Battalion to leave bivouacs at 8_0 am.
   ROUTE. Via track through field occupied by the SOUTH LANCASHIRE REGT. ;D.;track.

4. Transport Lines and Quartermaster Stores will remain in their present location.

5.. Company Commanders will report their arrival in new billets to Battalion Headquarters.

6. Transport will arrange:-
   (a) To move all kits, Cooking utensils etc from Bivouacs by 1 pm. and take them to new billets.
   (b) To move all kits, cooking utensils and Stores from Battalion Headquarters at Doncaster Camp by 2 pm. and take them to BIRR BARRACKS.

7. Advance party of 1 N.C.O. per company and 1 man per platoon to report to the Assistant Adjutant at BIRR BARRACKS at 2 pm.

8. Captain H. W. House will detail a Subaltern to hand over the Bivouacs. He will also obtain the certificate- that the area occupied by the Battalion is left in a clean and sanitary condition.

9. O.C.Companies will detail a Party of 1 N.C.O. and the sanitary men of each company to clean camp. This party should report to the subaltern of C. Company.

       (Signed.) R. D. Allsopp.
          Lieut. & Adjt.
       7th. East Lancashire Regiment.

Issued at 12 noon.
  Copy to
    No. 1. 56th. Bgde.
      2. C. O.
      3. Adjutant.
      4. O.C.A Coy.
      5. O.C.B Coy.
      6. O.C.C Coy.
      7. O.C.D Coy.
      8. Lewis Gun Officer.
      9. Transport & Qomr.
     10. R.S.M.
     11. M.O.
     12. War Diary.
     13. File.

Appendix 2

Secret.　　　　　　　East Lancashire Regiment.　　　　　Copy No. 13

OPERATION ORDER NO. 18.

Reference Map Sheet 28 S.W. 1/20,000.　　　　　　　　18/7/17.

1. The Battalion will move into CENTRE SUPPORT LINE tonight. This Sector is at present unoccupied.

2. On completion of move C & D Coys will be situate in BLUE LINE O.8.c, A & B Coys in RED LINE O.7.d. and Battalion Headquarters at N.17.c.9 o.

3. Companies will move off in the following order C,D,A,B Coys and Headquarter Section. First named Company to leave BIRR BARRACKS at 5-30 p.m. Distance of 150 yards between Platoons to be maintained. Transport will move in rear of Battalion.

4. Route via BUTTERFLY FARM-BEAVER CORNER-SIEGE FARM-YORK HOUSE- thence by track to ONRAET WOOD.

5. Dress - Fighting Order with canteens under haversack.

6. Packs will be dumped at Quartermaster Stores at 2-30 p.m.

7. Mess Cart, Maltese Cart, Limbers and Pack Ponies for Officers Mess and other stores for the line will report at Headquarters at 4-30 p.m.

8. Officers Kits and stores not for the line will be dumped outside Officers Quarters by 4-30 p.m.
Company stores not for line will be dumped near Guard Room by 4-30 p.m.

9. Cookers will not go with Battalion into line. Dixies will be used for cooking purposes.

10. Advance Party of 2 N.C.Os per Company and 1 N.C.O. for Hdqrs will report to Major Morrison outside Officers Quarters at 4-30 p.m. This party will guide Companies to their respective positions

11. All empty Tommies Cookers tins to be returned daily by Ration Party to Quartermaster Stores to be refilled.

12. A certificate that all Huts etc. are in a clean and sanitary condition to be rendered to Orderly Room by 4-30 p.m. to-day.

13. 2nd. Lieut. R. B. Hoggett will hand over the camp to incoming Battalion and receive usual certificate that camp was handed over in a clean and sanitary condition.

14. Sgt. Stevens, Cpl Walsh and all Sanitary men of Companies & Hdqr. Section will parade at Orderly Room at 5-0 p.m.
They will rejoin their respective units in their new positions after the vicinity of the camp has been thoroughly cleaned up.

15. Trench Stores will be carefully checked and lists of same sent to Orderly Room by 9-0 a.m. on 20th. inst.

16. Companies will notify Adjutant by Runner that move is complete
　　　　　　　　Signed. R. D. Allsopp. Lieut. & Adjt.
Issued at 2-0 p.m.　　　　East Lancashire Regt.
Copy No. 1 56th. Infy. Bgde.　　8. O.C. B Coy.
　　　　2 Commanding Officer.　　9. O.C. C Coy.
　　　　3.Major W.Morrison.　　10. O.C. D Coy.
　　　　4.Medical Officer.　　11. Transport Officer.
　　　　5.Signalling Officer.　　12. File.
　　　　6.Lewis Gun Officer.　　13. War Diary.
　　　　7.O.C. A Coy.　　14. R. S. M.

Secret. Appendix 3   East Lancashire Regiment.   Copy NO. 10

Operation Orders. NO. 19.

Reference Map Sheet 28 S. W.

1. The Battalion will be relieved to-night and on relief will move to Camp about N.16.b.9.3.
    C. Company will move to Camp N.16. b.9.3. under orders of the South Lancashire Regiment.
    A. Company of the South Lancashire Regiment will remain in line until night 23/24th and will until that time be under orders of 10th. Worcester Regt. One Company of 10th. Worcesters will remain in Camp N.16.b.9.3. until night 23/24th.

2. Guides of D and B Companies for incoming Battalion will be at DOME HOUSE at 9-45 p.m.
   Guides of A Company to be at IN DE STERKTE CABARET by 9-45 p.m.

3. Advance Party of 2 N.C.Os. per Company will report to Sergt. Sandham at Headquarters at 3-0 p.m. to take over new Camp.

4. All Officers Mess and other stores will be dumped at DOME-HOUSE at 7-0 p.m. The Transport Officer will arrange transport for same.
   2 Limbers for Lewis Guns will be at DOME HOUSE at 11-0pm

5. Trench Stores will be carefully checked and receipts sent to Orderly Room by 12-0 noon 23rd. inst.

6. The Quartermaster will arrange for Officers Kits, Rations and Cookers to be at New Camp.

7. A. D. & B Companies will report completion of relief by runner to Battalion Headquarters.

8. Acknowledge.

                        Signed. R. D. Allsopp. Lieut. & Adjt.
   Issued at 11-45 a.m.   7th. East Lancashire Regiment.

        Copy No. 1. Transport Officer.
                 2. Brigade.
                 3. Commanding Officer.
                 4. O.C.A.Company.
                 5. O.C.B.   "
                 6. O.C.D.   "
                 7. O.C.A.Coy.South Lan.R.
                 8. O.C.C.Coy.East Lan. R.
                 9. Major Morrison.
                10. War Diary.
                11. O.C.10th. Worcester Regt.
                12. File.

Appendix 4/109

SECRET   EAST LANCASHIRE REGIMENT   Copy No ...

OPERATION ORDER NO. ...

                                                    ...th July 1917.

Reference Map Sheet ...

1. The Battalion will move into the Trenches, SECTOR SUBSECTOR, tomorrow relieving the WORCESTER REGT. Present Camp to be cleared by 8 A.M.

2. Companies and Hdqr Section will move off in the following order and at the following times and on completion of relief will be disposed in the line as under:—
    A Coy   ... p.m.   to RIGHT SUPPORT LINE
    B Coy   4.15 p.m.   to LEFT SUPPORT LINE
    Hdqr Section   4.30 p.m.   to Hdqrs ROYAL WOOD
    D Coy   5 p.m.   to LEFT FRONT LINE
    C Coy   5.30 p.m.   to RIGHT FRONT LINE

3. GUIDES for Front Line Companies will be at ENGINEER CORNER at 6.30 p.m

4. MOVEMENTS to be by X track ...
   Distances of ... yards between Platoons W of Ridge and 100 yards between Sections E of RIDGE to be observed. and 100 yards between Platoons by NIGHT. From Line Coys. move to East of RIDGE before 10 p.m.

5. DRESS   Fighting Order.

6. In order to practice wearing the small box respirator on the march the Divisional Commander directs that all relief and working parties marching up to the trenches are to wear the box respirator with the mask fully adjusted for ten minutes whilst on the march.
   When possible the practice will be carried out east of the YPRES–ASSE BEEK.
   At the end of the practice the inside of the mask should be carefully dried as the condensation of moisture on metal parts of the eye pieces and nose clips causes rusting which corrodes the fabric of the facepieces.

7. On completion of the relief R.Lan R. will extend their left flank so as to take over from this Battalion up to the N.E corner of the small wood at O.17.d.55.65. This will be carried out by 3 a.m on the morning of the 30th inst. On completion of this adjustment to be reported by dash by messenger to Battalion Hdqrs.

8. (1) Transport for Arms,Shoemakers and Tailors Tools and Orderly Room Stores will report at Hdqrs at 10.30 a.m. All above articles to be dumped at Orderly Room by 10 a.m.
   (2) Transport for Officers Kits and Surplus Stores (Mess) will report at 3 p.m. Same to be dumped at Orderly Room by ... p.m.
   (3) Maltese Cart, Mess Cart,1 Limber for C.Q.M. Sgts L.Gs and One for A & B Coys, also Limber for Hdqrs Stores will report at 3 p.m.

9. Rations for B & Hdqr Section will be dumped at HALF CUBE by 6 p.m and for A Coy at HALF STRINGY CABARET at same time. C & D Coys. rations at CREMAILLE CORNER B.25.a.9.7 at 7.30
   C.Q.M.Sgts will issue Rations to Companies as they pass by.

10. All surplus personnel will report to the R.S.M at 4 p.m to clean up the camp. On completion they will be marched to Advanced Stores where they will report to Lt.Telquret who will arrange for their accommodation.

11. S.A.A., Grenades,Shovels &c will be issued with rations.

12. Trench Stores will be carefully checked up list thereof same sent to Orderly Room by 10 a.m on 30th inst.

1.

Operation Order No 30 continued.

2.

13. On completion of relief Companies will send code word "SAXON" to Bn Hdqrs by runner.

.... Lieut & Adjt
THE EAST LANCASHIRE REGIMENT.

ISSUED AT

Copies to:-
1. 88th Infantry Brigade
2. 10th Worcesters
3. Commanding Officer
4. Major Morrison
5. O.C A Coy
6. O.C B Coy
7. O.C C Coy
8. O.C D Coy
9. Transport Officer
10. Quartermaster
11. L.G.Officer
12. Signalling Officer
13. M.O
14. Adjutant
15. R.S.M
16. File
17. War Diary.

B + H6h. — DOME HOUSE.
A — IN DE STERKTE CABT.
C . D — ESTAMINET CORNER
O. 20. a. 3½. 9.

Appendix 5

7th BN. EAST LANCASHIRE REGIMENT
INSTRUCTIONS FOR THE OFFENSIVE

GENERAL PLAN 1. The IXth Corps in conjunction with the Corps on the Right and Left is to undertake offensive operations on a Zero day to be notified later.

OBJECTIVE OF 56TH INFANTRY BRIGADE. 2. The objective allotted to the 56th Infantry Brigade is that portion of the BLUE LINE marked on the map shown to Company Commanders between the following boundaries
On the Right
   The road from O.33.a.3.3 to O.23.b.2.4 (inclusive to the Battalion on the Right)
On the Left
   A line drawn from O.11.a.8.1 to O.11.b.55.00 FORRET FME being inclusive to Brigade on the left.

ASSEMBLY OF 56th INFANTRY BRIGADE 3. (a) The boundaries between battalions in the assembly position will be
   7/R.Lan R. RIGHT O.23.a.8.4 - VAN HOVE FME - POLKA ESTAMINET - Bend in road O.21.central.

   7/E.Lan R Right at S.E of small wood at O.17.c.33.68 thence due westward.

   7/N.Lan.R Right at Junction of present Front line and ROOZEBEEK thence due westward.

   The above 3 battalions will assemble in the present Front Line and the line of supporting points in rear.

   7/S.Lan R will assemble in the Old British Front Line.

PLAN OF ATTACK 4. At Zero hour to be notified later the three leading battalions of the Brigade will advance under an artillery barrage which will move forward in lifts of 100 yards according to Map shown to all Officers.

The boundaries between Battalions on the objective will be
7/R.Lan R and 7/E.Lan R Point in the Blue line due West of house at O.17.3.60.75.
7/E.Lan R and 7/N.Lan R Road Junction at O.17.b.3.8 (inclusive to 7/E.Lan.Rgt.

7/R.Lan R, 7/E.Lan R and 7/N.Lan R will each have four Companies in the Line. Each Company being on a frontage of two half platoons. The first line will move in extended order, and the second line will move in sections in file. The two lines comprise the first wave which will assault the objective. The third line will also advance by parties in file and will be detailed for Mopping up. The remaining platoon of each Company will be detailed for carrying.

PLAN OF 7TH E. LAN RGT ATTACK. 5. The Battalion will carry out the assault within the Battalion boundaries in the following order from Right to Left
   C Coy   A Coy   B Coy   D Coy
Each Company will attack on a front of 150 yards. Each Company will be responsible for mopping up the area over which it advances with the exception that "D" Coy will be responsible for dealing with the low lying ground lying between the left of their advance and the ROOZE-BEEK including GYM FME and the adjoining dugouts O.17.b.30.95.

2.

Each Company will consolidate the objective allotted to it work being commenced as far as possible during daylight. The line consolidated will be approximately along the BLUE LINE but the new trench will be dug at least 70 yards in front of or behind any conspicuous landmarks e.g hedges or houses.

In order to assist them in finding the line of the objective where there are no clear landmarks Companies will arrange to find their approximate positions on the BLUE LINE by means of measured strings pulled out as they advance.

CONSOLIDATION will be carried out on the following lines

FRONT LINE   Fire bays will be dug first, each about 8 yds long with gaps 3 yds wide between each fire bay. These gaps will subsequently be made into traverses. Shell holes will be improvised and eventually linked up.

This front line will be consolidated by the leading wave who will also be responsible for finding a covering party (two Lewis Guns per Company should be sufficient for this) and also for the sending out of patrols after the capture of the objective. One patrol consisting of 1 N.C.O and 2 men per Company should be sufficient for this. The patrols must act boldly, searching all dead ground or places where the enemy is likely to collect. The role of these patrols is to get in touch with the enemy and give warning to the Companies in case of attack.

WIRING The front line will be well wired. The utmost energy must be expended in this. French concertina wire well be interlaced with barbed wire will be available for this. Care should be taken that this wire is anchored down. The most important features should be wired first.

SUPPORT LINE will be dug at first as a series of small posts which will not be connected until the digging and wiring of the new front line are well advanced.

The digging of these posts will be commenced by the carrying platoons from each Company and will afterwards be taken over by the mopping up platoons on completion of the mopping up tasks.

M.G.COMPANY	6.	2 Vickers Guns will be attached to B & C Coys respectively and will be accommodated in the strong points to be constructed by the R.E. Prior to the construction of these strong points these guns will be pushed well forward along the central spur running eastwards in order to cover consolidation.
TRENCH MORTAR BATTERY	7.	½ Section, 56th T.M.B will be attached to the Battalion and will be used primarily to assist in the reduction of enemy strong points. The two mortars affiliated to the 7/E.Lan R temporarily augmented by those of 7/S.Lan R will be in a position in GREEN WOOD prior to Zero hour to assist the advance in the centre of the line. The ½ Section affiliated to the 7/E.Lan R will advance with "B" Coy.
ARTILLERY AND M.G.BARRAGE	8.	The advance will be covered by an Artillery and hopping barrage as well as a Machine Gun Barrage.
HEADQUARTERS	9.	19th Division SCHERPENBERG 56th Infy Bde DAMHSTRASSE (O.9.c.3.8) 7/R.Lan R POLKA ESTAMINET (O.22.a.3.2) 7/E.Lan R Dugouts at O.16.d.1.6 7/N.Lan R Dugouts in RAVINE O.10.d.15.55 7/S.Lan R Dugout near House at O.15.c.50.95

COMMUNICATIONS 10.

PRINCIPLES

1. Inter communications during the operations will be in accordance with the principles laid down in S.S 148 "Forward intercommunication in Battle"

2. The following methods will be employed
   (a) Telephone   (c) Power Buzzer & Amplyfier
   (b) Visual   (d) Runners
         (e) Pigeons

FORWARD STATIONS

Three Brigade Forward Stations will be established with any of which it is optional for units to communicate. Messages sent to these stations will be forwarded under Brigade arrangements. There is a buried cable head at COURAGEUX FME.
These stations will not move forward
(a) Central Station (Code call G.Z)
From this station the following methods will be available forward
    Telephone   to all Battalions
VISUAL   On an Arc of 45° - 180° (T.B) formed
The Southern limit of visibility being formed by the crest of the ridge from 0.16.d.P.9 - 0.17.c.3.3

AMPLIFIER & POWER BUZZER to two stations (b) & (c) below.

Runners

(b) Right Station (Code Call T.R)   0.16.d.90.25
(c) Left Station   (Code Call O.L)   0.10.d.3.5)
Both stations (b) and (c) are fitted with visual and Amplyfier and Power Buzzer.
    The above three stations will open at 5 p.m on "Y" day.

DIVISIONAL VISUAL STATION

Divisional Visual Station will also be open at KEMMEL. Code Call Y.S In order to assist units to pick up this station at night a Green light will be shown every half hour.
    Units working to KEMMEL by night will use a red glass.

BATTALION FORWARD STATION

A Battalion Forward Station will be established in GREEN WOOD dugout about 0.17.a.70.55
A telephone line and visual will be established here to communicate with Battalion Hdqrs
Telephone Lines will also be run out to C & B Coys
All messages handed in at the Battalion Forward Station will be forwarded under Battalion arrangements.

DUMPS

11. GRENADE   )
    S.A.A   )   0.16.a.4.5
    R.E   )
    WATER   )
        Water not to be drawn from this dump before Zero hour.

    Forward Dump of Wire)   0.17.a.1.3
       & Pickets   )

12. Regimental Aid Post   0.16.c.4.5

13. Prisoners of War   - near IN DE STERKTE CABARET

14. A dump of Signal stores will be available after cable head.

26/7/17   T. Eastham Lt & Adjt

7/E. Lewis R
June 16.17

- MAKE USE OF PARAGRAPHS AS REQUIRED. -

GIVE MAP REFERENCE OR MARK
ON MAP AT BACK.

1. I am at ....
2. I am at .... and am consolidating.
3. I am at .... and have consolidated.
4. Am held up by M.G. at ....
5. I need:-   Ammunition.
             Bombs.
             Rifle Grenades.
             Water.
             Very Lights.
             Stokes Shells.
6. Counter-attack forming up at ....
7. I am in touch with .... on Right at ....
                                  Left
8. I am not in touch on Right
                        Left
9. Am being shelled from ....
10. I estimate my present strength at .... rifles.
11. Hostile (Battery   )
            (Machine Gun) active at ....
            (Trench Mortar)
12. General information:-

Time............ m.   Name.............................
Date.............   Platoon...........................
                           Company...........................
                           Battalion.........................

WAR DIARY
INTELLIGENCE SUMMARY

Army Form C. 2118.

(Erase heading not required.)

Instructions regarding War Diaries and Intelligence Summaries are contained in F. S. Regs., Part II. and the Staff Manual respectively. Title Pages will be prepared in manuscript.

Place	Date	Hour	Summary of Events and Information	Remarks and references to Appendices
In the line	1/8/17		Battalion carried on with consolidation after attack of 31st July 1917. - No enemy counter attacks.	
—	2/8/17		— ditto —	
—	3/8/17		— ditto —	
BIRR BARRACKS LOCRE	4/8/17		Battalion relieved in line by R. Bear R. and moved by lorry to BIRR BARRACKS LOCRE - Casualties - 2nd Lt. P.K. Smedley previously reported killed, now reported wounded and missing. OR's killed, wounded and missing 50.	APP I
—	5/8/17		Battalion engaged in cleaning up equipment and clothing.	
—	6/8/17		— ditto —	
CAMP M.13.B.8.9 NR WESTOUTRE SHEET 28. 1/40.000	6/8/17		Battalion moved to camp near WESTOUTRE M.13.6.8.9	APP II
	7/8/17		Battalion carried out training.	
	8/8/17		— ditto —	
	9/8/17		— ditto —	
NIELLES EN BLEQUIN	10/8/17		Battalion moved by rail from BAILLEUL to WIZERNES area and then marched to NIELLES EN BLEQUIN from LUMBRES.	APP III
HENNEVEUX	11/8/17		Battalion marched to HENNEVEUX.	APP IV
	12/8/17		Battalion carried out training.	
	13/8/17		— do —	
	14/8/17		— do —	
	15/8/17		— do —	
	16/8/17		— do —	
	17/8/17		Battalion was taken by lorry to ECAULT to bathe. Spent a very enjoyable day.	
	18/8/17		Battalion practised "march past" with remainder of Brigade for Brit General inspection.	
	19/8/17		Massed Brigade Church Parade carried out, followed by presentation of medal ribbons to those awarded same in action of June 7/17 (Wytschaete) awarded for Ribbons:- 6413 Cpl. E. Robinson, 13037 L.Cpl A. Hilpin, 11688 Pte J. Zuilleman, 12798 C.S.M J. Lovell M.C., 13100 L/Sgt J. McAuley, 13828 Pte J. Sutton.	

Army Form C. 2118.

WAR DIARY
INTELLIGENCE SUMMARY
(Erase heading not required.)

Instructions regarding War Diaries and Intelligence Summaries are contained in F. S. Regs., Part II. and the Staff Manual respectively. Title Pages will be prepared in manuscript.

Place	Date	Hour	Summary of Events and Information	Remarks and references to Appendices
HENNEVEUX	19/8/17		and 23493 Pte (S.M. Fitzpatrick) by the G.O.C. 19th Division (Major General G.T. Bridges) followed by a Brigade Lunchland.	
"	20/8/17		a Brigade "march past" for inspection by F.M Sir Douglas Haig. Training carried out	APP V
"	21/8/17		ditto	
"	22/8/17		Battalion carried out Training	
QUESQUES	23/8/17		Battalion marched to Billets at QUESQUES	
"	24/8/17		Battalion carried out Training	
"	25/8/17		Battalion practised along with remainder of Brigade "march past" for inspection by F.M. SIR DOUGLAS HAIG.	
"	26/8/17		Battalion along with remainder of Brigade and 58th Brigade inspected by F.M. SIR DOUGLAS HAIG. Brigade moved to NIELLES LEZ BLEQUIN on return to IXth Corps Reserve Area.	
"	27/8/17		Battalion carried out training	
"	28/8/17		ditto	
"	29/8/17		Battalion moved by bus to WIZERNES, by rail to BAILLEUL and by march route to WESTOUTRE AREA. Camp at M.20.d.S.S. Sheet 28. 1/40.000.	APP VI
M.20 d.S.S Sheet 28 1/40.000	30/8/17		Battalion carried out training	
	31/8/17		Battalion employed on tactical parties at ZEVENCOTE and MONT NOIR.	

SECRET.   EAST LANCASHIRE REGIMENT.   Copy No 7

OPERATION ORDER No 21.   3/8/17.

The Battalion will be relieved tonight in the left Subsector by the Worcestershire Regiment and on completion of relief will move to BIRR BARRACKS, LOCRE.

Route :- Companies will use their own discretion as to course of route to cross roads at VIERSTRAAT.

Motor Lorries will convey all ranks to destination from Cross Roads VIERSTRAAT.

These lorries which commence to arrive at VIERSTRAAT VILLAGE N. 11. c. 9.9. at 12-45 a.m. will be under orders of Staff Captain 55th Infantry Brigade and they will be allotted by him as men arrive.

Complete parties of men from one Battalion will be carried on each journey.

GUIDES :- No 1 Coy (RIGHT Coy) and 2 RIGHT POSTS of No 2 Coy (LEFT Coy) will be relieved by C Coy Worcester Regt.

No 2 Coy (LEFT Coy) less two right hand posts will be relieved by part of B Coy Worcester Regt.

O.C. Left Coy will arrange to have 1 guide per post (for his two right hand posts) at O. C. No 1 (RIGHT Coy) HDQRS to guide up to relief.

1 Guide per platoon will be at GOUDEZEUNE FARM at 9-30 p.m. Special care should be taken that guides are fully acquainted with route. i.e. ROSE WOOD then overland.

Trench stores, Lewis Gun drums and large entrenching tools will be handed over on relief.

All stores to be dumped at DOME HOUSE by 8 p.m.

Transport Officer will arrange for transport for stores to be at DOME HOUSE by 8 p.m. and Pack Mules for Lewis Guns by 11 p.m.

On relief O. C. Coys will report to HDQRS by runner.

(Sd) R. D. Allsopp
Lt and Adjt
East Lancashire Regiment.

Copy No 1. 55th Brigade.
2. Commanding Officer.
3. O. C. A Coy
4. O. C. B Coy
5. O. C. C. Coy
6. O. C. D Coy
7. War Diary.
8. File.

EAST LANCASHIRE REGIMENT.

SECRET　　　　　OPERATION ORDER　No 22.　　　　Copy No 14.

6-8-17.

Reference Map Sheets　　28 S.W.　1/20=000.
　　　　　　　　　　　　27　　　 1/40,000.
　　　　　　　　　　　　28　　　 1/40,000.

1. Battalion will move into Camp M. 13. b. 8.9. today.
   ROUTE :-　CANADA CORNER - WESTOUTRE.

2. Battalion will be formed up in column of route in the following order :-
   　　Drums, A, B, C, D and Headquarters.
   　　Transport in rear of Battalion.
   The head of column to be on road outside Orderly Room facing EAST at 2-0 p.m. ready to march off at 2-15 p.m.
   DRESS :- Full Marching Order. Steel Helmets to be worn.
   Officers Chargers report at 2-0 p.m.
   Maltese Cart, Mess Cart, 2 limbers for Lewis Guns, one for Hdqrs Stores, one for Canteen, one for Orderly Room and Signallers and 3 for Officers Mess Stores and kits to report at 1-0 p.m.
   　　Headquarters and Coy Stores to be dumped outside Orderly Room by 1-0 p.m. and Officers Valises and Mess Stores outside Messes by 1-0 p.m.
   　　Advance Party of 1 N.C.O. and 2 men per Coy, 1 N.C.O. for Hdqrs 1 N.C.O. for Depot and Transport to report to Lt C.D. Gray at Orderly Room at 8-30 a.m.
   　　O. C. Coys will see that huts and vicinity are left in a clean and sanitary condition.

　　　　　　　　　(Sd)　　R. D. Allsopp,
　　　　　　　　　　　　　　Lt and Adjutant,
　　　　　　　　　　　　　　East Lancashire Regiment.

Copy No 1　　　55th Infantry Brigade.
　　　　 2　　　Commanding Officer.
　　　　 3　　　Major Morrison M.C.
　　　　 4　　　O. C. A Coy.
　　　　 5　　　O. C. B Coy.
　　　　 6　　　O. C. C Coy.
　　　　 7　　　O. C. D Coy
　　　　 8　　　Lt C. D. Gray.
　　　　 9　　　Transport Officer.
　　　　10　　　Lt and Quartermaster.
　　　　11　　　R. S. M.
　　　　12　　　File.
　　　　13　　　Medical Officer.
　　　　14　　　War Diary.

SECRET.   OPERATION ORDER No 23.   Copy No 12.

EAST LANCASHIRE REGIMENT.

8/8/17.

Reference Map Sheet HAZEBROUK 5a 1/10,000.

1. The Battalion will move to QUESQUES tomorrow.
    Entraining at BAILLEUL.
    Detraining at WIZERNES.
Proceeding by No 2 Train.

2. Battalion will be formed up on main road outside Camp facing West ready to move off at 5 a.m. in the following order
    Drums, Hdqrs, C, D, A, B Coys.
Route :- SCHAEXHEN X ROADS - St JAN CAPPEL - BAILLEUL.
10 minutes halt will be observed on the march at 10 minutes to each clock hour.

3. Dress :- Full marching order, steel helmets to be worn, water bottles to be filled and haversack ration to be carried.

4. Transport will proceed by No 1 Train and will pass SCHAEXHEN X Roads at 5-25 a.m. and will follow same route as Battalion.
    It will march under orders of 2nd Lt J. M. Colvin.

5. On arrival at WIZERNES Battalion will march to QUESQUES. Detailed orders later.

            (Sd)   R. D. Allsopp,
                    Lt and Adjutant.
                    The East Lancashire Regiment.

        Copies to   No 1   55th Infantry Brigade.
                        2   Commanding Officer.
                        3   Major Morrison.
                        4   Adjutant.
                        5   O. C. A Coy.
                        6   O. C. B Coy.
                        7   O. C. C Coy
                        8   O. C. D Coy
                        9   Lieut C. D. Gray.
                       10   Quartermaster.
                       11   Transport Officer.
                       12   War Diary.
                       13   File.

SECRET.   EAST LANCASHIRE REGIMENT   Copy No 13.
             OPERATION ORDER No 24.

Map Sheet HAZEBROOK 5a and CALAIS 13   1/10,000.

                                                    10/8/17.

1. The Battalion will move to HENNEVEUX tomorrow.

2. The Battalion will be formed up on NEILLES - COULOMBY ROAD North of Railway Line ready to move off at 9-30 a.m. in the following order D, A, Drums, Hdqr Sectn, B, C Coys and Transport.

    Reveille 7-0 a.m.
    Sick Parade 7-30 a.m.
    Breakfasts 8-9 a.m.

3. All stores to be loaded by 7-0 a.m.

4. Route COULOMBY - HARLETTES - BOULOGNE ROAD - LONGUEVILLE - HENNEVEUX.

                (Sd)   R. D. ALLSOPP,
                        Lt and Adjutant,
                        The East Lancashire Regiment.

        Copy No 1 55th Infantry Brigade.
             2 Commanding Officer.
             3 Major W. Morrison.
             4 Adjutant.
             5 O. C. A Coy.
             6 O. C. B. Coy.
             7 O. C. C. Coy
             8 O. C. D Coy
             9 Lt C. D. Gray.
            10 Transport Officer.
            11 R. S. M.
            12 Medical Officer.
            13 War Diary.
            14 File.

NO. 7/340.
Secret.

EAST LANCASHIRE REGIMENT.
OPERATION ORDER NO. 25.

Copy No. 13

21/8/17

Reference Map Sheet CALAIS 13.   1/100,000.
                HAZEBROUCK 5a.   1/100,000.

---

1. The Battalion will move to the QUESQUES area tomorrow.

2. The Battalion will be formed up in column of route on the HENNEVEUX - BRUNEMBERT Road in the following order :- Drums, D, C, Hdqrs, B, A Coys and Transport, head of column to be opposite D. Company's Headquarters ready to move off at 9-0 a.m. One Marker per Company and Headquarters to report to the Regimental Sergeant Major outside D. Company's Headquarters at 8-30 a.m.

3. Dress. Full Marching Order. Steel Helmets to be worn.

4. All Officers and other stores to be stacked outside Company Headquarters by 8-0 a.m. Transport will be detailed by Transport Officer to collect same.

5. Training Grounds will be left in their present condition. Practice Trenches and Ranges will not be filled in.

6. 2nd. Lieut. McChesney and 1 responsible N.C.O. per Company will be left behind to hand over the present billets. On completion of this duty their will rejoin their Company's in QUESQUES area.

7. Present Billets must be left in a clean and Sanitary condition

Signed. R. D. Allsopp.
Lieutenant & Adjutant.
7th. East Lancashire Regiment.

Issued at 12.15 p.m.

Copy No. 1. 56th. Infantry Brigade.
        2. Commanding Officer.
        3. O.C.A. Company.
        4. O.C.B. Company.
        5. O.C.C. Company.
        6. O.C.D. Company.
        7. Lieut. C.D. Gray.
        8. M.O.
        9. T.O.
       10. Quartermaster.
       11. Adjutant.
       12. R.S.M.
       13. War Diary
       14. File.

SECRET.   EAST LANCASHIRE REGIMENT.   Copy No 14

OPERATION ORDER No 26.   26/8/17.

Reference Map Sheet   CALAIS 13.
                           HAZEBROUCK 6a.
                           SHEET 28 S.W.

1. The Battalion will move into Reserve Area near WESTOUTRE by bus, rail and road tomorrow.

2. The Battalion will move as follows :-
   All Transport will be formed up under Orders of 2nd Lt S. WHEAL ready to move off at 9-0 a.m.
   They will proceed by most direct route to WIZERNES and be ready to entrain there at 3-30 p.m. punctually.
   All Stores (with the exception of 4 Camp Kettles per Company) will be stacked outside Company Headquarters ready for loading on motor lorry by 8 a.m. Lorry will call for same.
   Drummers will stack their packs and rifles with these stores.
   The Battalion will be formed up outside Orderly Room by 4-15 pm and will embuss under the Orders of 2nd Lt J. H. McChesney. 20 busses will be available. Busses will proceed to WIZERNES where Battalion will entrain for BAILLEUL.
   On arrival at BAILLEUL, Companies will be formed up outside Station in column of route in the following order Drums, Hdqrs, A,B,C and D Companies.
   Route :- BAILLEUL - ST JAN CAPPEL - Road ½ mile W of C in Croix de POPERINGHE - MONT NOIR - to Camp at M. 20. d.5.9.

3. All billets to be left in a clean and sanitary condition.

4. Entraining states to be rendered to Orderly Room by all Companies, Hdqrs, Depot and Transport (Transport to show number of horses and vehicles) by 7-0 a.m. tomorrow.

                .... Lieut and Adjutant,
                7th Bn East Lancashire Regiment.
Issued at 5 p.m.

        Copy No 1.   36th Infantry Brigade.
                 2.   Commanding Officer.
                 3.   Major Morrison.
                 4.   O. C. A Coy.
                 5.   O. C. B Coy.
                 6.   O. C. C Coy.
                 7.   O. C. D Coy.
                 8.   Lt and Quartermaster.
                 9.   2nd Lt S. Wheal.
                10.   Medical Officer.
                11.   Adjutant.
                12.   Hdqr Coy (Lt Gray).
                13.   R. S. M.
                14.   War Diary.
                15.   File.

WAR DIARY
INTELLIGENCE SUMMARY
(Erase heading not required.)

Army Form C. 2118.

Place	Date	Hour	Summary of Events and Information	Remarks and references to Appendices
INKERMAN CAMP WESTOUTRE. SHEET 28 SW.	1/9/17		Battalion paraded for Divine Service.	
	2/9/17		Working parties were supplied for work at ZEVENCOTE DEPOT and MONT NOIR.	
	3/9/17		Working parties supplied and training as able carried out.	
	4/9/17		do	
			One officer and 25 other ranks attached to 61st Field Coy RE for duty. Working parties supplied for work at WALBSDEN JUNCTION	
	5/9/17		Training of specialists carried out. Practice trenches at M.19.d. utilised.	
WAKEFIELD HUTS, LOCRE. M.29.A.G.1.	6/9/17		"B" Coy attached to IX Corps Heavies for work. Battalion moved from Inkerman Camp to WAKEFIELD HUTS LOCRE. Working parties found.	SEE APPENDIX 1
	7/9/17		Battalion supplied working parties	
			ditto	
	8/9/17		"B" Coy rejoined Battalion from IX Corps Heavies.	
			Divine Service (Voluntary)	
	9/9/17		ditto	
	10/9/17		All available officers and men training	
	11/9/17		ditto	
	12/9/17		Battalion prepared to move to KEMMEL SHELTERS but orders for move were cancelled.	SEE APPENDIX 2
	13/9/17		Reinforcements - 31 other ranks. One Company (D) attached to 1st Canadian Tunnelling Coy - digging for electric cables.	
			Reinforcements - 22 other ranks. Baths at LOCRE allotted to Battalion.	
	14/9/17		Battalion supplied working parties. All available officers and men training.	
			Reinforcements - 53 other ranks.	
	15/9/17		Battalion supplied working parties. All specialist training.	
			Reinforcements 53 other ranks. Casualties 1 O.R. killed 4 wounded.	
	16/9/17		Divine Service (Voluntary)	
			Battalion supplied working party. Specialist training.	
	17/9/17		Battalion supplied working parties. Specialist training.	
			Casualties 1 O. Rank killed 3 wounded	

Army Form C. 2118.

WAR DIARY
INTELLIGENCE SUMMARY.
(Erase heading not required.)

Instructions regarding War Diaries and Intelligence Summaries are contained in F. S. Regs., Part II. and the Staff Manual respectively. Title pages will be prepared in manuscript.

Place	Date	Hour	Summary of Events and Information	Remarks and references to Appendices
WAKEFIELD HUTS LOCRE.	16/9/17		Battalion carried on parades and prepared for move. A Coy rejoined Bn. from 1st Canadian Tunnelling Coy. Battalion moved from Indefield Huts to IRISH HOUSE.	SEE APPENDIX 3.
IRISH HOUSE	19/9/17		Battalion moved to assemble positions BOIS CONFLUENT. Surplus Personnel moved to Chin at KARINE VIERSTRAAT. 60 o.Rks attached to 58th Field and an Shelter Reserve.	SEE APPENDIX 4.
BOIS CONFLUENT	20/9/17		Battalion moved into Reserve at the BLUFF. Canal Embankment. Carrying parties found for forward area.	
CENTRE SECTOR I.36.b LINE	21/9/17		Redkes moved into the Line, relieving 9th Cheshire Regiment and 10th Worcester Regiment. B and D Coys holding line. C Coy in support and A Coy in Reserve. Casualties 6 O.Rks wounded.	
RIGHT SECTOR I.36.	22/9/17		Battalion occupied as in trench manual. Heavy shelling by both sides. Casualties. 1 Officer (2nd F. POTTER) Dvd. 2 o.Rks wounded.	
	23/9/17		Battalion carried on trench manual. At night Battalion Headquarters fronts and relieved Kings own in Right Subsector (which lies at between POTSDAM EME – HESSIAN WOOD – LOCRE. Canadian Capt. Ist B. relief wounded.	SEE APPENDIX 5.
	24/9/17		Usual warfare carried out. Casualties 5 o.Rks killed. 7 O.Rks wounded.	
	25/9/17		Usual Trench Warfare carried out. Casualties – 2 O.Rks Killed. 3 O.Rks wounded.	
	26/9/17		Battalion relieved in line by 1/Kings Own and moved into Reserve at SPOIL BANK and GASPARS CLIFF.	SEE APPENDIX 6.
	27/9/17		B and C Coys had baths and clean change at SIEGE FARM and afterwards hot dinners at Camp KAERE VIERSTRAAT	
	28/9/17		HDQRS, A and B Coys —— ditto ——	
N.22.a.2.4. Sheet 28.S.W.	29/9/17		Battalion moved into Divisional Reserve to Camp at N.22.a.2.4. Sheet 28.S.W.	SEE APPENDIX 7.
	30/9/17		Battalion found working parties and attended voluntary Church Parades –	

SECRET COPY NO. 14.

APPENDIX. 1

EAST LANCASHIRE REGIMENT
OPERATION ORDER NO. 37
5th September 1917.

Reference Map Sheet 28 S.W. 1/20.000

1. The Battalion (less B Coy) will move to WAKEFIELD HUTS N.29.a.6.1 tomorrow

2. The Battalion will be formed up in Column of Route on the road South of the Camp ready to move off at 9.45 a.m in the following order:- Drums HdQrs A,B,C and D Companies.
   1 Marker per Company will report to the Regimental Sergeant Major at Medical Inspection Room at 9.15 a.m

3. Dress :- Full marching Order, Steel Helmets to be worn.

4. Route:- Via Road Junction N.31.a.6.6 - MONT ROUGE - LOCRE.

5. All Stores, Officers Valises &c to be stacked outside the Quartermasters Stores by 8.30 a.m
   The Transport Officer will arrange for the removal of same to new Camp.
   Drummers will stack their packs and rifles with these stores.

6. 1 N.C.O per Company, Depot and HdQrs will report to 2nd Lt. R.D.Hoggett with bicycles at 8.30 a.m. They will proceed ahead as Billeting Party.

7. 1 N.C.O per Company, Depot and HdQrs will remain behind along with one Officer of C Company to hand present Camp over to incoming Unit of 87th Infantry Bde.

8. Present Camp must be left in a clean and sanitary condition List of Camp Stores and Furniture on charge of Companies will be forwarded to Orderly Room by 7.30 a.m.

.... Lieut & Adjt
7th Bn East Lancashire Regiment.

Issued at 2.10 p.m.

Copy No. 1 to   36th Infantry Bde.
        2.   Commanding Officer
        3.   Adjutant
        4.   O.C A Coy
        5.   O.C B Coy
        6.   O.C C Coy
        7.   O.C D Coy
        8.   Transport Officer
        9.   Medical Officer
       10.   2nd Lt. Hoggett
       11.   Lt & Qrmr Hilbert
       12.   R.S.M
       13.   Lt.C.D.Gray
       14.   War Diary
       15.   File.

SECRET.   EAST LANCASHIRE REGIMENT.   Copy No. 15

Operation Order No. 28.

11/9/17.

Reference Map Sheet 28 S.W.

1. The Battalion will move to KEMMEL SHELTERS tomorrow.

2. The Battalion (less Working Parties) will be formed up in column of Route on ground outside Orderly Room ready to move off at 2-45 p.m. in the following order:- Drums, Headquarters, A, B, C and D Companies.
Markers will report to the R.S.M. at 2-45 p.m.

3. ROUTE via HOSPICE-Cross Road M.30.b.2.9. road junction N.19.c.9.0.

4. On completion of work, working parties will join at New Camp.

5. All stores, Officers' valises etc. to be stacked near Guard Room by 1-0 p.m. Packs of Drummers and Working Parties will be dumped at same time and place.

6. Usual advance Party will report to 2nd. Lieut. R.B. Hoggett at Orderly Room at 12-0 noon.
Rear party of one Officer of B Company and 1 N.C.O. per Coy. will be left behind to hand over Camp.

7. Transport Lines will be at N.16.c.2.9.

8. Present Camp to be left in a clean and Sanitary condition. List of stores to be forwarded to Orderly Room by 11-0 a.m.

Lieutenant & Adjutant.
East Lancashire Regiment.

Issued at 8 p.m.

Copy No. 1. 66th. Infantry Brigade.
2. Commanding Officer.
3. Major Morrison.
4. O.C. A. Company.
5. O.C. B. Company.
6. O.C. C. Company.
7. O.C. D. Company.
8. Lieut. C.D. Gray.
9. Lieut. & Qmr.
10. Transport Officer.
11. R.S.M.
12. 2nd. Lieut. R.B. Hoggett.
13. Medical Officer.
14. Adjutant.
15. War Diary.
16. File.

SECRET.   APPENDIX J   EAST LANCASHIRE REGIMENT.   Copy No. 15

Operation Order No.29.

REFERENCE MAP SHEET 28 S.W. 1/20,000.

1. The Battalion will move to IRISH HOUSE today.

2. Companies will be formed up in column of route on ground in centre of Camp head of column to be 25 yards short of Guard Room, in the following order :- Hdqurs., A, B, C & D Coys; ready to move off at 6.0 p.m. Dress:- ~~Full marching order~~ fighting order, steel helmets to be worn.

3. ROUTE:- via LOCRE HOSPICE - Cross Roads at N.1 c 6.0, and KEMMEL.

4. Distance of 500 yards between Companies will be maintained.

5. Officers' valises, Company and other Stores to be stacked near Guard Room by 4.0 p.m. T.O. will arrange transport. All surplus kit of Officers and men will be dumped at DONCASTER HUTS by 3.0 p.m., it must be clearly marked with Regt.No., Rank, Name and Coy.

6. Cookers and watercarts will proceed with Battalion.

7. Present Camp to be left in a clean and sanitary condition.

8. 1 N.C.O. per Coy and Headqurs will report to 2/Lieut.R.B.Hoggett at Orderly Room at 4 p.m. to take over new Camp.

9. 1 N.C.O. per Coy, Hdqrs and Transport will remain behind to hand over present Camp to incoming Battalion, and will report to 2/Lieut. V.Kirby at Orderly Room at 6.0 p.m.

                           Lieut. &
                           Adjutant,
             7th East Lancs.Regt.,

Issued at 1040 a.m.

      Copy No.1.   55th Infantry Brigade,
           2.   Commanding Officer,
           3.   Major Morrison,
           4.   O.C. A Company,
           5.   " B "
           6.   " C "
           7.   " D "
           8.   Lieut.C.D.Gray,
           9.   Lieut. & Qmr.,
          10.   Transport Officer,
          11.   R. S. M.,
          12.   2/Lt. R.B.Hoggett,
          13.   Medical Officer,
          14.   Adjutant,
          15.   War Diary (2)
          16.   File.

APPENDIX 4.

Para 3 is cancelled, and the following substituted :-

3. Battalion will pass starting point S.23.a.60.45 as follows :-
   Hdqrs 8.0 p.m.,
   A Coy. 8.10 ,
   B ,   8.20 ,
   C ,   8.30 ,
   D ,   8.40 ,

SECRET.   EAST LANCASHIRE REGIMENT.   Copy No. 15

Operation Order No. 37.

1/8/17.

REFERENCE MAP ISSUE No.S.1.

1. The Battalion will move forward to the assembly position in BOIS CONFLUENT today.

2. Battalion will be formed up in column of route in the following order - H.Q., A, B, C & D Coys. Head of column to be at road junction M21 d.B.c.66.45 at 3.0 p.m.

3. Hot onouts at 5 o FARMS DUMP 100 yards between Coys. After FARMS DUMP 100 yards between platoons.

4. Company Commanders will ensure that a slow pace is maintained on the march - 10 minutes halt will be observed in every half hour, i.e. 10 minutes past and 10 minutes to each clockhour.

5. ROUTE is via Road junction No.b.d.7 FARMS DUMP - track running along west own edges of GRAND BOIS and BOIS QUARANTE.

6. Surplus personnel will parade on the road outside Hqrs ready to move off at 6 p.m.

7. All Officers valises and Stores not for the line will be stacked on F end opposite O.R. by 2.30 p.m.

8. Stores etc. for the line will be stacked outside O.R. by 7 p.m.

9. In the event of the R.Lan.R. not having vacated BOIS CONFLUENT on Batn. arriving they will wait outside the wood until camp had been vacated.

10. Present camp to be left in a clean and sanitary condition.

(s) R Dalrymph Lieut. &
                      Adjutant,
                 East Lancs.Regt.

Issued at 11 a.m.

Copy No.1   58th Infantry Brigade,
       2   Commanding Officer,
       3   Major Harrison,
       4   O.C. A Coy.,
       5   " B   "
       6   " C   "
       7   " D   "
       8   Lieut.C.D.Gray,
       9   Lieut & Q Mr.
      10   Transport Officer,
      11   R. S. M.;
      12   L/Lt .R.B.Muggett,
      13   Medical Officer,
      14   Adjutant,
      15   War Diary (s)
      16   File.

APPENDIX 5.

SECRET.   Copy No.10.

            East Lancashire Regiment.   23-9-17.

OPERATION ORDER NO.31.

1. The Brigade Front will be re-adjusted tonight and on completion of re-adjustment the Battn. will hold the line as follows reading from left to right.
   POTSDAM FME to HESSIAN WOOD to LOCK 6. "D" Coy. on left, "A" Coy. in Centre, "C" Coy. Right, and "B" Coy. in Reserve.

2. Coys. will relieve as follows :-
   One platoon of "C" Coy. E.LAN.R. will relieve "A" Coy. KING'S OWN in the advanced posts on right.
   One platoon of "C" Coy. E.LAN.R. will relieve platoon of "C" Coy. KING'S OWN in Strong Point.
   "C" Coy. Headquarters will be near advanced posts.
   1 Platoon of "A" Coy. E.LAN.R. will relieve one platoon of "B" Coy. KING'S OWN in the advanced Posts on left.
   One platoon of "A" Coy. E.LAN.R. will relieve 1 platoon of "C" Coy. KING'S OWN in Strong Points.
   "A" Coy. Headqrs will be in Strong Point.
   Strong Points which will be held by "C" and "A" Coys. run from O.6.b.7.4. to O.6.b.95.45.
   "D" Coy. E.LAN.R. will stand fast in present position.
   "B" Coy. will be relieved by "B" Coy. S.LAN.R. and will then relieve "D" Coy. KING'S OWN in Reserve Dugouts in Railway Embankment about I.36.c.3.1.; also in 2 points near LOCK 6 on left Bank of Canal.
   Dispositions of advanced Posts have been given verbally to Coy. Commanders concerned.
   Battn. Hdqrs will be situate in Dugouts at present occupied by Hdqrs. KING'S OWN at I.36.c.3.1.

3. Guides will meet "C" Coy. at junction of OAK AVENUE and Railway Line at 8.30 p.m. and 9 p.m. respectively.
   Guides for "A" Coy. at same place at 9.30 p.m.
   Platoon of "A" Coy. E.LAN.R. taking over advanced Posts will march direct.
   "B" Coy. E.LAN.R. will arrange for 4 guides per platoon to be at "C" Coy. Hdqrs at 8.30 p.m. to guide in "B" Coy. of S.LAN.R.

4. Rations will be drawn from Railway Cutting at I.36.c.2.3. about 8.30 p.m. The platoons in support of "C" and "A" Coys. will carry rations, and water for themselves and platoons in advanced posts.
   Men detailed to carry rations will wait at Dump for them if they have not arrived and will then follow up at least half an hour after advanced Posts have moved off.
   "B" Coy. will carry their own rations and water.
   "D" Coy. will send two guides under a good N.C.O. to report at Ration Dump at 8.30 p.m. to guide Surplus Personnel to their Coy. Surplus Personnel will carry rations for "D" Coy.

5. S.A.A. and other stores in possession of 2 forward Coys. will be left in Strong Points by KING'S OWN.

6. Reports on completion of relief to Battn. Hdqrs. by Runner.

          (Signed)   R. D. ALLSOPP, Lieut.& Adjt.,
                           East Lancs. Regt.

Issued at 3.0 p.m.
          Copies to 1. C.O.,
                  2. King's Own,
                  3. O.C. A Coy.,
                  4.   , B ,
                  5.   , C ,
                  6.   , D ,
                  7. Adjt.,
                  8. M.O.,
                  9. File,
                  10. War Diary.

APPENDIX No 6.

Secret   East Lancashire Regiment   Copy No 12

OPERATION ORDER No 32.   26/9/17.

1. The Battalion will be relieved by the KINGS OWN tonight.

2. Companies will be relieved as follows:-

    "C" Company King's Own will relieve "C" Coy E.L.R. in Right Forward Posts and Right Strong Points.

    "D" Company King's Own will relieve "A" Coy E.L.R. in centre Forward Posts and left Strong Point.

    "B" Coy King's Own will relieve "D" Coy E.L.R. in Left Forward Posts and Intermediate Line.

    "A" Coy King's Own will relieve "B" Coy E.L.R. at Railway Embankment.

    Reliefs in following order:-
    C. B. D. A. HdQRS.

3. Empty Petrol Tins will be carried out by Coys and left at Ration Dump.

4. Receipts for Trench Stores will be taken and forwarded to Orderly Room by 12 NOON, 27th inst. On completion of relief Coys will move as follows:-

    A Coy   }   To SPOIL BANK (N.E) on Canal Bank
    C -   }   between PONTOON and NORFOLK BRIDGES
    D -   }   MOVE VIA OAF AVENUE
    HdQRS }

    B Coy to GASPARS CLIFF

    March direct under Company arrangements.

6. All movements by ½ Platoons at 100 yards distance.

7. Reports by Coy Commanders on completion of relief to present Battalion Headquarters.

               (Sd) R.D. ALLSOPP
               Lt and Adjutant
Issued at 5.15 p.m   East Lancashire Regiment

Copies No 1. 56th Infy Bgde
      2. C.O.
      3. O.C. A Coy
      4. - B -
      5. - C -
      6. - D -
      7. - HdQRS.
      8. Adjutant.
      9. Medical Officer
     10. King's Own Regiment
     11. File
     12. War Diary.

Appendix 7.
4/10.

EAST LANCASHIRE REGIMENT.   Copy No.10.
SECRET.
                OPERATION ORDER No.33.   29/9/17.

                Reference Map Sheet 28.S.W.

1. The Battalion will be relieved by units of the 58th Brigade today and on relief will move to Camp at ROSSIGNOL WOOD.

2. "B" and "D" Coys. will be relieved by Royal Welsh Fusiliers, and Hdqrs by 6th Wilts Regt. "A" and "C" Coys.will not be relieved but will move off at an hour to be notified later.

3. All movement East of YPRES ST.ELOI Road by sections at XXX 200 yards distance. West of that Road by platoons at 300 yards distance.

4. All stores to be loaded on limbers by 1.15 p.m.

5. Coy.Commanders will report on arrival at New Camp.

                (Signed)   R.D.Allsopp, Lieut.&
                                          Adjutant,
                                 East Lancashire Regt.

        Copies to.   1. 58th Brigade,
                     2. C.O.,
                     3. O.C. A Coy.,
                     4. , B ,
                     5. , C ,
                     6. , D ,
                     7. Hdqrs.,
                     8. M.O.,
                     9. Adjutant,
                    10. War Diary.
                    11. File.

    Issued at 10.15 a.m.

WAR DIARY
INTELLIGENCE SUMMARY.
(Erase heading not required.)

Army Form C. 2118.

7 E Lane 28
Vol 24

Place	Date	Hour	Summary of Events and Information	Remarks and references to Appendices
ROSSIGNOL WOOD	1/10/17		Battalion carried out training. Particular attention being paid to specialists, Lewis Gunners, Grenadiers etc. Lt E.J.G. Chapman joined Battalion. Instructions in B and P.T. under C.S.M. Joyce A.G.S.	
—	2/10/17		Battalion carried out training. Particular attention being paid to specialists, Lewis Gunners, Grenadiers etc. Lt J.M. Gibbs joined Battalion. Instructions in B and P.T. under C.S.M. Joyce A.G.S.	
—	3/10/17		Battalion carried out training. Particular attention being paid to Lewis Gunners, Grenadiers etc. Instruction in B and P.T. under C.S.M. Joyce A.G.S. NCOs practised in communication drill. Reinforcement 21 O.Ranks.	
—	4/10/17		Battalion paraded for Divine Service. Major W. Morrison took over command of Battalion.	
—	5/10/17		Battalion relieved 10th Worcester Regiment in Right Subsector. A, C and D Coys in Front Line, B Coy in Reserve. Conveyed to Feb 8 by motor lorry. Captain W. Flint wounded. 1 O.Rank wounded.	APPENDIX 1.
RIGHT SUBSECTOR.	6/10/17		Usual Trench Routine carried out. Trenches renovated. Duckboards laid and provision made for shelter of troops against weather. 10 O.Ranks wounded.	
—	7/10/17		Ditto	
—	8/10/17		Battalion relieved by Kings Own R.L. Regiment on completion, was disposed as follows:- A and C Coys and HdQrs at Hope-60, D Coy Essex Keep, B Coy I platoon T.35.c.9.5, I platoon I.30.J.1.5	APPENDIX 2.
SUPPORT (RIGHT)	9/10/17		Battalion cleaned up after four in line and had clean change of socks & Boots cleaned and improved working and carrying parties found for R.E's.	
—	10/10/17		Ditto. 2 O.Ranks wounded.	
—	11/10/17		Battalion relieved K.O.R.L. Regt in Right Subsector in the evening and was disposed as follows:- C and B Front line, D Company Reserve, A Coy IMAGE RESERVE T.30.2.1.5	APPENDIX 3.
RIGHT SUBSECTOR	12/10/17		Usual Trench Routine carried out. Pots and trenches bailed out and duckboards laid. 4 O.Ranks wounded.	
—	13/10/17		Ditto. 2 O.Ranks wounded.	
CAMP N.6.d.1.7	14/10/17		Battalion relieved by North Staffordshire Regiment and on relief moved to Camp at N.6.d.1.7. 1 O.R died from wounds.	APPENDIX 4.
—	15/10/17		Battalion devoted day to cleaning up after tour in trenches. Camp improved.	
—	16/10/17		Battalion worked. BATHS at SIEGE FARM. Supervision Parades afternoon devoted to Camp Improvement.	

WAR DIARY
INTELLIGENCE SUMMARY
(Erase heading not required.)

Army Form C. 2118.

Instructions regarding War Diaries and Intelligence Summaries are contained in F.S. Regs., Part II. and the Staff Manual respectively. Title pages will be prepared in manuscript.

Place	Date	Hour	Summary of Events and Information	Remarks and references to Appendices
CAMP N.6.2.1.7.	17/10/17		Battalion carried out Training, improved Camp, and supplied working parties.	
-	18/10/17		— Ditto —	
-	19/10/17		Battalion moved to KENNEL SHELTERS. Transferred to 9th Division. Reorganised - 15 teams H.C.	APPENDIX 5.
KENNEL SHELTERS	20/10/17		Battalion carried out training. Instruction in Band P.T. under C.E.M. Joyce A.G.S.	
-	21/10/17		Battalion fanned out for Divine Service. Afternoon devoted to Sport.	
-	22/10/17		Battalion carried out training. Special attention given to Lewis Gunners and other Specialists. Instruction in Band P.T. under C.S.M. Joyce.	
-	23/10/17		— Ditto — Special attention given to Lewis Gunners — Cpl Green A.G.S.	
-	24/10/17		— Ditto — Special attention given to Lewis Gunners — Cpl Green A.G.S.	
-	25/10/17		2/1 Yorkshire Yeo - 2/1 Queens Own - 2/1 Greenwich Bn - 2/1 Navet - Joined Battalion. Brentwood Lewis Guns at Kemmel.	
-	26/10/17		Battalion carried out training. Special attention given to Lewis Gunners. Cpl Green A.G.S.	
-	27/10/17		Battalion attended Baths at LOCRE. Training carried out. Instruction in B and P.T. under Cpl Green A.G.S.	
LEFT SUPPORT	28/10/17		Battalion moved into Left Support and and disposed as follows:- HQ RFs and D Coy at Watt Coy - B and C Coys at Speck Bank. A Coy at LARCH WOOD.	APPENDIX 6.
-	29/10/17		Battalion supplied working and carrying parties and improved Billets &	
-	30/10/17		— Ditto —	
LEFT SUBSECTOR	31/10/17		Battalion moved into Line relieving K.O.R.L. Regt. and was disposed as follows. A Coy LEFT FRONT. B Coy CENTRE FRONT. D Coy RIGHT FRONT. C Coy PT. SUPPORT.	APPENDIX 7.

APPENDIX No 1

East Lancashire Regiment.   Copy No.12.

SECRET.   OPERATION ORDER NO.34.
                                             4/10/17.

REFERENCE MAP SHEET ZILLEBEKE.

1. The Battalion will relieve the 10th Worcester Regiment in the Right Subsector of Left Brigade Front tomorrow night.

2. Companies will be disposed in the line as follows relieving corresponding Companies of Worcesters :-
    Right of line   "C" Coy.,
    Centre   "A"   ,
    Left   "D"   ,
    Reserve   "B"   ,

3. Companies will be conveyed to LOCK No.8 by lorry and will then move off by sections at 200 yards interval. ROUTE: via tramline from YPRES-ST.ELOI Road at I.32.a.9.4 - BLAUWE POORT FME - PLANK ROAD at I.28.a.20 - VEERBRANDEN MOLEN in following order - "D" "A" "C" "B" HDQRS. First Company not to pass LOCK 8 before 8.15 p.m.

4. 2 guides per platoon from Worcesters will be at RIFLE DUMP 100 yards West of new Battn.Hdqrs. at 9.15 p.m.

5. DRESS: Haversacks will not be carried but packs with greatcoat, waterproof sheet, and rations for 6th inst.

6. 2 Hdqr.runners will proceed to line with each Coy.to ascertain position of Coy.Hdqrs. These will be sent back with a Company runner, one with Relief Report and one with Disposition Report. The first Coy.runner will be sent back to Company with the Coy. runner bringing Disposition Report.

7. All stores etc. not for the line to be dumped at Battn.Hdqrs.at 6 p.m.

8. All stores for trenches to be dumped at Battn.Hdqrs.with Lewis Guns at 5 p.m.

9. Men not proceeding to line will parade under C.S.M.Dollery at Orderly Room at 6 p.m.

10. Reports on completion of relief to Battn.Hdqrs. by runner.

                    (Signed). R.D.ALLSOPP, Lieut.&
                                            Adjutant,
                               7th Battn.East Lancashire Regt.

Issued at 11.0 p.m.

Copy No.1, 58th Brigade,
     2, C.O.,
     3, O.C."A" Coy.,
     4, ,   "B" ,
     5, ,   "C" ,
     6, ,   "D" ,
     7, Lt.C.D.Gray,
     8, 2/Lt.R.B.Hoggett,
     9, Adjutant,
    10, M.O.,
    11, R.S.M.,
    12, War Diary (2),
    13, File,
    14, Lt.& Q.M.,
    15, Transport Officer.

Copy No.12.

ADMINISTRATIVE INSTRUCTIONS.

SECRET.

With reference to Operation Order No.34.

1. Busses for conveyance of troops to the trenches will report at Hdqrs. at 6.45 p.m. tomorrow.
   Companies and Hdqrs. will be formed up in MASS in field in rear of Regimental Canteen ready to embus at 6.45 p.m.
2. 2/Lt.F.Morris, "B" Coy., will proceed with the first bus and supervise the debussing of Battalion. On completion of this duty he will rejoin his Company.

2. Trench Stores will be carefully checked and list sent to Battn. Hdqrs. by 9.0 p.m. on 6th inst. All water tins will be handed over by units of 57th Bgde.

3. Salvage will be collected at RIFLE DUMP J.25.c.80.35.

4. Sgt.Sandham will hand over present Camp and obtain receipts for stores and as to cleanliness.

5. One man per Coy.(Surplus Personnel) will report to CSM Dollery at Battn.Hdqrs. at 11 a.m. to take over Camp at KEMMEL SHELTERS for Surplus Personnel from 10th Warwicks.
   Surplus Personnel will be as already notified to Coys.
   Names of all N.C.O's and men to be left out of line to be forwarded to Orderly Room by 12 noon tomorrow 5th instant.

6. DUMPS. The main Brigade Dump for S.A.A. Grenades and R.E. materials will be at RIFLE DUMP J.25.c.80.35.
   There are also Dumps of S.A.A. and Grenades at
       HEDGE ROW DUMP   I.34.a.3.4,
       SHERWOOD DUMP,   I.29.d.Central.
   There are Dumps of R.E. material at:-
       JACKSONS DUMP I.28.b.5.2.
       MOLEN DUMP.   I.35.a.2.5.

7. Aid Posts of all Battalions are situate to all Headquarters. The A.B.S. is at ZWARTELEEN.

8. Two extra runners per company will report at Headquarters with rations for tomorrow at 9-0 a.m.

                        Signed R.D. Allsopp, Lt & Adj.,
                            7th Bn. East Lancashire Regt.

Issued at 11-0 p.m. to
all recipients of O.O. 34.

APPENDIX No 2.

SECRET. East Lancashire Regiment. Copy.No.12.

OPERATION ORDER No.35.

7/10/17.

1. The Battalion will be relieved tomorrow night by KINGS OWN ROYAL LANCASTER REGT.,
   "C" Coy. K.O.R.L.Regt., relieving "C" Coy., E.L.Regt.,
   "B"   ,   ,   ,   "A"   ,   ,
   "D"   ,   ,   ,   "D"   ,   ,
   "A"   ,   ,   ,   "B"   ,   ,
   (Strength of K.O.R.L.Regt. = 2 platoons per Company).

2. Four guides per Coy. to be at RIFLE DUMP at 7.30 p.m.

3. On completion of relief Company Commanders will report in person at present Battalion Hdqrs.

4. Work report to be rendered to Adjutant before daylight tomorrow. All empty petrol tins to be brought to RIFLE DUMP.

5. Usual receipts for trench stores to be obtained and rendered to Orderly Room by 6 p.m. 9th instant.

6. On completion of relief the Battalion will take over Dug-outs from NORTH LANCASHIRE REGIMENT as follows :-
   Battn.Hdqrs.)
   "A" Coy.,   )   Hill 60.
   "C"   ,   )
   "D" Coy.,   -   Corner House,
   "B"   ,   -   1 platoon at J.25.c.9.5, and
                   1 platoon at I.30.d.1.5.

7. Advance party of 1 N.C.O. per Coy. to report to Lt.C.D.Gray at present Battn.Hdqrs. before daylight tomorrow.

                    (Sgd).   R.D.ALLSOPP,
                                        Lieut. &
                                        Adjutant,
Issued at 2.0 p.m.   East Lancashire Regiment.

Copies to No.1, 55th Infy.Bgde.
         2, C.O.,
         3, Adjutant ,
         4, Lt.C.D.Gray,
         5, M.O.,
         6, O.C. "A" Coy.,
         7,   ,   "B"   ,
         8,   ,   "C"   ,
         9,   ,   "D"   ,
        10. K.O.R.L.Regt.,
        11. Q.M.,
        12. War Diary,
        13. File.

APPENDIX No 3

Copy.No.12.

SECRET.   East Lancashire Regiment.

OPERATION ORDER No.36.   11/10/17.

1. The Battalion will relieve KINGS OWN ROYAL LANCASTER REGT.
   in right Subsector tonight :-
      "C" Coy. E.L.Regt. relieving "C" & "B" Coys.K.O.R.L.Regt.,
      "B"   ,   ,   ,   "D" Coy.,   ,
      "A"   , &)
      Coy.Hdqrs.) ,   moving to IMAGE RESERVE I.30.d.1.5.
      "D" Coy.,   ,   relieving "A" Coy., K.O.R.L.Regt.

2. Companies will move off at the following times :n Hdqrs.5.0 p.m.,
   "A" Coy. 4.45 p.m., "C" & "D" Coys.5.30 p.m. "B" Coy.6.0 p.m.

3. Guides will be at RIFLE DUMP at 6 p.m.

4. Gumboots in bulk will be issued and carried by all Coys.

5. Tunnels to be left thoroughly clean. Debris to be buried by
   5.0 p.m.

6. Trench Store Lists to be sent to Battn.Hdqrs. as early as
   possible.

7. Reports to Battalion Hdqrs.by runner on completion of relief.

                (Sgd). R.D.ALLSOPP,
                              Lieut. &
                              Adjutant,
                         East Lancashire Regiment.

Issued at 2 p.m.

Copies to No.1, K.O.R.L.Regt.,
          2, 55th Infy.Bde.
          3, C.O.,
          4, Lt.C.D.Gray,
          5, Medical Officer,
          6, O.C. "A" Coy.,
          7,   ,   "B" ,
          8,   ,   "C" ,
          9,   ,   "D" ,
         10, File,
         11, Lt.& Q.M.,
         12. War Diary,

APPENDIX N° 4

Copy No.11.

SECRET.

East Lancashire Regiment.

OPERATION ORDER No.37.   14/10/17.

1. The NORTH STAFFORDSHIRE REGIMENT will relieve East Lancashire and South Lancashire Regiments tonight,
East Lancashire Regiment being relieved as follows :-
"C" Coy.E.L.Regt. and 3 Rt) .... ("B" Coy.NORTH STAFFS
Posts "B" Coy.E.L.Regt.,   ) being relieved by (less 2½ platoons.
"B" Coy.E.L.Regt.less 3 Rt.) .... ("C" Coy.NORTH STAFFS
Posts & platoon in support,) ,   ,   , (less 3 platoons.
"D" Coy.E.L.Regt.,   ,   ,   , 1 platoon "C" Coy.& 2½ platoons "B" Coy.NORTH STAFFS.
Battn.Hdqrs.E.L.R.being relieved by Hdqrs.NORTH STAFFS.
    The following will not be relieved but will march to new Camp at 6 p.m.
"A" Coy.,   "C" Coy's post at Princes House;   "B" Coy's support platoon.
O.C."A" Coy.to report by runner when Coy. has moved off.
The NORTH STAFFS REGT. who will move into the line as follows -
Hdqrs, "B" & "C" Coys. will take over as arranged by officers attached to front line Companies on night 13/14th.

2. On completion of relief, Battalion will take over Camp at N.6.d.1.7 from Royal Welsh Fusiliers.
ROUTE: MULE TRACK - HILL 60 - VEERBRANDEN MOLEN - BOIS CONFLUENT.
Guides for Companies will wait at LOCK 8 to guide to New Camp.

3. Guides for relief will report at Battn.Hdqrs.at 5.30 p.m. Company Commanders to report in person at present Battn.Hdqrs.when relief is complete.

4. Mules for "A" Coy.will report at IMAGE RESERVE at 6 p.m. and at RIFLE DUMP at 6.30 p.m. for Stores of Hdqrs and "D" Coy.
A limber for "B" & "C" Coys. will be waiting at A.D.Station on the Mule Track near HILL 60 to convey Lewis Guns etc.to new Camp.
    Greatcoats will not be worn but carried in valise.

5. Gumboots, - O.C.Companies will pay strict attention as to the return and handing over of gumboots on return to Camp. Any deficiency to be made good by men concerned.

6. The Quartermaster will arrange to take over new Camp, providing Billeting Party from Surplus Personnel who will rejoin Battalion there.

7. Usual Trench Store Receipts to be rendered to Orderly Room by 12 noon tomorrow.

                (Signed).   R.D.ALLSOPP, Lieut.&
                                         Adjutant,
Issued at 2.0 p.m.   East Lancashire Regiment.

Copies No.1, 56th Infy.Bde.,
       2, C.O.,
       3, Lt.D.D.Gray,
       4, O.C."A" Coy.,
       5,   , "B" ,
       6,   , "C" ,
       7,   , "D" ,
       8, Lt.& Q.M.,
       9, North Staffs,
      10, File,
      11, War Diary.

APPENDIX No 5

East Lancashire Regt.

SECRET.

Copy No. 13

OPERATION ORDER No.18

18/10/17

REFERENCE MAP SHEET 28.N.E. 1/40000.

1. The Battalion will move to KEMMEL SHELTERS tomorrow.

2. The Battalion will be formed up in column of route in the following order - H.Q., "A" "B" "C" & "D" Coys. Head of column to be at entrance to Camp ready to move off at 1.45 p.m.

3. ROUTE - via BRANDHOEK, NINE ELMS, KEMMEL.

4. Distance of two yards between Companies to be observed.

5. Blankets to be rolled in section bundles and dumped near Orderly Room by 10.0 a.m.

6. All Stores and Officers' kits to be dumped near Orderly Room by 1.30 p.m. Transport Officer will arrange for carriage of all Stores etc.

7. Lieut. C.D.Gray, Lieut.E.H.Shepham, and one N.C.O. per Coy. and R.E. will parade at Orderly Room at 10.0 a.m. and will proceed to KEMMEL SHELTERS in advance to take over Camp. Lt.C.D.Gray to report to Adjutant for instructions.

8. Camp to be left in a clean and sanitary condition. Certificates to be rendered to Orderly Room to this effect by 1p.m.

9. Lists of Camp Stores and furniture to be handed in to Orderly Room by 11 a.m. List of kit ones to be forwarded to this office at same time.

10. One Officer of "D" Coy. and one N.C.O. per Coy. and H.Q. will be left behind to hand Camp over to incoming Battalion and obtain receipts as to cleanliness and for stores etc.

11. Acknowledge.

S.Wheat
Lieut. & Adjt.,
East Lancashire Regiment.

Issued at 7.45 p.m.

Copies to -
No.1. Brigade,
2. O.C.,
3. Major Garrison,
4. O.C. "A" Coy.,
5. " "B" "
6. " "C" "
7. " "D" "
8. Lt.C.D.Gray,
9. M.O.,
10. T.O.,
11. L.M. & G.O.,
12. S.B.O.,
13. For Diary,
14. File

APPENDIX N° 6

EAST LANCASHIRE REGIMENT.

Secret.   Copy No. 15

OPERATION ORDER. No. 39.

Reference 1/10,000 Sheet. HOLLEBEKE.   26/10/17
          1/40,000 Sheet. 28.

1. The Battalion will move into LEFT SUPPORT tomorrow and will be disposed as follows.

    Hdqr. and D Coy.   at HILL 60
    B and C Coys.   at SPOIL BANK, N. BANK of CANAL.
    A Coy   at LARCH WOOD.

2. The Battalion will move off in the following order - Hdqrs, D, A, B and C Coys. by platoons. All movements S.W. of YPRES-ST.ELOI Road by platoons at 400 yards distance. N.W. of that point by Sections at 100 yards distance. First platoon to leave Camp at 12-30 PM
    DRESS:- Marching Order.

3. ROUTE:- Lock 8 - TOWSEYS TRACK- CLEMSONS LANE and TRENCHES and TRACKS N. of HILL 60.

4. 4 guides from B and C Coys will be at BRICKSTACKS SPOIL BANK at 3-0 p.m. 6 guides for Hdqrs, A, and D Coys will be at Clemsons Lane at 3-0 p.m.

5. All stores, Officers valises, etc., not for the line to be stacked at Officers Mess by 12-0 noon.

6. All stores for the line to be stacked at Officers Mess by 12-0 noon.

7. Transport Officer will arrange for carriage of all stores.

8. Trench Stores etc. to be carefully checked before taking over and lists sent to Orderly Room by 12-0 noon 28th inst.

9. The L.G. teams of A and B Coys. will be relieved not later than 2 p.m tomorrow by 57th Brigade at KLIEN VIERSTRAAT and will then rejoin their Coys.

10. Reports to Orderly Room by runner on completion of relief.

                        Sgd S Wheal, Lt & A/Adj.,

                        East Lancashire Regt.

Issued at 7-15 P.M.

Copies to 1 56th Bgde.
          2 Cheshire Regt.
          3 C.B.
          4 Major Morrison.
          5 Adjt.
          6 O.C. A Coy
          7 -   B -
          8 -   C -
          9 -   D -
         10 M.O.
         11 T.O
         12 Q.M.
         13 R.S.M.
         14 File.
         15 War Diary

SECRET.
Copy No.10.

APPENDIX 7

East Lancashire Regiment.

OPERATION ORDER NO.40. 30/10/17.

REFERENCE HOLLEBEKE SHEET 1/10,000.

1. The Battalion will relieve the King's Own in the line tomorrow and will be disposed as follows :- "A" Coy. on left front, "B" Coy. Centre front, "D" Coy. right front, and "C" Coy. in support.

2. Companies will relieve corresponding Companies of King's Own and will move off in the following order and at following times :-
   "B" Coy., 3.45 p.m.   NOTE:
   "A"   ,   4.45 p.m.   Leading Coy. to reach
   "D"   ,   5.15 p.m.   CORNER HOUSE at 5 p.m.
   H.Q. ,   5.30 p.m.
   "C"   ,   5.30 p.m.

3. Guides for Companies will be at CORNER HOUSE at 5 p.m. for platoons at Battn.H.Q. and for posts at Company H.Q. in the line.

4. All movements by sections at 100 yards distance.

5. Stores and the following days rations to be carried in with Companies.

6. Company cooks of front line Companies will be accommodated at Battn.Hdqrs., and will cook and send up hot food at night. 2 dixies per Coy. to be taken by Cooks.

7. Rations will be delivered to Companies tomorrow as usual.

8. Trench Stores to be carefully checked and lists forwarded to Battn.Hdqrs. by 8 p.m. on 1st Novr. Companies will also take over anti-aircraft posts from King's Own.

9. Situation, Casualty, and Intelligence Returns to be at Battn. Hdqrs. by 8 p.m. each day.

10. Reports by runner on completion of relief to Bn.H.Q.

(Signed). SAM WHEAL, Lt. &
A/Adjutant,
Issued 4.30 p.m.   East Lancs.Regt.

Copy No.1, Bde,
     2,   Kings Own,
     3,   C.O.,
     4,   O.C. "A" Coy.,
     5,   "B"   ,
     6,   "C"   ,
     7,   "D"   ,
     8,   M.O.,
     9,   File,
    10.   War Diary.

WAR DIARY
INTELLIGENCE SUMMARY.
(Erase heading not required.)

Army Form C. 2118.

Instructions regarding War Diaries and Intelligence Summaries are contained in F. S. Regs., Part II. and the Staff Manual respectively. Title pages will be prepared in manuscript.

Place	Date	Hour	Summary of Events and Information	Remarks and references to Appendices
IN THE LINE SCHERSNBURY FOREST SHEET 28 N.W	1917 Nov 1		Trench Routine carried out. 2 killed 3 wounded. Other ranks 2nd Lt J Bawden 2/Lt R J Sheppard 2/Lt W.A. Rocket & 2/Lt J.C Redding joined Battalion.	
- do -	Nov 2		Trench routine carried out - "Kings Own" (R.L.) Regiment carried out a raid on the German trenches at 7.26 from our subsector and captured 6 prisoners. Enemy retaliated with a few gas shells. 1 Other rank wounded.	
- do -	Nov 3		Trench Routine carried out.	
- do -	Nov 4		Trench Routine carried out - In the evening the Battalion was relieved by the 8th S. Staffs on the line and moved to close reserve at BEGGARS REST near VIERSTRAAT Sheet 28 S.W 1/20,000	APP. I
BEGGARS REST SHEET 28 SW 1/20,000 Nov 5			In close reserve. Working parties found. Bn. bathed at SIEGE FARM. 2/Lt E.C Fox joined Battalion	
- do -	Nov 6		- do -	
- do -	Nov 7		- do -	
- do -	Nov 8		Bn. moved to WAKEFIELD HUTS N.R LOCRE. Sheet 28 1/40,000 into Divisional Reserve.	APP. 2
WAKEFIELD HUTS N.R LOCRE	Nov 9		Bn. moved to INKERMAN CAMP at M.20.a.5.5. Sheet 28 1/40,000	APP. 3
INKERMAN CAMP	Nov 10		Bn. moved by road and rail to training area near EBBLINGHEM. Bn. billeted at SERCUS Sheet 36a. Square C.9.	APP. 4
SERCUS	Nov 11		Battalion engaged cleaning up. Voluntary Church parades.	
- do -	Nov 12		Battalion carried out training.	
- do -	Nov 13		- do -	
- do -	Nov 14		Battalion inspected by G.O.C. 56th Infantry Brigade.	
- do -	Nov 15		Battalion carried out training.	

WAR DIARY

INTELLIGENCE SUMMARY.

(Erase heading not required.)

Army Form C. 2118.

Place	Date	Hour	Summary of Events and Information	Remarks and references to Appendices
SERCUS	Nov 16		Battalion carried out training. Battalion bathed at BLARINGHEM.	
do	Nov 17		do	
do	Nov 18		Battalion paraded for Divine Service. 2/Lt. G. Ellingham joined Battalion.	
do	Nov 19		Battalion carried out training.	
do	Nov 20		Battalion carried out training. BATHS at BLARINGHEM.	
do	Nov 21		do	
do	Nov 22		do 2/Lt W. Stiles-Bryan joined Battalion.	
do	Nov 23		do	
do	Nov 24		do	
do	Nov 25		Battalion paraded for DIVINE SERVICE.	
do	Nov 26		Battalion carried out training.	
do	Nov 27		do	
do	Nov 28		do	
do	Nov 29		do	
do	Nov 30		do	

A. L. Kenton Lt Col
1/5th The East Lancashire Regt

SECRET.   EAST LANCASHIRE REGIMENT.   Copy No 11.

APPENDIX No 1

OPERATION ORDER No 41.   3/11/17.

Reference Map Sheet HOLLEBEKE 1/10,000.
                    28 S.W. 1/20,000.

1. The Battalion will be relieved in the line tomorrow by the 8th NORTH STAFFS REGt and on relief will move to Camp at BEGGAR'S REST, Near BRASSERIE.

2. Order of relief will be notified later. The North Staffs have 4 platoons to a Company.

3. One guide per platoon from A, B and D Companies will report to Battalion Headquarters just before dawn. Guides of C Coy will be at Corner House at 5-0 p.m. tomorrow. Guides for posts will be at Company Hdqrs.

4. Companies will carry out their stores to A.D.S. near Hill 60 where limbers will be detailed to carry same.

5. No man must come out of the line wearing gum-boots. Company Commanders will ensure that the same number of gum-boots are carried out of the line as were taken in. Gum-boots will be dumped at new Orderly Room at 12 noon 5th inst.

6. On arrival at new Camp, Company Commanders will see that each man has his feet rubbed and a clean change of socks.

7. Trench Stores will be carefully checked and lists forwarded to Orderly Room by noon on 5th inst.

8. C Coy will take over the following anti-aircraft posts by 9-0 p.m. tomorrow, 4th inst.
    1 pair L.G. at O.3.a.5.8.
    1 -   L.G. at I.33.d.5.2.
Relieving team of King's Own. Only half teams required.

9. O. C. Coys will hand over anti-aircraft posts and details of work done and contemplated to incoming Battalion.

10. Company Commanders will report completion of relief by wiring or sending by runner to Headquarters the word "DONE"

                        (Sd) R. D. Allsopp,
                              Lieut and Adjutant,
                              East Lancashire Regiment.
Issued at 4-30 p.m.

            Copies to :- 1. 56th Brigade.
                          2. Commanding Officer.
                          3. O. C. A Coy.
                          4. O. C. B Coy.
                          5. O. C. C. Coy.
                          6. O. C. D. Coy.
                          7. Medical Officer.
                          8. Q'Master & T. O.
                          9. N. Staffs.
                         10. Adjutant.
                         11. War Diary.
                         12. File.

APPENDIX No 2

SECRET.   East Lancashire Regiment.   Copy No. 11

OPERATION ORDER No. 32.

REFERENCE MAP 28 S.W. and SHEET 28.
        1/20,000.   1/40,000.

7/4/17

1. The Battalion will move to INKERMAN CAMP (H.30.d.35) tomorrow.

2. Companies (less "A" Coy) will be formed up in column of route on BRANDHOEK ROAD in the following order :- Drums, H.Q., "B" "C" & "D" Coys., Transport, ready to move off at 11.15 a.m. Transport not moving off with Battalion will join it on HALLEBAST ROAD.
DRESS: Full marching order; jerkins to be worn.

3. ROUTE: via HALLEBAST - MILLEKRUISSE - LA CLYTTE - SCHERPENBERG.

4. Usual 10 minutes halt at ten minutes to each clock hour will be observed on the march.

5. Distances of 800 yards between Battalions, 100 yards between Companies (including Transport which will count as a Company) will be observed.

6. "A" Coy. will proceed in advance to pitch tents for Battalion and for Brigade Headqrs. This Company will move off at 6 a.m.

7. All Stores, Blankets, etc, will be dumped, by Companies, at Guard Room by 8.30 a.m.
Officers' valises, Mess Stores, and Cooking utensils to be dumped at Guard Room at 10 a.m.

8. Transport Officer will arrange for collection of Stores etc., and for Officers' chargers.

9. Rear party of 2/Lt. J.A.Tinsley and two N.C.O's per Coy. and H.Q. will be left behind to hand over Camp. On completion of this duty they will rejoin Battalion.

10. Camp to be left in a clean and sanitary condition. Certificates to this effect to be forwarded to Orderly Room by 10 a.m.

                                    Bradburn   Lieut. &
                                                Adjutant,
                                    East Lancashire Regiment.

Issued at 7.30 p.m.

        Copies to, 1. Brigade,
                    2. C.O.,
                    3. O.C. "A" Coy.,
                    4. " "B" "
                    5. " "C" "
                    6. " "D" "
                    7. Lt. C.D.Gray,
                    8. M.O.,
                    9. R.S.M.,
                   10. Adjutant,
                   11. War Diary (2),
                   12. File.

NOTE:-
The Battalion moved to WAKEFIELD HUTS NR LOCRE on 8/4/17 and not to INKERMAN CAMP.

SECRET.   East Lancashire Regiment.   COPY NO. 14

                OPERATION ORDER NO. 43

                                                    8/11/17.
        REFERENCE MAP SHEET 28.S.W. 1/40,000.
                    SHEET NO.   1/40,000.

1. The Battalion will move to INKERMAN CAMP tomorrow.

2. Battalion (less "A" Coy) will be formed up in column of route on road outside Camp facing LOCRE ready to move off at 10.0 a.m., in the following order :- Drums, H.Q., "D" "C" "B" Coys., Transport. Dress as for today.

3. ROUTE: via MONT NOIRE.

4. All stores, Officers' valises, etc. to be stacked near Guard Room by 9.15 a.m.

5. Distances and halts on the march as ordered for today.

6. Camp to be left in a clean & sanitary condition.

                                            Lt. & Adjt.,
Issued at :- 7.45. p.m.   East Lancashire Regt.

    Copies to: 1. Brigade,   7. Lt. C.D.Gray,
                2. C.O.,   8. M.O.
                3. O.C. "A" Coy., 9. Adjt.,   13. War Diary.
                4. ,   "B" , 10. Lt. & R.M.   14. File.
                5. ,   "C" , 11. T.O.,
                6. ,   "D" , 12. R.S.M.

SECRET.   East Lancashire Regiment.   Copy No. 13

OPERATION ORDER NO. 44.

REFERENCE MAP SHEET HAZEBROUCK 5.a., 36.a.N.W.

Appendix No. C
9/11/17

1. The Battalion will move to SERCUS Area by rail tomorrow. H.Q. at
   C.6.c.4.8.

2. Battalion will be formed up in column of route on road outside Camp
   facing S.W., ready to move off at 8.40 a.m., in the following order-
   "A" "C" XXXX Drums, H.Q. "D" "B" Coys. Same distances and halts
   to be observed as for today.

3. DRESS: Same as for today. Troops to entrain with unconsumed
   portion of day's rations and waterbottles to be filled.

4. All Stores, Officers' valises, blankets, etc. to be dumped at Q.M.
   Stores by 7.30 a.m.

5. Transport will move in accordance with orders issued separately.

6. Camp to be left in a clean and sanitary condition.

                                          Lieut.& Adjt.,
Issued at 6 p.m.   East Lancashire Regt.

   Copies to - 1. Bde,   8. M.O.,
               2. C.O.,   9. Adjt.,
               3. O.C."A" Coy., 10. Lt.& Q.M.,
               4.   "B" ,   11. T.O.,
               5.   "C" ,   12. R.S.M.,
               6.   "D" .   13. War Diary,
               7. Lt.C.D.Gray, 14. File.

WAR DIARY

INTELLIGENCE SUMMARY.

(Erase heading not required.)

Army Form C. 2118.

7 E Kane R

Place	Date 1917	Hour	Summary of Events and Information	Remarks and references to Appendices
Serrecat	Dec 1		Training carried out	
	2		Battalion paraded for Divine Service	
	3		Battalion carried out training	
	4		— do —	
	5		— do —	
	6		Major N.B. Callard 7/S.L.W.R took over command of Battalion from Lieut Col H.J. Jones DSO To Clear Paris Third Army Area entraining at	
BAILLEULMONT	7		Battalion moved by rail to St Leger and place to Third Army Area entraining at	
	8		STEENBECQUE Battalion arrived at BAILLEULMONT	
LOUVERCELLES	9		Battalion moved by march route to COURCELLES LE COMTE	
LE COMTE	10		ETRICOURT 2/Lt Burton + 1 Baton joined	
ETRICOURT	11		Battalion carried out training / Lt Col R.L. Beasley R.W.Kent Regt took over command of	
	12		Battalion moved by route march to RIBECOURT (HINDENBURG LINE) with Battalion Reserve	
RIBECOURT	13		Battalion in Divisional Reserve	
FACI S/6	14		— do —	
	15		— do —	
	16		Battalion moved into front line such formed part of Battalion becoming N. STAFFS REGT	
	17		Battalion in line 2 prisoners captured on patrol by A.Coy	
	18		Battalion in line took over front line on right of Salient from 6th W. Rid Regt	
	19		— do — Raid carried out successfully by B.Coy on enemy line	
	20		— do — 5 prisoners and 1 machine gun captured 1 other rank wounded	
	21		Battalion relieved in line by 7 Hampshire Regt and moved into Brigade Reserve at	
	22		RIBECOURT In Brigade Reserve	
	23		— do —	
	24		— do — 2/Lt M. Jeffryes joined	

26W
2 About

Op May (illegible)
7 (illegible)

WAR DIARY
or
INTELLIGENCE SUMMARY.
(Erase heading not required.)

Army Form C. 2118.

Instructions regarding War Diaries and Intelligence Summaries are contained in F. S. Regs., Part II. and the Staff Manual respectively. Title pages will be prepared in manuscript.

Place	Date	Hour	Summary of Events and Information	Remarks and references to Appendices
RIBECOURT	26/12/17		In Brigade Reserve. Battalion moved into line in the evening relieving	
MOEUVRE	27/12/17		Battalion in the line 7/Kings Own Regt	
	28ᵈ		— do —	
	29		Battalion moved into Divisional Reserve near RIBECOURT (HINDENBURG LINES)	
	30		Battalion in Divisional Reserve. 3 other ranks wounded by shell fire	
	31		Battalion in Divisional Reserve	

Co Gray Lieut for Adjutant
1/5ᵗʰ Bn. East Lancashire Regt.

WAR DIARY
INTELLIGENCE SUMMARY.
(Erase heading not required.)

Army Form C. 2118.

Place	Date	Hour	Summary of Events and Information	Remarks and references to Appendices
France	January 1918 Tues. 1st		9Bn - in Bde Res. in HINDENBERG LINE. Enemy fired Gas shells in vicinity. no casualties.	27.W 5 wheels
	Wed 2nd		"	
	Thurs 3rd		"	
	Frid 4th		" Relieved by 9 RWF at 11.30 p.m. marched to camp at HAVRINCOURT WOOD. All coys settled in about 3am (Sat)	
	Sat 5th		Orders about 9am to move at 2 p.m. Bn moved into Bde Res in another part of HINDENBERG LINE. Bde took over ground to S.E. on right. Enemy	
	Sun 6th		In Bde Res. Enemy machine guns active during night on all open ground near trenches.	
	Mon 7th		Thaw started. Trenches already in very bad condition. Intermittent shelling of area by enemy during the day. 2/Lt Thompson awarded M.C. 2 O.Rs. Army awarded D.C.M.	
	Tues 8th		Front line trenches still very bad. Intermittent shelling as yesterday. Enemy machine guns active during night on open ground near trenches. Still in Bde Reserve. Few inches of snow fell during day.	

WAR DIARY
or
INTELLIGENCE SUMMARY.
(Erase heading not required.)

Army Form C. 2118.

Instructions regarding War Diaries and Intelligence Summaries are contained in F. S. Regs., Part II. and the Staff Manual respectively. Title pages will be prepared in manuscript.

Place	Date	Hour	Summary of Events and Information	Remarks and references to Appendices
In the field	1918 January Wed 9th		Batt'n in support about 2070 yds in rear of front line. Clear morning, many enemy aircraft flying over our lines. Enemy shelled trenches and ground near ration dump during day. Snow and strong wind in afternoon. Ground & forward line reconnoitred for line of advance for counter attack	
	Thurs 10th		Batt'n in support. During day enemy shelled vicinity of Batt'n and ration dump slightly. Heavier fire than usual. Our artillery fired hard during night. Notice received yesterday that enemy attack might be expected at 5" warned to be ready for counter attack	
	Fri 11th		B'n in support. Our artillery fired heavily on enemy aircraft. Please etc for about 20 minutes early this morn. Last night heavy gunfire on left of Salient. Trenches were not communicated to Colt. G.P.A. watched enemy to long post present than Batt'n being used most of day for carrying, sandbag protection. Last night fairly quiet. Usual machine gun fire and intermittent shelling of area.	
	Sat 12th		Carrying parties furnished again (about B'n SI-P) in support. Movement of large body of enemy reported on 10th. Attack was expected on Corps front. Batt'n relieved by 10.Worc.Regt Proceeded by Beaumelle Ry from Toccault to Lecheux Camp near YTRES. Settled in camp at midnight	

M6945 Wt W14925/M160 35,000 12/16 D. D. & L. Form/C/2118/14.

Army Form C. 2118.

WAR DIARY
or
INTELLIGENCE SUMMARY.
(Erase heading not required.)

Instructions regarding War Diaries and Intelligence Summaries are contained in F. S. Regs., Part II. and the Staff Manual respectively. Title pages will be prepared in manuscript.

Place	Date	Hour	Summary of Events and Information	Remarks and references to Appendices
In the field	January 1918			
	Sun 13		Billets for Bn at Neuville St V in Divisional Reserve	
	Mon 14		Div. Reserve. General inspection and exercise of clothing & equipment etc.	
	Tues 15	"	" Divine Service in camp. Remainder of Bn working parties	
	Wed 16	"	" Working parties. Heavy rain turned	
	Thurs 17	"	" Reconnaissance of new line by officers. Mud very bad in trenches	
	Frid 18		Bn went into front line relieving R.W.F. Little shelling on approaches to line during night.	
	Sat 19		Enemy aircraft very active. Line was shelled at intervals during day. Trench mortars active especially against right and centre Coys. Luckily only two casualties. Part of trenches impossible owing to heavy mud. Work can only be carried on by night, going along the top.	
	Sun 20th		Enemy aircraft active. Trench mortars active against Farwood posts. Shelling in vicinity of trenches and approaches heavier.	
	Mon 21st		Shelling intermittent during last night. Have casualties. Trench mortars not quite so active. Relieved by 6th Punjaby 7th N. Lanc Regt. Bn went to Hindenberg lodge in Bde Reserve.	

WAR DIARY
or
INTELLIGENCE SUMMARY.

(Erase heading not required.)

Army Form C. 2118.

Place	Date	Hour	Summary of Events and Information	Remarks and references to Appendices
In the Field	January 1918 Tues 22nd		Relief last night was not interfered with by enemy fire. Before relief his fire was active on all approaches & batteries from our S.P. Two Coys in a very bad trench & one Coy in Hindenburg Line.	
	Wed. 23rd		Did a great amount of work on the trenches which were in a very bad state. Trenches first were not shelled by enemy artillery.	
	Thur 24th		Relieved 7th Bgd Yorks. Lancashire Regt. in Support. Relief carried out without any great incident.	
	Fri 25th		Found that in very bad state. Kept amount of work done then Coys undertaking greatly.	
	Sat 26th		Matters of importance to report. Hostile bombardment possible improvement to line.	
	Sun 27th		Nothing to report.	
	Mon 28th		Enemy Artillery very active during 27/28th. Enemy putting down an intense barrage at 7.00 pm of 7.5" Heavy (Gas) (probably) Rgt & rear cams head of HAWES CAMP, W637 & HAVRINCOURT WOOD.	

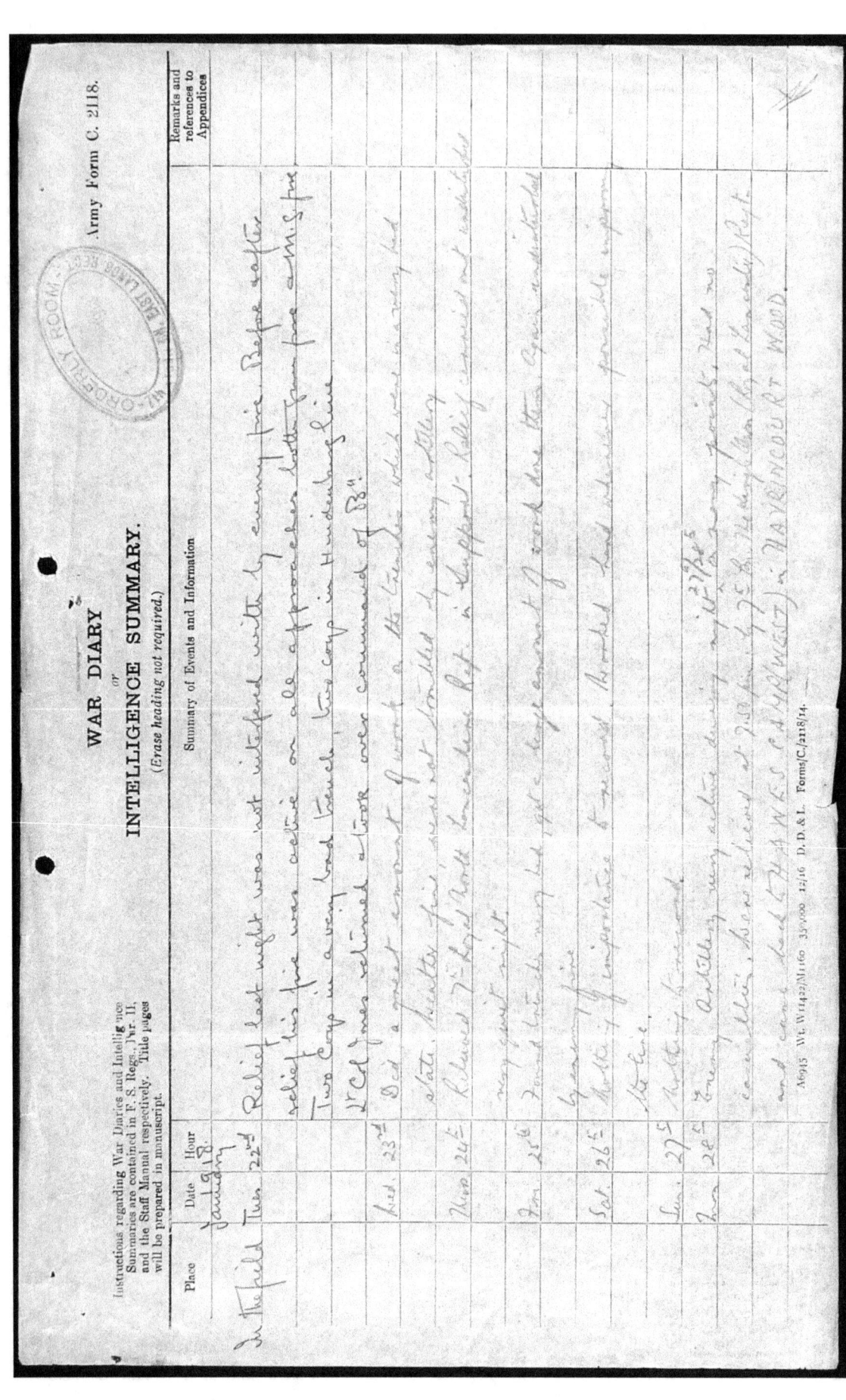

Army Form C. 2118.

WAR DIARY
or
INTELLIGENCE SUMMARY.
(Erase heading not required.)

Instructions regarding War Diaries and Intelligence Summaries are contained in F. S. Regs., Part II. and the Staff Manual respectively. Title pages will be prepared in manuscript.

Place	Date	Hour	Summary of Events and Information	Remarks and references to Appendices
In Field	January 1918			
	Tues. 29th		Spent the day cleaning up and stabled & looking to sports ground	
			the lub for authorised sports.	
	Wed. 30th		Got huts for whole battalion and used the working parties round huts.	
			Enemy aircraft very active at night bombing	
	Thurs. 31st		Camouflaged huts with twigs & string & coloured the working parties	
			round the huts.	
			About 6 offrs. & 120 of proud and of O.R.s other Ranks on the ground the battn.	
			rest of the men in supporting up for the move up to the Line. Battalion	

A. L. Rendel
Lieut/Col.
7/8. the East Lancs. Regt.

www.ingramcontent.com/pod-product-compliance
Lightning Source LLC
Chambersburg PA
CBHW082006220426
43670CB00014B/2565